Supporting Direct Contact after Adoption

Supporting Direct Contact after Adoption

Elsbeth Neil, Jeanette Cossar, Christine Jones, Paula Lorgelly and Julie Young

Published by British Association
for Adoption & Fostering
(BAAF)
Saffron House
3rd Floor, 6–10 Kirby Street
London EC1N 8TS
www.baaf.org.uk

Charity registration 275689 (England and Wales)
and SC039337 (Scotland)

© Elsbeth Neil, Jeanette Cossar, Christine Jones,
   Paula Lorgelly and Julie Young, 2011

British Library Cataloguing in Publication Data
A catalogue record for this book is available
from the British Library

ISBN 978 1 907585 05 0

Editorial project management by Miranda Davies, BAAF Publications
Designed by Helen Joubert Design
Typeset by Avon DataSet Ltd, Bidford on Avon
Printed in Great Britain by TJ International
Trade distribution by Turnaround Publisher Services,
Unit 3, Olympia Trading Estate, Coburg Road,
London N22 6TZ

BAAF is the leading UK-wide membership
organisation for all those concerned with
adoption, fostering and child care issues.

Contents

List of tables

List of figures

Acknowledgements

This study and report could not have been completed without the large number of people outside of the immediate research team who generously gave their help, support and expertise. We are very grateful to the Department for Children, Schools and Families for sponsoring this study and, in particular, Caroline Thomas for her continued patience and support.

We would like to thank colleagues at the Centre for Research on the Child and Family: Jo Connolly, Michelle Cooper, Nick Healey and Dr Clive Sellick, who all participated as team members at some point in the process, and many other academic and administrative colleagues at the University of East Anglia who assisted and supported us along the way.

We are also indebted to our research advisory group, who enabled us to benefit from their invaluable wisdom and advice throughout the course of the project: Jennifer Castle, Lyndsay Davison, Jenny Gwilt, Isabella Craig, Julie Selwyn, John Simmonds, Chris Smith, Carol Vella and Doreen Ward. Additionally, we are grateful for comments and support from our academic colleagues overseas: Professor Harold Grotevant (on project design and quantitative measures), Dr Lynn von Korff (on statistical analysis) and Marta Reinoso Bernuz (on 'coping with adoption' and CBCL coding).

Special thanks must also go to our team of service-user consultants who gave considerable time at many points throughout the study, providing invaluable feedback and suggestions based on their own experiences: Zoe Boreham, Judy Blowers, Claire, Robert Claxton-Ingham, Anne Cooper, Imogen Cooper, Nina De'ath, Ian Eskriett, Zoë Eskriett, Geoff, Becky Hawthorn, Bernadette James, Angela Jenner, Kiri Joseph, David Leaver, Roma Meah, Lzetwicia Oscar-Jackman, Rachel Taylor, Rachel Victor-Sampson, David and Sally Wood and Tracey. Thanks also to Alison Flack and Doreen Ward, who were extremely helpful in giving us advice on involving service users in research and in facilitating the meetings with these consultants.

We are also grateful to Martin Howard, who took on board our service-user consultants' suggestions and helped us design effective recruitment leaflets, and to Nicole Hamilton, who helped in the presentation of the final manuscript of this report.

Our thanks must also go to those who, for reasons of confidentiality, cannot be named: the many people in local authorities and adoption agencies who were prepared to participate in and support this study, despite the demands on their already pressurised time. We would particularly like to thank the social workers and administrative assistants who helped us with recruitment and completed our questionnaires.

Most of all, we would like to thank the adoptive parents and birth relatives who took part in our interviews. Without their willingness to share their own personal stories, emotions and vulnerabilities, this report could not have been written. We sincerely hope that this report does justice to their experience and feelings.

Notes about the authors

Elsbeth Neil is a senior lecturer in social work at the University of East Anglia (UEA), Norwich. Her research career began in 1996 when she started a longitudinal study of children having contact after adoption. She has directed the "Supporting contact" study and its sister project the "Helping birth families" project exploring support for birth relatives in adoption (also part of the Adoption Research Initiative and published by BAAF). She is the author of several journal articles and book chapters in these two fields, including the BAAF book (co-edited with David Howe) *Contact in Adoption and Permanent Foster Care: Theory, research and practice* (2004) and *International Advances in Adoption Research for Practice* (co-edited with Gretchen Wrobel, Wiley, 2009). Elsbeth can be contacted by e-mail at e.neil@uea.ac.uk.

Jeanette Cossar is a lecturer in social work at the University of East Anglia, Norwich. In addition to her contributions to the "Supporting contact" project, Jeanette has worked on the parallel UEA study looking at support for birth relatives in adoption. Her other research interests and experiences are in relation to children's views of the child protection process, and the experiences of gay and lesbian young people in care.

Christine Jones is a lecturer in social work at the University of Durham. Prior to this appointment she undertook an ESRC Postdoctoral Fellowship at the University of Edinburgh. She completed her PhD at Durham in 2009. Her doctoral research was entitled "What makes adoptive family life work: adoptive parents' narratives of the making and remaking of adoptive kinship". Her research interests include adoption and fostering, the application within social work of sociological and anthropological theories of family and kinship, and service-user perspectives. Chris joined the UEA "Supporting contact" research team to help with qualitative data analysis and write-up. Chris is also an adoptive parent.

Paula Lorgelly has worked since January 2010 at the Centre for Health Economics at Monash University in Melbourne. Prior to this she has held academic posts in the UK at Nottingham, Glasgow, and at UEA. Paula's research interests are varied, but generally centre on the methodological issues of economic evaluations. She directed the economic evaluation aspect of the "Supporting contact" and "Helping birth families" studies.

Julie Young is a senior research associate at the University of East Anglia, Norwich. After several years of experience in the fields of education and counselling, she joined UEA in 2001 to work on the "Contact after adoption" study. She has co-authored book chapters with Elsbeth Neil on the topic of post-adoption contact, including a chapter in *The Child Placement Handbook* (BAAF, 2009). As well as her role as a key researcher on the "Supporting contact" study, Julie has worked on a range of projects at UEA exploring the experiences of parents involved with children's services.

The Adoption Research Initiative

This series brings together the research studies in the Adoption Research Initiative (ARI), a programme of research on adoption funded by the former Department for Children, Schools and Families (DCSF). It is designed to evaluate the impact of the Labour Government's adoption project, including the Adoption and Children Act 2002 and various related policy initiatives. The research initiative is examining how these objectives are being translated into local policies, procedures and practice.

There are seven studies within the Adoption Research Initiative. They address four broad themes: permanency planning and professional decision-making; linking and matching; adoption support; and the costs of adoption. They also complement other recently reported and current research on the full range of placements for looked after children, including kinship care, foster care, residential care, private fostering and return home.

More information on the Adoption Research Initiative is available at www.adoptionresearchinitiative.org.uk.

Published by BAAF:

- *Enhancing Adoptive Parenting: A test of effectiveness*, Alan Rushton and Elizabeth Monck, 2009
- *Linking and Matching: A survey of adoption agency practice in England and Wales*, Cherilyn Dance, Danielle Ouwejan, Jennifer Beecham and Elaine Farmer, 2010
- *Pathways to Permanence for Black, Asian and Mixed Ethnicity Children*, Julie Selwyn, David Quinton, Perlita Harris, Dinithi Wijedasa, Shameem Nawaz and Marsha Wood, 2010
- *Special Guardianship in Practice*, Jim Wade, Jo Dixon and Andrew Richards, 2010
- *Helping Birth Families: Services, costs and outcomes*, Elsbeth Neil, Jeanette Cossar, Paula Longelly and Julie Young, 2010
- *Belonging and Permanence: Outcomes in long-term foster care and adoption*, Nina Biehal, Sarah Ellison, Claire Baker and Ian Sinclair, 2010

Executive summary

Aims of this study

This study was commissioned to explore the provision of adoption support services to help birth and adoptive families manage direct post-adoption contact arrangements. The Adoption and Children Act 2002 (s.4) and its accompanying regulations [reg.3(5)] specify that adopted children, birth relatives and adoptive parents all have the right to ask for an assessment of their needs for post-adoption support, and that support for contact must be made available to them. A significant minority of adopted children are likely to have direct contact with a sibling, birth parent, grandparent or other member of the extended birth family.

In an earlier stage of this research project we carried out a survey that mapped services to support contact, using data from 135 questionnaires, 60 interviews with adoption support staff and two focus groups (Sellick, 2007). This survey showed that contact support services were mainly provided in-house by local authorities and that supporting letterbox contact was the predominant activity. Most agencies were supporting only small numbers of direct contact cases, usually organising this support on a case-by-case basis rather than via dedicated staff or formal systems. We examined social workers' attitudes towards supporting contact (Neil, 2007a). The results of this suggested that agencies have a strong focus on the child's needs, but may not always recognise or meet birth relatives' or adoptive parents' needs for support in managing the psychological complexities of contact. The needs of birth relatives in particular may be overlooked and intervention with relatives focused on controlling risk rather than support or enablement.

The aims of the current study were to explore services provided to support post-adoption contact in complex cases. 'Complex' contact was defined as direct contact where agencies had an ongoing role in relation to the contact. This excludes, therefore, contact arrangements managed entirely between the birth family and the adoptive family, or between adoptive parents and parents or carers of the adopted child's siblings. The specific research questions were:

- What are the characteristics of adoptive parents, adopted children and birth relatives who are involved in complex direct contact arrangements?
- What are the experiences of adoptive parents and birth relatives of direct contact arrangements?
- What types of services to support contact do birth relatives and adoptive parents report using?
- What are adoptive parents' and birth relatives' experiences of using contact support services?
- How much do support services for direct contact cost?

In terms of the value base underpinning the research, there is no assumption that direct contact is always a good thing. Contact needs to be judged in terms of whether it promotes or impedes the child's developmental progress, including the developmental tasks specific to adoption. In understanding its quality, contact is conceived of theoretically as a relationship-based process that is both dynamic and transactional, and that adopted children, adoptive parents and birth relatives all contribute to the nature and quality of the experience (Neil and Howe, 2004).

Study design

This study was conducted in collaboration with eight agencies: one adoption support agency, six local authorities and one consortium of local authorities. The study used both qualitative and quantitative methods to answer the above questions. A group of adoptive parents and a group of birth relatives were recruited to act as consultants to the research process. They advised the research team about recruiting participants and data collection methods, data analysis and implications for practice. The research involved three strands.

The adoptive families study

We interviewed 51 adoptive parents and four long-term foster carers (these were carers of a sibling of an adopted child). We then followed up these parents approximately 16 months later, and 53 people (96%) took part at the second stage. Interviews focused on one index child and one direct contact arrangement with birth relatives. All except two of the children had been in public care before being adopted. The majority had experienced high levels of adversity in their early lives and 84 per cent had a history of abuse and neglect.

The average age at which children were placed for adoption was 3.7 years and the mean length of time that children had been with their adoptive families was 4.8 years. Five adoptive parents were from minority ethnic groups (9%), as were 14 of their index children (25%). Seven people were single parents (13%) and the rest were part of a couple. About half of the index children (49%) were having contact with a birth parent, grandparent or aunt. Just under one-third of children (31%) were having contact with birth siblings. One in five (20%) children had contact meetings that included both adult birth relatives and siblings. Most contact was once or twice a year and lasted between one and five hours. In over three-quarters of cases there had been no exchange of identifying information between birth family members and adoptive families. Our analysis focused first on the strengths and risks of adoptive families, in particular:

- whether or not the child had emotional or behavioural problems;
- adoptive parents' perceptions of the child's feelings about adoption;
- the relationship between the adoptive parent and the child, as reported by the adoptive parent;
- the adoptive parent's openness in communicating about adoption;
- the child's age at placement;
- whether or not contact involved a birth relative who had been the child's main carer and involved in the neglect or abuse of that child.

Adoptive parents' views of contact and contact support were studied as follows:

- the 'adoptive parent views of contact' measure;
- the adoptive parent's perception of the child's comfort with contact;
- the adoptive parent's comfort with contact;
- the adoptive parent's satisfaction with their relationship with the birth relative;
- the satisfaction of adoptive parents with their contact support;
- whether contact was "working very well" overall.

3

The birth relatives study

Thirty-nine birth relatives spanning three generations in the birth family took part in interviews: 21 birth parents, nine grandparents, seven adult siblings and two aunts. Most of these relatives (87%) were from the maternal birth family. Just over half had been the child's main carer prior to adoption. In all cases except one, the child had been adopted from the care system. Fifteen per cent of the sample was from a minority ethnic group. Ninety per cent took part in the second round of interviews. There was an overlap between the birth relative sample and the adoptive parent sample – of the 94 people we interviewed in total, 55 of these had a connection via contact to another person in the study.

We looked at the strengths and risks of birth relatives, focusing on the following factors:

- "coping with adoption": interview data were used to develop a three-dimensional measure looking at how people were coping with adoption. The three dimensions were "acceptance of dual connection", "feelings about the outcomes of adoption for the child" and "living with the impact of adoption on self";
- mental health (measured using the Brief Symptom Inventory);
- whether the birth relative had been the child's main carer prior to adoption.

We explored birth relatives' views in relation to:

- their satisfaction with contact;
- their satisfaction with contact support.

The economic analysis

The economic analysis aimed to estimate the cost of providing contact support services to birth relatives and adoptive parents over a 12-month period. Case workers completed diaries to enable us to estimate the amount of time spent providing each of the various services to support contact. From these, the monetary cost of providing different types of support was estimated by using published unit costs (Curtis, 2007). Agencies then provided information about the number and type of services that each birth relative and adoptive parent in the interview sample was provided with over one year. The costs of support services were combined with individuals' use of support services to calculate the costs for individual service users. Four different models of contact support were compared in terms of their costs.

Summary of key findings

What are the characteristics of adoptive parents, adopted children and birth relatives who are involved in complex direct contact arrangements?

- Adoptive parents, adopted children and birth relatives varied widely in terms of their strengths and risks, suggesting that contact is likely to be more complex in some cases than in others.
- Many children in the study were continuing to struggle with the impact of their early histories and had ongoing psychological or developmental problems that could make them vulnerable in terms of handling complex contact situations. For example, 44 per cent of children had emotional or behavioural problems, over half (51%) were reported by their parents to have very complicated feelings about their birth family and their status as an adopted person, and 29 per cent had problems in their relationship with their adoptive parents.
- Over half of children (51%) were having direct contact with the birth relative who had been their carer and who had neglected or abused them.
- The adoptive parents in the study generally scored very high on a measure of adoption communication openness, suggesting they bring a number of resources to the contact situation.
- A combined risks/strengths score was computed to quantify the risks that both adoptive parents and children brought to the contact situation. A minority of families (11%) had many more risks than strengths, one in five families (38%) had a mixture of strengths and risks, and just over half had many more strengths than risks (51%).
- In the birth relative sample, four relatives had been a carer for the child but had not been involved in neglect or abuse. Eighteen birth parents

had been the main carer and the child had been removed because of concerns of neglect or abuse. Seventeen birth relatives had never been the main carer for the child.

- Over half of the birth relatives (55%) had scores on the Brief Symptom Inventory within the clinical range.
- On the "coping with adoption" measure, over 70 per cent of the birth relatives scored mainly high or very high on "acceptance of dual connection". Three-quarters felt very positive about how the adoption had worked out for the child. On the dimension of "dealing with the impact of adoption on self", 60 per cent of birth relatives still had some or quite significant problems in managing the negative consequences of adoption, e.g. dealing with difficult feelings and re-engaging with wider life activities.
- Using coding from all three factors (mental health, coping with adoption, previous history of being the child's main carer), combined risks/strengths scores were calculated for birth relatives. A minority had many more risks than strengths (19%), 39 per cent had a mixture of strengths and risks, and 42 per cent had more strengths than risks.

What are the experiences of adoptive parents and birth relatives of direct contact arrangements?

- In the adoptive parent sample, contact arrangements were classified as "working very well" where very few problems had been experienced and where parents were very positive about the comfort and value of contact for themselves and their child. A second category, called "unresolved issues", included cases where adoptive parents had largely positive experiences but some difficulties had been experienced, through to very unsatisfactory cases where contact had stopped or was of very poor quality. Between 43 and 45 per cent of cases were "working very well" and between 55 to 57 per cent of cases had "unresolved issues".
- Contact "working very well" was significantly associated with the following factors:
  - the child not having emotional and behavioural problems ($p<.05$);
  - the child being under age two at placement ($p<.05$);

- the child not having contact with a person who had been their main carer and who had abused or neglected them (p<.01);
- higher adoption communication openness scores of adoptive parents (p<.01)
- higher adoptive family strengths (p<.01).

In addition, the child having a positive and unproblematic relationship with their adoptive parent was not statistically significant (p = .051), but future research is needed to examine this further, as it may be an important factor:

- Just over half of birth relatives (53%) were mainly satisfied with contact, 18 per cent expressed mixed feelings of satisfaction and dissatisfaction and 29 per cent were dissatisfied with many or most aspects of contact.
- Birth relatives' scores on the "coping with adoption" measure significantly predicted whether or not they were satisfied with contact. Relatives who were coping better with adoption were more likely to be satisfied than those who were coping less well. Satisfaction with contact was not significantly associated with whether or not relatives were scoring in the clinical range on the mental health measure (the Brief Symptom Inventory). Neither was having been the main carer for the child significantly associated with birth relatives' satisfaction with contact.
- Qualitative analyses of interviews with adoptive parents and birth relatives suggests that direct post-adoption contact is complex in different ways in different cases, but there are several key needs or challenges for people involved in having such contact. These include building and sustaining relationships, understanding one's role and the role of others, making sense of family boundaries, coping with the strangeness of the event and dealing with complex feelings.
- All contact arrangements appear to involve some level of challenge, and in all cases some level of benefit was apparent. The balance between these two sets of factors was very different in different cases.

What types of services to support contact do birth relatives and adoptive parents report using?

- From adoptive parents' reports of services received, five different types of contact support activity were coded according to the function they appeared to serve, as follows:
  - co-ordination and administration;
  - relationship-building;
  - protecting or promoting interests;
  - reviewing arrangements and planning;
  - providing emotional or therapeutic support.

Birth relatives also identified the five types of contact support that adoptive parents received. In addition, they identified a sixth category of intervention: "risk management and minimisation". This refers to interventions by the agency designed to minimise risks that birth relatives may present to the child or adoptive parents.

- The type of support activity most frequently received by adoptive parents was co-ordination and administration, followed by protecting or promoting interests. About one-third of parents received services related to reviewing and planning, about a quarter received emotional support and only one in five reported relationship-building activities.
- The service received by the most birth relatives was co-ordination and administration. Relationship building, reviewing and planning and emotional support were received by only a minority. Less than one in five birth relatives felt they had received services aimed at "protecting or promoting" their interests. About a third felt they had received interventions focused on risks they were perceived to present.
- The research identified four different models of contact support. *Administrated contact* was (in most cases) where the agency retained control of the setting up of contact meetings, but did not attend meetings or facilitate contact further by offering emotional support, relationship building or review and planning. The second model, *facilitated contact*, was again where families met without the support worker but the agency was intervening outside of the contact meeting in terms of emotionally supporting people, helping build relationships,

or planning and reviewing the contact. In the third model, *supervised and facilitated* support, workers attended the contact meetings and provided input aimed at relationship building, reviewing and planning, or emotional or therapeutic support. The fourth model, *supervised contact*, was where the agency arranged and supervised the contact but did not actively facilitate its working; they exercised control, but made little contribution to managing the dynamics of contact.

- About half of the adoptive parents received supervised and facilitated contact support. The remaining adoptive parents received, in roughly equal measures, one of the other models of contact support.

- Eight per cent of the birth relatives received administrated contact support, 25 per cent had facilitated contact support, 44 per cent received supervised and facilitated contact support and 22 per cent received supervised contact support.

What are adoptive parents' and birth relatives' experiences of using contact support services?

- Just over half of the adoptive parents (56%) were mainly satisfied and just under half (44%) had concerns about the support offered. Five factors were associated with satisfaction with contact support:
  - a relationship with a consistent worker who was caring, empathic and approachable;
  - workers who were professionally competent, and experienced in understanding and managing the dynamics of adoption and contact;
  - the agency striking the right balance between controlling the contact arrangements and allowing adoptive parents to be in control;
  - contact support that addressed not just their and the child's needs, but also the needs of the birth relatives;
  - support that was organised and forward thinking, anticipating rather than merely responding to challenges and changes in the contact.

- Just over half of the birth relatives (54%) were very happy with the contact support services they had received; the remainder (46%)

expressed several anxieties or concerns. Birth relatives were more likely to be happy with contact support where:

- they had a good relationship with the worker and the worker was an effective intermediary between them and the adoptive family, i.e. taking everyone's needs into account;
- contact support was planned and predictable and involved them in decision-making;
- clear explanations were given about the need for rules and boundaries, and any such boundaries made sense to the birth relative in terms of the risks they presented to the child;
- an element of emotional support was provided.

How much do support services for direct contact cost?

- The "average" adoptive family was estimated to have used 12 support services over a 12-month period at an average cost of £999 (range £0–£4,052). This includes services provided to adoptive parents and adopted child.

- The average birth relative received 8.9 services and the average cost over the 12-month period was £757 (range £0–£1,984).

- For adoptive families, the model of support with the highest costs was supervised and facilitated contact (an average cost of £1,371) and the cheapest model was administrated contact (an average cost of £395 per year). For birth relatives, the most expensive model was supervised contact (costing on average £1,004) and the least expensive model was administrated contact (£246 on average per year). Although the data presented are exploratory, they do suggest that some models of contact support are more expensive than others and that, therefore, it is important that services are targeted appropriately to needs.

- As well as differing in terms of cost, other differences between the four models of contact support are reported in terms of the strengths and risks of families receiving the models, the satisfaction of adoptive parents and birth relatives with support, birth relatives' satisfaction with contact, and whether or not contact was "working very well" according to adoptive parents.

- No one model of contact support emerged as the best overall, suggesting that different models of support may each be best in different cases.

Implications for practice

- How well contact arrangements progressed seem to be influenced by a number of factors to do with the child, adoptive parents, birth relatives and the relationships between these people. Taking account of these strengths and risk factors when planning contact, and when planning contact support, is likely to lead to more case-sensitive decision-making.
- Important roles that contact support services can play include helping people manage emotions, building and maintaining relationships between people, negotiating and managing risk and offering practical help.
- Suggestions for the provision of contact support services include:
  - ensuring that the model of contact support is matched appropriately to the needs and wishes of families and the strengths and risks in the case;
  - including families in the assessment of contact plans and contact support plans;
  - ensuring that attention is paid to the needs of all parties;
  - recognising the dynamic nature of contact;
  - where it is necessary for direct contact to be stopped, supporting people through and after this process.

Evaluation of the research

- Strengths of the research include:
  - data were collected from a number of key informants: adoptive parents, birth relatives and service providers. The retention of service users over the follow-up period was exceptionally high, as was the return of data from case workers;
  - distinct models of contact support were identified and costed;
  - adoptive parents and birth relatives were successfully involved as consultants in the research process.

- Limitations of the research include:
  - the unit costs employed on the project may underestimate the true cost of contact support;
  - the views of adopted children and young people were not included;
  - the research did not include contact support provided by specialist services in the independent sector.
- Future research could build on the current study by systematically evaluating the comparative benefits of the different models of contact support identified in this study. A much larger sample size would be needed to take account of all the relevant factors. In any such research where the outcomes of contact are to be studied, it will be important to seek the views of adopted children and young people.

1 Introduction: the policy context and literature review

Introduction to the research

The research summarised in this book is part of a larger study, the Researching Adoption Support project, the aims of which were to map, cost and evaluate services to support the birth relatives of adopted children and services to support post-adoption contact in complex cases. The study began with a mapping survey that jointly explored both of these areas of service provision; a brief summary of this stage of the project is provided in this chapter. The larger project then split into two branches: the "Supporting contact in complex cases" study, the subject of this book; and the "Helping birth families" study, the findings of which are explored in a separate book (Neil *et al*, 2010). These two studies were carried out by the same team, and much of the design and methods were shared between the two projects.

The Researching Adoption Support project is one of a number of studies funded by the Department for Children, Schools and Families (DCSF, now the Department for Education) in their Adoption Research Initiative. This study, like others in the initiative, was commissioned to explore issues relating to the implementation of the Adoption and Children Act 2002. This Act contained important changes in relation to the provision of post-adoption support services. One such change was the duty imposed upon local authorities to carry out an assessment of need for adoption support at the request of adopted children, adoptive parents and birth relatives (section 3). Support for all parties with post-adoption contact was specified as one of a range of adoption services that ought to be available.

The aims of the current study were to examine services provided to support direct post-adoption contact. The research explored the characteristics of adoptive and birth family members involved in direct contact arrangements, and the experiences of the adults involved about these contact meetings. The types of services people had received to enable them to maintain contact were explored and costed. The research was carried out in collaboration with eight agencies involved in providing contact support services (one adoption support agency, six local authorities and one consortium of local authorities). Fifty-one adoptive parents, four foster carers, and 39 birth relatives took part. The study employed both qualitative and quantitative methods.

In the remainder of this chapter, the legal and policy framework for contact will be discussed, including the important reforms made by the Adoption and Children Act 2002. Theoretical perspectives on adoption and contact will then be outlined. The particular challenges for all involved in contact when children have been adopted from the care system will be discussed. The research evidence about the impact of contact on adopted children and the potential benefits and risks is then examined. The chapter concludes with a consideration of research on adoption support services and services aimed specifically at supporting contact.

Legal, policy and practice background to the research

Currently, adoption in England and Wales primarily concerns the place-ment of children from public care, mostly those at the younger end of the in-care population age range (the average age for children adopted in 2008–09 was three years nine months and 74 per cent were aged four or under – DCSF, 2009). The need to maintain existing relationships between some older adopted children and birth relatives has been recognised. Direct contact has been seen as one way of achieving this. Statistics about rates and types of post-adoption contact are not routinely collected, but research suggests some form of contact with birth relatives after adoption is now the norm for at least 70 per cent of children (Parker, 1999; Performance and Innovation Unit, 2000). An ongoing exchange of letters and/or cards and photographs between adoptive parents and birth relatives mediated by the adoption agency, and usually referred to as 'letterbox contact', is the most common arrangement (Neil, 2000). A substantial minority of children will have face-to-face contact with members of their birth family. In Neil's survey of children under four (Neil 2000, 2002a), 17 per cent were having face-to-face contact with a birth parent or grand-parent after adoption. Face-to-face contact seems to be more common for older adopted children or between siblings. In Lowe *et al*'s (1999) study of children adopted over the age of five, 39 per cent of children were having direct contact with an adult birth family member. In a sample of older children adopted from care (the children were on average 5.7 years when the adoption plan was agreed), 31 per cent had face-to-face contact with a birth parent and 90 per cent with birth siblings in their first year after placement; these figures fell to 17 per cent and 55 per cent respectively at the time of follow-up seven years later (Selwyn, 2004). Research also suggests that it is more common for children to have contact with maternal relatives than paternal relatives and that this can result in gaps in children's knowledge about their birth fathers and extended family (Fratter, 1996).

Adoption agencies have a crucial role both in determining what contact an adopted child should have with their birth family members and in managing and supporting any post-adoption contact. A movement towards the acceptance and promotion of openness by adoption agencies has taken place over the past 20 years or so for both relinquished infants in the USA (Henney *et al*, 2003) and older children adopted from care in the UK and USA (Fratter *et al*, 1991; Parker, 1999; Frasch *et al*, 2000). Although there has been a general movement away from closed adoptions, there is evidence from the UK of considerable variation in the type and extent of post-adoption contact planned for children according to the agency making the placement (Neil, 2002a). The survey of 168 children placed by ten different agencies in England found that rates of children having face-to-face contact with adult birth relatives varied from nought to 33 per cent. Even among cases where face-to-face contact had been planned, differences in social workers' attitudes to the plan were apparent. Some insisted on contact (even when adoptive parents were reluctant), others mutually agreed contact with adoptive parents, and yet others opposed contact plans proposed by adoptive parents (Neil, 2002a).

Adoption and Children Act 2002: contact plans

The Adoption and Children Act 2002 modernised the legal framework for adoption in England and Wales and clarified the role of adoption agencies in planning and supporting post-adoption contact (Smith *et al*, 2006 provide a full summary). The Act does not include any presumption of contact for adopted children, but did introduce a new demand that contact must be considered and decided upon (s.46(6)), and that proposed arrangements must be set out in the child's placement plan. As Pearce suggests, 'the intention is to ensure that the issue is actively addressed and not sidelined' (Pearce, 2006, p 145). Decisions about contact should take account of the principle that the child's welfare throughout their life should be the paramount consideration.

The Act also introduced changes to the adoption process, abolishing freeing orders and introducing placement orders which authorise an adoption agency to place a child for adoption. Importantly, the court may make directions for contact under a placement order (ss. 26 and 27). Birth relatives can apply for contact with a child who is subject to a placement order. Any provisions made come to an end when the adoption order is made, at which point applications for contact would be dealt with under section 8 of the Children Act 1989. While section 26 orders cease at the point that an adoption order is granted, they ensure the continued involvement of the court in the period between placement order and adoption and thus may influence the search for adopters, contact during the early stages of placement and possibly the outcome of an adoption order application. Potentially, therefore, the Adoption and Children Act may provide more clarity about arrangements for contact during the transitional phase between a care order and an adoption order. However, it remains to be seen how the courts will exercise their powers.

A recent Appeal Court judgment (*re P 2008 EWCA Civ 535*) included guidance on this question and that of post-adoption contact. It concerned a case where, among other issues, it was considered vital for two siblings to have continued direct contact. The court considered it essential to make section 26 orders concerning contact for the period that the placement order was in force. With regard to post-adoption contact, the judgment included a summary of preceding case law, concluding that it has been rare to impose contact orders on prospective adopters as enforced contact is unlikely to be in the best interests of the child. However, in relation to the case in question, the Appeal Court concluded that 'in our judgment the question of contact between D and S, and between the children and their parents, should henceforth be a matter for the court, not for the local authority, or the local authority in agreement with prospective adopters' (para 147). Wall summed up as follows:

> *We do not know if our views on contact on the facts of this particular case presage a general sea change in post-adoption contact overall. It seems to us, however, that the stakes in the present case are sufficiently high to make it appropriate for the court to retain control over the question of the children's welfare throughout their respective lives under sections 1, 26, 27 and 46(6) of the 2002 Act; and, if necessary, to make orders for contact post adoption in accordance with section 26 of the 2002 Act, under section 8 of the 1989 Act. This is what Parliament has enacted. In section 46(6) of the 2002 Act Parliament has specifically directed the court to consider post-adoption contact, and in section 26(5) Parliament has specifically envisaged an application for contact being heard at the same time as an adoption order is applied for. All this leads us to the view that the 2002 Act envisages the court exercising its powers to make contact orders post adoption, where such orders are in the interests of the child concerned.* (para 154)

This judgment provides an interesting benchmark in case law, although it remains to be seen how courts will adjudicate in the future, and in what circumstances the court will take the view that a legal order to enforce contact is in the best interests of the child.

Adoption and Children Act 2002: post-adoption support

One of the aims of the Adoption and Children Act 2002 was to strengthen provisions for post-adoption support for children, adoptive parents and birth relatives. Local authorities have been given a duty to undertake an assessment of need for adoption support services on behalf of adopted people, adoptive parents and birth parents. They are required to provide assistance, including mediation services, in relation to contact arrangements between adopted children and their birth relatives. The Act also specifies that when a children's services department agrees upon a plan of adoption for a child in its care, the birth parents of this child must be offered independent support from a worker who is not the social worker for their child. While this stipulation could be met by simply providing a different worker from within the same agency, in 2005 over two-thirds (68%) of local authorities had chosen to buy or commission independent birth relative support services from voluntary adoption agencies or adoption support agencies (Sellick et al, 2006; Neil et al, 2010).

The Act clarifies who is responsible for providing support, for example, when adoptive parents move to a new area or when interagency placements are made (i.e. when the local authority seeking an adoptive home for a child in their care places the child with adoptive parents recruited and approved by another adoption agency). The local authority placing the child remains responsible for providing post-adoption support for three years after the child is legally adopted, although they may con-tract the provision of such services to other bodies such as other adoption agencies (e.g. another agency with whom they have placed the child), health or education services or adoption support agencies. Beyond this three-year period, adoption support becomes the responsibility of the local authority where the adoptive family reside. Adoption support agencies (organisations that do not make adoption placements but who provide post-placement support) must be registered and approved under this new legislation.

Theoretical perspectives on adoption and contact

Adoption has been theorised as a phenomenon that requires adopted people, adoptive parents and birth parents to negotiate lifelong psycho-logical challenges that are different from, or additional to, the challenges in non-adoptive families (Brodzinsky, 1987; Triseliotis et al, 1997). For the adopted child, the first challenge is to form an attachment to new parents, a process that is particularly complicated if a child's prior experi-ence of relationships is poor (Howe, 1998). The next challenge is to manage overt issues of loss and separation from established attachment figures (e.g. a birth relative or foster carer), and covert issues of loss such as the loss of biological connection to the adoptive parents, the loss of genealogical continuity, and the status loss of being different from non-adopted peers (Brodzinsky, 1990). Children need to retain a sense of connection to their birth family but also need to be fully integrated into their adoptive family (Schofield and Beek, 2006). Finally, the adopted child may face additional challenges in achieving a healthy sense of identity because of their disconnection from their birth family, a lack of background information and the need to make sense of *why* they were adopted (Hoopes, 1990; Grotevant, 1997). For the birth parents of the adopted child, the key psychological challenges are coming to terms with the loss of the child and understanding their role as a "biological" but not "psychological" parent (Brodzinsky, 1990; Thoburn, 1996; Neil *et al*, 2010). Psychological challenges for adoptive parents involve building a relationship with a child they have not given birth to and integrating this child fully into their family, while at the same time recognising that the child has different needs because they are adopted (Kirk, 1964). Adoptive parents need to be open to considering the meaning of adoption, for both themselves and their child, and should be willing to promote communication about adoption both within and beyond their family – these qualities being labelled by Brodzinsky (2005) as 'communicative openness'.

The approach to child adoption characterised as a "clean break and fresh start" has, over time, been revealed to be a problematic model for practice. Evidence has emerged of the potentially damaging consequences of secrecy for adopted children and the enduring need for some to discover their biological roots and the reasons for their adoption (Triseliotis, 1973; Howe and Feast, 2003). There has been a move towards a more open model of adoption involving a spectrum of practices aimed at adopted adults, including access to records, the adoption contact register and intermediary services for relatives seeking reunion. For children, life story work may be undertaken and children may have access in their adoptive placements to life story books, memory boxes and later-life letters. Contact (both direct and indirect) between adopted children and birth relatives has emerged as one potential way to meet the ongoing needs of adopted children.

Contact in itself is neither good nor bad. What is important is the extent to which it promotes or impedes the child's capacity to address the psychological challenges of adoption. The needs of the child must be considered paramount when decisions are made about contact, but they cannot be adequately assessed in isolation from the adults involved. Contact is a dynamic, transactional process and all parties can influence and be influenced by the contact arrangements (Neil and Howe, 2004). It is very clear that both birth parents and adoptive parents have a crucial role to play in supporting the experience of the child. Adoptive parents who are communicatively open (Brodzinsky, 2005) are empathic and undefended in supporting the child to retain their birth family connection. Such parents are likely to work hard to sustain successful post-adoption contact plans (e.g. Fratter, 1996; Berry *et al*, 1998; Lowe *et al*, 1999; Sykes, 2000; Brodzinsky, 2005, 2006; Neil, 2007b, 2009). Similarly, when birth relatives can allow the child to make new relationships and be fully part of the adoptive family – accepting that the adoptive parents are the psychological parents, while at the same time remaining caring and concerned about their child's welfare – contact is likely to be a positive experience for adoptive parents and children (Festinger, 1986; Grotevant *et al*, 1999; Lowe *et al*, 1999; Smith and Logan, 2004; Neil, 2007c, 2009). In thinking about the quality of contact, the individual characteristics of adoptive parents and birth relatives are undoubtedly important, but equally important is the relationship between the two sets of adults. Mutual trust and empathy, collaborative and proactive approaches to any difficulties that might arise, a shared commitment to the values and purposes of contact, and an ability to transcend individual differences and difficulties to place the interests of the child first have all been identified as central to beneficial and sustained contact (Grotevant *et al*, 1999; Macaskill, 2002; Logan and Smith, 2005; Grotevant, 2009; Neil, 2009). Conversely, where relationships between adults are strained contact may prove hard to sustain. Neil (2009) studied 30 contact cases where adoptive parents and birth relatives were both interviewed. When adoptive parents did not have an open attitude, and birth family members did not approve of the adoption, contact tended to confirm unfavourable views that the adults had of each other, leading to downward spirals of mutual negativity and a diminution of commitment to maintaining contact. In the following section, the particular complexities of contact for children adopted from the care system will be considered.

Contact in complex cases

The more complicated the adoption placement, the more challenging contact issues are likely to be (Barth and Berry, 1988; Neil and Howe, 2004). For relinquished infants whose birth mothers had few problems, a major US study found no evidence that face-to-face contact resulted in detrimental developmental outcomes for the child (Von Korff *et al*, 2006). In another study of children placed from difficult backgrounds, for those who were young and did not have established relationships with birth relatives, direct contact generally appeared positive and safe when children were followed up in middle childhood (Neil, 2004a). For older children with established relationships with birth relatives, the cost of cutting contact (in terms of the loss for the child) is highest, yet it is in just these cases that establishing positive contact may be most difficult (Macaskill, 2002; Neil and Howe, 2004; Selwyn, 2004). The psycho-logical challenges of managing adoption for all parties in the adoption triangle are arguably most complicated when older children are adopted from public care.

Older children adopted from care are a particularily vulnerable group. Selwyn, in a study of 130 children aged three to 11 with a best interests decision for adoption, found that nearly all the children had experienced at least one form of abuse and over two-thirds had experienced multiple forms of abuse. Thirty-eight per cent had been actively rejected by their parents, often suffering sadistic treatment. Just under half had physical injuries involving broken bones, head injuries, bite marks or burns (Selwyn, 2004). Rushton (2009), in his review of adoption support services, draws attention to the complex needs of adopted children.

Attachment theory suggests that infants have an innate drive to seek protection when frightened or distressed (Bowlby, 1988). When they are subjected to a stimulus that frightens them they will seek proximity to their principle caregiver. Once comforted, the attachment system is de-activated and the child is free to explore. Crucially, infants depend upon the caregiver to regulate their distress. Over the first years of life, the child develops selective attachments to specific caregivers. From repeated experiences with the caregiver, the child develops expectations of rela-tionships and what is likely to happen in times of need. Where children are neglected or abused they are unable to rely on their caregivers to protect and comfort them, or they are placed in a paradoxical situation where the very person from whom they seek protection is the cause of the distress (Main and Hesse, 1990). In such a situation, rather than the child being calmed there is no means of regulating intense emotional arousal. If children are exposed to prolonged experiences of abusive care they will develop maladaptive strategies to try to regulate arousal and control the environment. Early experiences of abuse and neglect can have long-term developmental consequences. Children who have experienced early neglect have more behavioural problems and difficulties in peer relationships than other children (Egeland *et al*, 1983). As adults they are at increased risk for a range of problems including anxiety, depression, eating disorders, substance abuse and criminal activity (Spertus *et al*, 2003). The effects of abuse are reviewed by Dozier and Rutter (2008) and include difficulty in forming a relationship with a caregiver (Milan and Pinderhughes, 2000), lack of empathy (George and Main, 1979), and later dissociative and externalising symptoms (Lyons-Ruth *et al*, 1993).

According to attachment theory, separation from the main caregiver is likely to be distressing for the child. With the exception of cases of severe institutional neglect, children who have been maltreated are still likely to have formed an attachment to their caregivers and to experience separation as a significant loss. Moreover, the ability of maltreated children to deal with separation will be compromised, compared to children who have received sensitive care in their early years. Children placed for adoption will bring the effects of their previous relationship history, plus the trauma of separation from their attachment figures, into their foster home and then adoptive placements. Contact can help to mitigate the effects of loss for adopted children but children with a history of maltreatment may be ill-equipped to deal with the emotions involved and will require sensitive support.

Children's histories and ongoing needs can pose challenges to adoptive parents in managing the connection with the birth family. The complex and sensitive nature of children's backgrounds, the need to present positive yet honest accounts of adoption and the different needs of different children in the same family can all make it harder for adoptive parents to be as communicatively open as they would like to be (Jones and Hackett, 2007). Adoptive parents may feel protective of their child and angry towards the birth relatives who abused or failed to protect the child. Where a child has particularly complex needs, the adoptive parents may feel undermined in their parenting role. Some adopted children are likely to be challenging to parent. There is evidence from studies of foster care that children presenting difficult behaviours elicit rejecting behaviours from caregivers (Dozier and Rutter, 2008). Children placed for adoption, particularly older children with a history of maltreatment, may have difficulty forming trusting relationships with their adoptive parents and may display a range of difficult behaviours. Rushton (2009) suggests that adoptive parents can have their 'confidence dented by a hard to manage child' (p 267). Sturgess and Selwyn (2007) point out that adoptive parents may be reluctant to ask for support, in case they are seen as failing in their role as parents. Contact reminds the adoptive parents of the child's connection with another family and may threaten their own sense of family identity (Lowe *et al*, 1999), particularly if the adoptive parents lack confidence in the parenting role.

A further complication of contact after adoption from care is that the birth relatives (especially birth parents) involved in such contact are likely to be living with a number of social and psychological difficulties, which can make positive participation in contact more difficult (Neil, 2007c). Birth parents of children adopted from care have very high levels of problems that indicate and lead to social exclusion. Neil's survey of 104 children adopted from care found almost half (45%) of birth mothers had a mental health problem, a third (34%) had a learning disability, over a quarter (28%) had a drug or alcohol problem and a quarter (23%) had a criminal record (Neil, 2000). There were high levels of social disadvantage; 68 per cent of birth mothers had never been employed and less than 5 per cent owned their own homes. These difficulties were central to why their children were removed from their care and placed for adoption. The removal of the child can precipitate a crisis for an already vulnerable parent (Neil *et al*, 2010). A report into services in Wales (After Adoption, 2007, p 13) described parents' lives 'spiralling out of control'. Parents' pre-existing problems may be exacerbated by the child being placed in care. They are ill-equipped to cope with the loss involved in having a child adopted.

Children adopted from the care system may have complex needs and may have experienced maltreatment within the birth family. Adoptive parents may have negative feelings towards the birth relatives who were responsible for placing the child at risk of harm. Birth relatives are disadvantaged and often have chronic difficulties. These factors make the psychological challenges posed by adoption harder to negotiate and make managing contact a complex task for all parties. Contact needs to be carefully considered – prioritising the needs of the individual child, but with an awareness that the relationships between the adults involved will influence the outcome for the child. Achieving a plan that is appropriate to the needs of the child and takes into account the needs of the adults is particularly difficult, given the context in which initial post-adoption contact plans are made.

Making decisions about and managing post-adoption contact is a challenging area of work for professionals. It can involve conflicts of interests between different parties and often raises ethical dilemmas about privacy and confidentiality, autonomy and paternalism, and deception and truth-telling (Harris and Lindsey, 2002; Reamer and Siegel, 2007). Different professionals may understand and interpret the same concepts (e.g. identity, the child's wishes and feelings, attachment, safety) in different ways (Harris and Lindsey, 2002). As Siegel (2003, p 417) argues, social workers may lack training in relevant skills and concepts and can be left 'to fly by the seat of their pants, guided only by uninformed intuition through a minefield of clients' intense emotions and issues'. The attitudes and assessments of other professionals involved in court proceedings (e.g. guardians ad litem, child mental health experts, judges) also contribute to the making of contact plans (Harris and Lindsey, 2002).

Contact planning is considered from the point when the child enters the care system and it forms part of the care plan for the child during legal proceedings. Post-adoption contact is planned at an extremely emotive time for birth relatives and adoptive parents. Freeman and Hunt (1998) studied the perspectives of birth parents in care proceedings and found that most felt marginalised, intimidated and confused by court proceedings. The legal process of care proceedings and adoption is inevitably adversarial and may result in birth relatives finding it hard to trust statutory services. Negotiating contact may feel tantamount to accepting the inevitability of the adoption at a point where birth relatives are still fighting to keep their child. In some cases, contact may even have been used as a bargaining tool to encourage birth parents to consent to the adoption (Richards, 1996).

Adoptive parents may not be included in the contact planning process. They may have been presented with a child for whom contact was planned and not felt able to voice their own qualms for fear of jeopardising the match (Logan and Smith, 2004). Logan and Smith found variation in the degree to which adoptive families felt involved in detailed contact planning. Adoptive parents in ten out of 61 families in the sample felt that contact planning was driven by the agency, the birth relative's solicitors or the guardian. They felt compelled to accept contact arrangements although they were unhappy with the contact plan. Similarly, Lowe *et al* (1999) suggest that when agreement with contact is a condition of approval or of a specific match, adoptive parents may agree without fully understanding the implications, or may voice agreement while not being fully committed to contact.

The impact of contact

Robust research evidence about the long-term outcomes of different types of contact is scant, particularly for children placed from public care (Brodzinsky, 2005; Quinton and Selwyn, 2006). Of central importance in guiding practice is the impact of contact on adopted children, although the experiences of the adults involved are also important, not least because adults' experiences of contact will affect the experiences of the children. There is evidence that contact can be beneficial for adoptive parents and birth relatives. For adoptive parents, there may be a greater sense of entitlement and increased sense of empathy for the child and birth family (Etter, 1993; Gross, 1993; Fratter, 1996; Berry *et al*, 1998; Lee and Thwaite, 1997; Grotevant and McRoy, 1998; Logan and Smith, 1999; Sykes, 2000; Neil, 2003a, 2007a) and greater satisfaction with the adoption process (Ge *et al*, 2008). For birth relatives, contact arrangements can help to assuage feelings of loss and promote their acceptance of the adoption (Etter, 1993; Christian *et al*, 1997; Cushman *et al*, 1997; Young and Neil, 2004; Neil, 2007c), and improve post-placement adjustment and satisfaction with the adoption process (Ge *et al*, 2008).

Children's satisfaction with contact

Studies of the views of adopted children and young people report general satisfaction among those having contact with birth relatives and a wish to continue contact (Thomas *et al*, 1999; Macaskill, 2002; Neil, 2004a, b; Adoption Policy Review Group, 2005; Logan and Smith, 2005). Where children expressed dissatisfaction with contact, it was often because they wanted increased contact in terms of the frequency of contact, mode of contact or number of birth relatives included (Thomas *et al*, 1999; Macaskill, 2002; Logan and Smith, 2005). The literature relating to children who are looked after by the state also reports a strong desire on the children's part to stay in touch with significant birth relatives if or when adopted (Harrison, 1999; Sinclair *et al*, 2005). Some adopted children view contact as an entitlement or human right (Fratter, 1996).

Contact with siblings has been reported to be very important to children in care (Harrison, 1999; Adoption Policy Review Group, 2005; Sinclair *et al*, 2005) and children have expressed fears about being estranged from siblings. This fear appears to be well founded (Thomas *et al*, 1999; Thoburn *et al*, 2000). For example, Thomas *et al* (1999) reported that 27 of the 41 children they interviewed had been placed separately from siblings but only 17 of the 27 had some form of contact (direct or indirect) with at least one sibling. Following adoption, contact between siblings is generally highly valued by children and experienced positively (Fratter, 1996; Macaskill, 2002).

Although many older placed children want to see their birth relatives after adoption, they may discriminate between different relatives and sometimes wish for contact to stop (e.g. Thomas *et al*, 1999; Macaskill, 2002; Wilson and Sinclair, 2004). There is evidence that those children who desire contact with birth relatives discriminate between meaningful and less meaningful relationships and between harmful and safe relationships. Children may, therefore, seek ongoing contact with some birth relatives and not others (Fratter, 1996) and do not typically wish to continue contact with hostile or abusive relatives. There is also evidence of the significance of relationships changing over time (Fratter, 1996). Some children with no contact are satisfied with this arrangement and a small proportion are highly averse to the suggestion of contact (Thomas *et al*, 1999; Thoburn *et al*, 2000). Overall, children feel strongly that they should be listened to and fully involved in decisions relating to contact (Adoption Policy Review Group, 2005; Fratter, 1996).

The benefits of contact

For children who are adopted from care, contact can be a complex experience. Even where children want to have contact, it may be emotionally demanding. Children typically report a complex mixture of feelings in relation to contact with birth relatives, including positive feelings of happiness and excitement at the same time as more negative feelings of anxiety (Macaskill, 2002; Neil, 2004a). Children have identified the benefits of contact, which include continuing relationships with birth relatives to whom they are emotionally attached, providing reassurance that a birth relative is safe (Macaskill, 2002; Smith and Logan, 2004), enabling them to understand the reasons why they were adopted (Thoburn, 2004) and increasing their understanding of a birth parent's difficulties, therefore reducing self-blame and assisting with identity issues, particularly when placements are transracial (Fratter, 1996).

Many of the benefits identified by children cluster around the theme of information. Children consider contact to be an important way in which to gain knowledge about why they were adopted, hear and discuss their life story first hand and learn about inherited traits (Fratter, 1996; Macaskill, 2002). It is important to adopted children that they receive information about their adoption and their family of origin, and not only historical information. A survey of over 200 adopted children and young people by the Children's Rights Director of the Commission for Social Care Inspection (Morgan, 2006) revealed that 71 per cent of children felt it was very important to be told about their life before being adopted. In addition, 29 per cent felt it was fairly important and 56 per cent very important to get "news" about their birth family. Of those children who wanted "news", some were seeking a general update about birth families while others wanted to be told about specific family events such as someone being born, someone dying, people getting married, someone falling seriously ill or birth relatives moving house. Some also needed explanations and reassurances from their birth relatives. There is some evidence to suggest that children with direct contact with birth relatives have access to more and better information relating to their adoption and their birth family and are more willing to seek out such information than those with indirect or no contact (Ryburn, 1995; Grotevant *et al*, 2008).

The risks and challenges of contact

There is evidence that in some cases contact meetings can disturb or unsettle children, especially where children have a background of abuse or neglect (Macaskill, 2002; Howe and Steele, 2004; Smith and Logan, 2004), indicating that careful consideration needs to be given to face-to-face contact between a child and relatives who have mistreated them. Selwyn (2004) reported that 21 per cent of children in a sample of those placed from difficult backgrounds were re-abused during unsupervised contact visits while in the care system and long-term foster care/adoptive placements. It has also been found that sibling contact after adoption can, in a small number of cases, introduce a risk of exposure to negative behaviours or sexual abuse (Head and Elgar, 1999; Macaskill, 2002). Children who have been abused or neglected may lack the emotional resources to deal with stressful situations. Howe and Steele (2004) argue that children who have suffered severe maltreatment may re-experience extreme states of emotional dysregulation during contact meetings. Where this is the case, contact is not advisable. However, Howe and Steele argue that adoptive parents who are emotionally available and respond sensitively to their child may, over the course of time, help the child to develop sufficient resilience to handle some renewed contact at a later date (Howe and Steele, 2004).

Wilson and Sinclair (2004), in their sample of children in long-term foster care who had suffered abuse, found that 31 per cent of placements disrupted where there were no prohibitions on contact, whereas 12 per cent disrupted when contact had been forbidden with at least one family member, although it was not necessarily the case that the child had no contact with any members of the birth family. This research suggests that in some circumstances forbidding contact with particular individuals can have a positive effect on placement stability. Wade *et al*'s (2010) study of fostered children found that the effect on placement stability of forbidding contact with at least one person in the birth family varied according to whether or not children had been maltreated. For maltreated children, forbidding contact with one person enhanced placement stability, but this was not the case for children who had not been maltreated. Where contact with certain individuals poses a risk to the child, it may be useful to consider whether contact with other members of the family would be beneficial. If contact with other relatives is planned, their ability to protect the child from the prohibited individual should be considered.

Contact meetings can be difficult for children because of the quality of interaction between the child and the birth relative. For example, in Macaskill's (2002) study, difficulties included rejecting or hostile behaviour by birth relatives towards the child, and distorted roles re-enacted in contact meetings. Children themselves have identified a number of scenarios that negatively affect contact, such as when a birth parent denies past abuse or avoids questions about the past, where birth relatives arrive late for contact or where siblings are unable to resolve feelings of guilt or anger relating to past abusive behaviours towards each other (Macaskill, 2002). In other cases, it may be that interactions are unsatisfactory because birth relatives and children simply do not know how to relate to each other anymore (Haight *et al*, 2002; Neil, 2002b). Children also find contact very challenging when tensions between adults are apparent and where these remain unresolved (Fratter, 1996; Macaskill, 2002). It is clear from these and other studies that while contact can have beneficial effects, positive outcomes are not inevitable and the quality of contact must be considered (Neil, 2003b; Neil and Howe, 2004; Grotevant *et al*, 2005; Quinton and Selwyn, 2006).

Key messages from research about adoption and contact support

Although research exploring support for direct contact after adoption is lacking, there is some literature about adoption support services in general, and Rushton (2009) provides a recent review of this topic. He argues that there is a lack of accurate information about how many adoptive families need a post-placement support service, and what form such services should take. However, he highlights the complex needs of many children adopted from the care system, and argues that mainstream services (e.g. child and adolescent mental health services – CAMHS) may lack both the capacity and adoption-specific understanding to help adoptive families. Hart and Luckock (2004) similarly argue for 'adoption competent' service provision. Rushton (2009) suggests that support workers need to recognise the challenges faced by some adopters in parenting a hard-to-manage child, and offer parents hope that they can improve the situation. Research by Sturgess and Selwyn (2007) illustrates that some adoptive parents may not want post-adoption support, or may feel hesitant about asking for help in case they are seen as failing. Rushton and Dance's (2002) survey of agencies in the UK suggests that service provision varies from area to area, and that few specialist services are available outside of urban centres.

In a survey of 873 adoptive parents carried out in the USA, Brooks *et al* (2002) found that less than 30 per cent of adoptive parents had used adoption support services. Parents who had adopted from public agencies (as opposed to private or voluntary agencies) were more likely to want clinical and specialist services, indicating greater needs of children adopted from care. Overall, these authors emphasise the needs of adoptive parents for information: information about the child's history and needs, and information more generally about dealing with adoption-related issues. They argue that these needs may not necessarily be apparent in the early stages of placement but can emerge over a period of years, sometimes as a result of the child's developmental changes.

Research by Atkinson and Gonet (2007) carried out in the USA suggests that adoptive parents value flexible adoption support services – that is, a range of different types of support (such as emotional support, advice and information, education, reassurance) that they can dip in and out of over many years as their needs and the child's needs change. The two types of adoption support service that parents in this study valued most were adoptive parent support groups and adoption-competent counselling. They wanted support from workers 'who have the capacity to view their world through an adoptive-sensitive lens' (p 100).

The research thus far discussed in this section is focused on adoption support services for adoptive families. There has been far less attention paid to support services for the birth relatives of adopted children. Some studies have suggested that social and emotional support following adoption is related to better adjustment for relinquishing birth mothers (Winkler and van Keppel, 1984; Bouchier *et al*, 1991; Howe *et al*, 1992). In relation to birth parents in contested adoption proceedings, Charlton *et al* (1998) argue that birth parents need advocacy, counselling and advice and information, and that these services are required before as well as after adoption. In our parallel study of birth relatives support services (Neil *et al*, 2010) we found that the aspects of support services that birth relatives particularly valued were the personal qualities of the worker, the independence and confidentiality of the service, and flexible and pro-active services. Independence and confidentiality were important because many birth relatives lacked trust and felt hostile towards statutory agencies. Flexible and proactive services were significant because the complex needs of birth relatives, together with their suspicion of pro-fessional involvement, meant that many people were "hard to engage" with service provision. However, our evaluation of support services found that for those birth relatives who did engage with services, the over-whelming majority of people expressed high levels of satisfaction with services. Birth relatives who had used support services appeared better able to cope with the adoption than those who did not, although the direction of effect was not established. The use of support services was related to improved mental health for birth relatives (Neil *et al*, 2010).

Systematic research into what works in supporting face-to-face contact in complex cases is lacking. A number of authors have highlighted the need for greater planning and support of direct contact arrangements (for example, Macaskill, 2002; Logan and Smith, 2004; Selwyn, 2004; Wilson and Sinclair, 2004). The need to take children's wishes and feelings into account has been identified, including the wish not to see certain birth relatives (Thoburn, 2004; Wilson and Sinclair, 2004). Very little is known about children's experiences of post-adoption contact support services. Macaskill (2002) reported that 23 of the 37 children she interviewed had experience of supervised contact. While 11 children identified benefits of such supervision – such as providing safety, maintaining control, ensuring the smooth running of contact and acting as an intermediary – nine children disliked supervision, considering it intrusive or stifling. Some authors have argued that contact support services must attempt to build working relationships between adults (Beek and Schofield, 2004) and that these relationships and the contact plans may need to be renegotiated over time (Grotevant *et al*, 2004). A few publications describe or suggest services that might help. These include: specialist mediation services where all parties have their own worker (Kedward *et al*, 1999; Macaskill, 2002; Sales, 2002); specialist contact venues with workers who are trained in facilitating meetings (Haight *et al*, 2002; Slade, 2002); individual casework support for birth parents (Crank, 2002; Haight *et al*, 2002, 2005) and financial support, especially for birth relatives (Millham *et al*, 1986; Macaskill, 2002). As Logan and Smith (2004, p 122) have described, 'Arranging contact is not a one-off event but the beginning of a process that involves complex work, negotiation and relationship building over time.'

Findings from the mapping survey of support for contact and support for birth parents

An earlier stage of the current research study carried out in 2005 involved the completion of questionnaires by 135 agencies, 60 telephone interviews with professionals involved in providing post-adoption support and two focus group meetings (Sellick *et al*, 2006; Sellick, 2007). The aims of this mapping exercise were to identify and describe the range and type of contact support and birth relative support services provided by local authorities, voluntary adoption agencies and adoption support agencies in England and Wales. This survey showed that, while the independent sector was heavily involved in birth relative support services, contact support services were mainly provided in-house by local authorities, necessitating an ongoing relationship between adoptive parents, birth relatives and these agencies. The activities of local authorities in relation to the provision of contact support services suggested that letterbox contact was the predominant activity. Many agencies had developed systems for supporting letterbox contact. In contrast, agencies were mainly supporting only small numbers of direct contact cases, usually organising this support on a case-by-case basis rather than via dedicated staff or formal systems.

Questionnaire respondents were asked to react to a case vignette, describing what action they would take to support contact in this case. The responses were examined in terms of workers' underpinning attitudes towards supporting contact (Neil, 2007a). This analysis suggested that workers have a strong focus on the child's needs. In contrast, the needs of birth relatives and adoptive parents to be supported in managing the psychological complexities of contact may not always be recognised or met. The needs of birth relatives in particular may be overlooked and proposed intervention with birth relatives often focused on control rather than support or enablement. Few responses to the case vignette suggested that agencies had embraced a systemic view of supporting post-adoption contact; contact support tended to be focused on the individual parties rather than on promoting communication and co-operation between the parties. This may not best meet children's needs, because if there is tension between adults in contact, meetings are unlikely to be comfortable for the child.

The aspect of the mapping study that examined support services for birth relatives suggested a number of ways in which support for contact and support for birth relatives were, or could be, linked in practice. Support for contact was identified as one dimension of supporting birth relatives and a useful way of engaging reluctant service users. Birth relative support services may indirectly benefit adopted children if they enable birth relatives to participate constructively in contact.

Summary

This chapter has summarised the aims of the research and set out the legal and policy framework underpinning contact. Relevant research literature concerning the psychological tasks involved in adoption, the complexities of contact for children adopted from the care system, the impact of contact on children and their families, and the role of adoption and contact support services has been reviewed. Key points are as follows:

- The research project aimed to explore the nature of, and evaluate, services provided to support direct contact arrangements between adopted children and members of their birth family. Ninety-four members of birth and adoptive families took part in two waves of interviews and data about service provision were also collected from case workers.

- New adoption legislation strengthens the position of both birth and adoptive families in relation to the provision of adoption support services, and services to support contact are among those that agencies should seek to provide.

- Direct contact can have benefits for adoptive parents, birth relatives and adopted children in helping them manage some of the psychological complexities that follow from adoption.

- Direct contact is more likely to be successful when birth family members support the child's membership of the adoptive family, and when adoptive parents support the child's membership of the birth family.

- Direct contact poses particular challenges when children are adopted from the care system. It is likely to be most difficult for children who are older at placement, who have established relationships with their birth family members or who are struggling with the ongoing impact of early neglect or abuse.

- Birth relatives whose children have been adopted from the care system may have complex social and psychological problems. They may struggle to cope with the loss of their child. They may not be involved in initial contact planning.

- Adoptive parents may have complex feelings about birth relatives who have harmed their children or put them at risk of harm. Adopters may have reservations about contact but feel obliged to accept proposals for fear of jeopardising the match.

- Direct contact for children adopted from the care system is usually valued by children and can have a range of benefits, including maintaining relationships, providing reassurance that a birth family member is safe and helping them to understand why they were adopted.

- In certain circumstances, contact may be experienced as difficult or harmful. It is important, therefore, that each case is carefully assessed to evaluate the potential benefits and risks involved.

- There is little directly relevant literature about "what works" in supporting direct contact. Messages from broader research about adoption support suggest that for both adoptive families and birth relatives the availability of support services is valued, and the use of support services can have beneficial effects.

- For both adoptive parents and birth relatives the use of support services may not be straightforward: adoptive parents may not wish to be seen as needy or vulnerable, and birth relatives may be mistrusting of statutory agencies.

- A survey by the current research team of the activities of local authorities and independent agencies in relation to supporting contact showed that most contact support is provided in-house by local authorities, with support for direct contact generally being organised on a case-by-case basis.

2 The supporting contact study: design, sample and methods

This chapter outlines our methodological approach, samples and research questions. Further details of our sample and methods are covered in the relevant chapters.

Research questions

The overarching aims of the supporting contact study were to explore and cost services to support direct post-adoption contact arrangements. The specific research questions we asked were as follows:

1. What are the characteristics of adoptive parents, adopted children and birth relatives who are involved in complex direct contact arrangements?
    - What are the pre-adoption backgrounds of children involved in direct contact arrangements?
    - How many children have emotional and behavioural problems as measured by the Child Behaviour Checklist or adoptive parent report?
    - What are adoptive parents' perceptions of their child's feelings about being adopted?
    - How are adoptive parent–child relationships described by adoptive parents?
    - How open are adoptive parents to thinking and communicating about adoption and contact?
    - To what extent do birth relatives support the child's position in their adoptive family (dual connection)?
    - How well are birth relatives coping with the impact of adoption?
    - How do birth relatives feel about the child's progress in the adoptive family?
    - What levels of psychological stress do birth relatives experience?

2. What are the experiences of adoptive parents and birth relatives of direct contact arrangements?
   - What is the nature of direct contact arrangements in terms of who is involved and the frequency, duration and location of meetings?
   - What do adoptive parents and birth relatives value or not value about direct contact arrangements and what are the issues they need support with?
   - How comfortable and satisfied with contact are adoptive parents and birth relatives?
   - How comfortable with contact do adoptive parents believe their child to be, and how do they describe their child's reactions to contact meetings?

3. What types of services to support contact do birth relatives and adoptive parents report using?
   - What are the different types of services that birth relatives and adoptive families receive to help them maintain direct contact arrangements?
   - Are there different models of contact support and, if so, what are they?
   - Are there differences in services provided to adoptive families versus those provided to birth relatives?

4. What are adoptive parents' and birth relatives' experiences of using contact support services?
   - What aspects of support services do adoptive parents and birth relatives value or not value?
   - How satisfied are adoptive parents and birth relatives with the contact support services they receive?

5. How much do support services for direct contact cost?
   - How much of a support worker's time does it take to support a birth relative or adoptive parent and what are the different costs of providing each support service?
   - How many and what types of different services did support agencies provide to each person in the study over a one-year period?

- What does it cost to support birth relatives and adoptive parents for a one-year period?
- Do different models of contact support incur different costs?

Our methodological approach

The study is underpinned by the assumption that contact may or may not benefit adopted children and that whether or not benefits are experienced depends on the quality of contact arrangements. Contact is conceived of theoretically as a relationship-based process that is both dynamic and transactional, and adopted children, adoptive parents and birth relatives all contribute to the nature and quality of the experience (Neil and Howe, 2004). In the words of Neil and Howe:

> *The value or otherwise of contact is determined by the views, thoughts, feelings and behaviours which the child, the adopters, and the birth parents bring to the conduct and management of the event. Because contact has the capacity to be a highly charged and stressful experience for one or more of the participants, their psychological strengths and weaknesses, including their coping skills, will be brought into play.* (p 229)

The overall theoretical model for our analyses therefore had three components. First, the characteristics of the adoptive parents, adopted children and the birth relatives – their strengths and risks; second, the services that people received – the support for contact; and third, the experience of contact and contact support, as reported by adoptive parents and birth relatives. This model is illustrated in Figure 2.1 below.

We recognise that the relationship between the characteristics of the people involved in contact and the experiences of contact in this model is likely to be bi-directional. In other words, the characteristics of adoptive parents, birth relatives and adopted children influence how contact progresses and is experienced, but these characteristics are also likely to be influenced and possibly changed by the experience of contact itself. As Figure 2.1 shows, our theoretical model also includes a time dimension. This is based on our understanding that contact is transactional and dynamic (Neil and Howe, 2004): contact is something that is liable to change as the people involved in the arrangement change.

Figure 2.1
The complexity of the contact experience

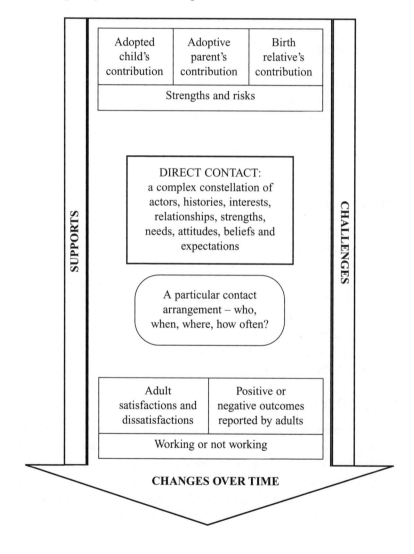

Summary of the study design

This study was conducted in collaboration with eight participating agencies. A mixed methodology using both qualitative and quantitative methods was employed. The study had a longitudinal design, following up birth relatives and adoptive parents over a time period and measuring the intervention they received over this time gap. The study focused on contact arrangements that were direct (defined as involving face-to-face meetings between the child and birth relative/s) and agency supported (where either the local authority or an independent agency had some involvement in the contact after adoption, i.e. contact arrangements that were entirely managed by families were excluded). The research involved three main strands: the adoptive families study, the birth relative study and the economic analysis. Reference groups of adoptive parents and birth relatives were consulted at the planning, analysis and results stages of the study.

Ethical approval and research governance

Prior to beginning the study, approval for the research was obtained from the Association of Directors of Social Services (in 2005). The study was also approved by the University of East Anglia's School of Social Work and Psychosocial Sciences ethics committee. Individual agencies then needed to give their approval. Two local authorities required us to complete formal research governance procedures before participation in the study would be agreed. The other agencies agreed to take part in the research without asking for these formal procedures, usually after detailed discussion with the research team, often including a visit to the agency.

The participating agencies

We conducted this research in collaboration with eight agencies, and the number of adoptive parents and birth relatives we recruited through each are detailed in Table 2.1 below. We invited agencies to help us with the study, bearing in mind the following criteria. First, we wanted to recruit people from a range of agencies to reflect variety in providing contact support. Second, we wanted to include larger agencies who were supporting relatively large numbers of face-to-face contact arrangements in order to efficiently recruit our target numbers of people. Third, we wanted to include agencies likely to be supporting contact for minority ethnic families. Fourth, we wanted to include different types of agencies: we knew that most contact support is managed by local authorities, and these agencies therefore are the largest group, but we also sought to include an adoption support agency and a consortium of local authorities.

The first six agencies listed in Table 2.1 were full participants in the study; that is, we asked them to put us in touch with all families they were supporting with direct post-adoption contact. To ensure we had a good representation of black and minority ethnic families, we recruited two further agencies working with very large minority ethnic populations (i.e. two inner-London boroughs) who agreed to put us in touch with minority ethnic families (defined as where the birth relative, the child or the

Table 2.1

Numbers of adoptive parents and birth relatives recruited via participating agencies

	Adoptive parents		Birth relatives	
	n	*%*	*n*	*%*
LA 1 (a large home county)	12	21.8	10	25.6
LA 2 (a consortium of five local authorities)	7	12.7	5	12.8
LA 3 (a large English county)	12	21.8	7	17.9
LA 8 (East London borough)	5	9.1	0	0
LA 9 (North London borough)	2	3.6	0	0
ASA 1 (an adoption support agency)	1	1.8	3	7.7
LA 7 (Inner London borough – South)	3	5.5	0	0
LA 4 (Inner London borough – North)	11	20	12	30.8
Other sources	2	3.6	2	5.2
Total	**55**	**100**	**39**	**100**

LA = local authority
Percentages may not add up to add due to rounding.

adoptive parent were of minority ethnicity). Two adoptive parents and two birth relatives were recruited into the study via agencies participating in our parallel "Helping birth families" study and these are represented in the table under the category of "Other sources".

Although we included a number of agencies in our research, we were not aiming to compare contact support practices between agencies. Our mapping survey did not suggest that agencies had developed discreet or particular models of contact support. We also considered it likely that the amount and type of contact support delivered to families could vary significantly within agencies. Our approach, therefore, was to develop typologies of contact support inductively from our data and to compare the costs and consequences of these.

Recruiting adoptive parents and birth relatives into the study

An extensive process of consultation with our birth relative and adoptive parent reference groups was undertaken before we attempted to recruit people into the study. The aims of this consultation exercise were to help us understand what might motivate adoptive parents and birth relatives to take part in the study and how to prepare the recruitment materials appropriately. Although we consulted with adoptive parents and birth relatives in separate groups, the key points of advice that we received from each were very similar and included:

- to make recruitment materials look professional and attractive;
- to keep the wording brief and clear;
- to emphasise that taking part in the study was an opportunity to help other adoptive parents/birth relatives;
- to include a freephone number via which people could contact us;
- to set up a website that potential participants could access;
- to try and resist agency attempts to screen who was or was not invited into the study – that birth relatives and adoptive parents should be allowed to make up their own minds about participation, not have the agency decide on their behalf.

We followed all of this advice and had leaflets professionally designed and accompanying websites set up. Invitation packs included leaflets, reply slips and postage-paid envelopes. Potential participants could contact us by post, the freephone number, email or an online form on the website. Most adoptive parents responded by post or phone but some used email or the online form. We asked the participating agencies to forward an invitation to take part in the study to all adoptive parents and birth relatives involved in direct contact arrangements that the agency had some role in supporting. Adoptive parents, foster carers and birth relatives who responded to the invitation to participate were contacted by phone, the study was explained further and their questions were answered. If people felt happy to proceed, a date was arranged for the interview. We suggested that the interview be done by phone, but made it clear to people that if they preferred a face-to-face interview we would be happy to arrange this. Our adoptive parent and birth relative consultants had advised us to offer the option of face-to-face interviews, and it turned out to be a preferred option for quite a number of people, especially birth relatives.

Our original aim was to recruit 45–50 contact cases, interviewing birth relatives and adoptive parents. This would have allowed us to compare the different perspectives of people in the same case. However, it quickly became clear that if we restricted ourselves only to cases where we could get the agreement of all parties to participate it would take us a long time to recruit our sample and we would lose the opportunity to interview many people who were willing to take part. Furthermore, cases where both sides agreed to participate may not have been representative of cases as a whole, e.g. if both sides were more likely to participate when contact was functioning well. We therefore revised our plans and aimed to interview approximately 90–100 people over all. Where contact was between two or more siblings (or sets of siblings) in different adoptive placements, we asked agencies to forward the invitation to both (or all) sets of adoptive parents. Where an adopted child was having contact with a birth sibling in a foster placement we asked the agency to forward the invitation to both the adoptive parent and the foster carer. Where an adopted child was having contact with an adult birth relative (birth parents, grandparents, adult sibling or other relatives) we asked for the invitation to be extended to the adoptive parents and these adult birth relatives.

Of the 94 people we interviewed, 55 had a connection to another person in the interview sample and the overlap between cases was quite complex. We interviewed (separately) 19 "pairs" of people (e.g. the adoptive mother and the birth relative). Other "matched" cases involved more complex networks of people (e.g. the adoptive mother, the birth mother and the grandmother). Three matched cases were particularly complex and all involved sibling group contacts (e.g. in one case where the contact arrangements involved nine siblings meeting together, we interviewed two adoptive parents, two adult siblings and one foster carer of an older sibling). In many cases, therefore, we heard about contact from more than one perspective. While this undoubtedly informed our thinking, we did not undertake any analysis specifically at the level of a contact case because of the small numbers of each type of matched case, the complexity of overlaps between cases and the fact that much of our coding required the identification of one child, one birth relative or one adoptive parent.

The adoptive families study: data collection

Two interviews were conducted with adoptive parents (on average) 16 months apart (range = 14–22, sd = 1.6). Fifty-one adoptive parents and four foster carers took part in the interviews at Time 1 – a total of 55 interviews. Fifty-three people (96%) took part again at Time 2. One adoptive parent did not respond to our contact and one foster carer did not take part because the placement of the adopted child's sibling with her had broken down. Almost all adoptive parents were happy to be interviewed over the phone: just one adoptive parent at Time 1 wanted a home interview and a different adoptive parent wanted this at Time 2. Adoptive parents were sent a store voucher to thank them for their participation. Full details of the parents in the adoptive families study are given in Chapter 4. For the sake of brevity and (in some places) to prevent cases being identified, foster carers and foster children are referred to as adoptive parents and adopted children throughout the report. Where we felt it was necessary to distinguish between the two, we have done so.

Semi-structured interviews with adoptive parents

Our interview schedule was designed in consultation with our adoptive parent consultancy group. A semi-structured but fairly open style of interview was used in order to allow parents to describe experiences in their own words. Most parents in the study had more than one adopted child (see Chapter 4) and one adopted child could be having more than one face-to-face contact arrangement with birth family members. Therefore, before conducting each interview we discussed with parents which child in their family (the index child) and which contact arrangement for this child (the target contact) the interview would focus on. Because we were aiming to study complex situations we asked adoptive parents to focus on the contact arrangement they felt was most difficult or problematic, especially in terms of difficulties for the child. The interview at Time 1 covered the following areas:

- descriptive information about the adoptive family, including reasons for adopting;
- the adopted child – their history prior to the placement for adoption;
- the adopted child's development and relationship with adoptive parents;
- family communication about adoption, including the child's feelings about and understanding of being adopted and the parent's behaviour and feelings about communicating about adoption;
- the contact – how plans had evolved and how contact was experienced by parents and child. This section of the interview included three closed questions where adoptive parents were asked to give a number from 1 to 10 to indicate how comfortable they believed their child to be with the contact, how comfortable they personally felt about the contact, and their satisfaction with their relationship with the birth relative involved in the contact (see Chapter 7);
- services to support contact – what support do parents receive from agencies or other sources and what are their experiences of this support.

The interview at Time 2 did not ask adoptive parents to repeat background information about their child's adoption. With other areas of the interview, parents were asked to provide an update on what had happened since the last interview and how they and their child were feeling about things now. Parents were asked again to answer the three closed questions requiring answers from 1 to 10.

Because our plan was to interview people by phone, consent to participate in the study was obtained verbally at the beginning of the interview and was recorded. People were asked to give permission for the interview to be recorded; they were informed about the confidentiality policy and were told about their right to withdraw, take a break or skip certain questions. People were informed about the intended goals of the study. Parents who were using support services in relation to post-adoption contact were asked to give their permission for us to ask the appropriate agency to fill in the service use diary (see below). Interviews were recorded either digitally or on tape. All interviews were fully transcribed.

The "adoptive parent views of contact" measure

Adoptive parents were asked to complete a 16-item Likert scale to measure their views of contact (see Chapter 7 for further details). This measure was based on the scale devised by Siegel (2003), with adapt-ations being made by the current research team. This measure was posted to adoptive parents at Time 1 and again at Time 2 and they were asked to send it back to the research team.

Child Behaviour Checklist

Adoptive parents were asked to complete the Child Behaviour Checklist (CBCL) for 6–18-year-olds (Achenbach and Rescorla, 2001). The CBCL is a questionnaire for the assessment of competencies and behavioural/ emotional problems, as reported by parents or guardians. It has 118 items that describe specific behavioural and emotional problems, plus two open-ended items for reporting additional problems. Two broad groups of symptoms, designated as Internalising and Externalising, and a Total Problems score can be obtained and these can be broken down into normal, borderline and clinical ranges. Parents were asked to complete the CBCL about their child at Time 1 and Time 2 and this measure was posted to people in advance of the interview.

The birth relative study: data collection

Two interviews were conducted with birth relatives (on average) 16 months apart (range = 13–20, sd = 1.8). Thirty-nine birth relatives took part at Time 1 and 35 were retained in the study at Time 2 (90%). Ten birth relatives at Time 1 (26%) and eight of those interviewed at Time 2 (23%) chose to be interviewed during a home visit; it was clearly good advice from our consultants to have this as an option. Full details of the birth relatives who took part in the interviews are given in Chapter 5.

Semi-structured interviews

The procedures for obtaining informed consent from birth relatives (including their consent to ask the agency to provide us with information about services provided) were the same as those described above for adoptive parents. Interviews were taped and transcribed and birth relatives were offered either a store voucher or, if we were making a home visit, a small cash gift as a thank you for participating in the study. The method of conducting the interviews was the same as described above for adoptive parents.

The interview schedule was again devised in consultation with our birth relative consultants group. A fairly open style of interview was felt to be most appropriate by both the research team and the birth relative consultants. The interview at Time 1 covered the following areas:

- basic details about self;
- the adopted child – how they came to be adopted;
- their relationship with the child's adoptive parents;
- contact arrangements with the adopted child;
- support for contact – from the agency or other sources and views of these;
- current feelings about the child and about the adoption, and their understanding of their role in the child's life;
- their current general welfare/functioning.

The interview at Time 2 did not ask relatives to repeat background information about their child's adoption. With the other areas of the interview, birth relatives were asked to provide an update on what had happened since the last interview and how they were feeling now.

Brief Symptom Inventory

The Brief Symptom Inventory (BSI) (Derogatis, 1993) is a 53-item self-report inventory that measures psychological symptoms (see Chapter 6 for further details). The test was administered at the end of the interview with birth relatives. If the interview was by phone, in most cases the person completed the measure over the phone with the interviewer. In a few cases, the measure was sent and posted back later. The test was administered at Time 1 and Time 2. The first BSI that birth relatives returned was used.

Data analysis in the adoptive family and birth relative samples

The analysis of data collected from adoptive parents and birth relatives took the following forms:

- Some interview data were analysed purely qualitatively using thematic analysis (Boyatzis, 1998). To assist this process, firstly a qualitative data analysis software package (Nvivo 2) was used and secondly, detailed case summaries were written for each interview.
- Other interview data were used to produce categories based on researcher ratings. For example, we used researcher ratings to code the types of support for contact people received, their satisfaction with contact support, birth relatives' satisfaction with contact, birth relatives' "coping with adoption", and adoptive parents' "adoption communication openness". These researcher ratings are described in more detail in the relevant chapters.
- The BSI and CBCL standardised measures were scored according to protocols described in their manuals.
- All quantitative data were entered into SPSS and, where appropriate, statistical analyses (as described in the findings chapters) were carried out. Where non-parametric or parametric statistics were used, the assumptions of each test were first checked.

The use of case material

Where we have used case material in this book, including quotes, we have changed people's names and in some cases other details that might enable families to be identified. We have not necessarily used the same names for cases throughout the report; this is to make cases less identifiable.

The economic analysis

Economic evaluation is the comparative analysis of alternative courses of action in terms of both their costs and their consequences (Drummond *et al*, 1997). The approach used in this study was to compare the costs of four different models of contact support (developed from the data in this study) with a range of benefits by presenting them in a tabulated form. This approach, termed a 'cost consequence analysis' (CCA) (Mauskopf *et al*, 1998), has been heralded as a good way to present (often confusing) economic information to decision-makers (Coast, 2004). The "consequences" we studied were: whether or not contact was working well from the adoptive parent perspective; whether or not birth relatives were satisfied with contact; whether or not birth relatives and adoptive parents were satisfied with contact support.

The economic analysis involved a number of stages as follows:[1]

1. **Estimating how much time it takes to support direct contact**
   Time diaries, referred to as case worker diaries, were developed to accurately estimate the amount of time taken for each service and activity provided by case workers to birth relatives and adoptive parents. These case worker diaries were designed to provide details of both direct activities (those involving meetings or phone calls with the service user) as well as indirect activities (including working indirectly with the service user via a letter or email, as well as travelling and administrative activities). Indirect activities are often overlooked, but without this preparation time it can be impossible to effectively provide the face-to-face services.

---

[1] Full details of the methodology of the economic analysis, including the measures used, can be obtained by contacting the first author.

The case worker diaries were used to provide an estimate of each respondent's average time commitment for each support service and activity combination. These were then further summarised to provide a representation of the average time commitment across the whole sample. Means, medians and the interquartile range were estimated in order to understand variation across the sample.

2. **Valuation of time**

The value of the time committed to providing each support service was estimated by applying published unit costs. The Personal Social Services Research Unit (PSSRU) estimated that in 2007, one hour of service user-related work for a social worker who earns an average annual salary of £26,748, costs £39 per hour (Curtis, 2007). Therefore, if it takes an average of 30 minutes to provide information and advice to an adoptive parent or birth relative, the estimated cost is £19.50 (39 x 0.5). An alternative approach would be to use the salaries of respondents (these were collected in the case worker diaries). However, using nationally prescribed costs makes the resulting costs more generalisable to the wider population of post-adoption service providers.

3. **Working out the amount of services used by individual service users**

In order to cost the provision of contact support, it was necessary to record the support provided (or not provided) to service users (adoptive parents and birth relatives). To undertake this task a service use diary was developed. This diary was to be completed for each birth relative and adoptive parent recruited to the study for a 12-month period. The service user's case worker logged which and how many of the services the person was offered/provided. The information collected in these diaries was aggregated for each type of support service. The total number of services provided to each service user was also estimated.

4. **Costing services to individuals**

The unit costs of support services (as estimated using the case worker diaries) were combined with the use of support services (as collected in the service use diaries). The total cost of providing post-adoption support services to birth relatives and adoptive parents was then estimated. The total cost of the "average" adoptive parent and birth relative was estimated, and analysis was undertaken to compare costs across agencies, specifically the four local authorities that provided the lion's share of the sample.

5. The cost consequence analysis

The final stage of the economic analysis was to work out the average cost of contact support services across the four contact support models identified in the study. This was done by averaging the costs of individual service users within each of the four contact support models. These average costs are reported alongside the outcomes of interest, as described above.

Summary

This chapter has summarised the aims and methods of the project. The aims of this study were to explore the nature of services provided to support post-adoption contact in complex cases, and to look at adoptive parents' and birth relatives' experiences of these. Key points are as follows:

- The study is underpinned by the assumption that contact may or may not benefit adopted children, and that whether or not benefits are experienced depends on the quality of contact arrangements. Contact is conceived of theoretically as a relationship-based process that is both dynamic and transactional, and that adopted children, adoptive parents and birth relatives all contribute to the nature and quality of the experience (Neil and Howe, 2004).
- The specific research questions we strove to answer were:
  1. What are the characteristics of adoptive parents, adopted children and birth relatives who are involved in complex direct contact arrangements?
  2. What are the experiences of adoptive parents and birth relatives of direct contact arrangements?

3. What types of services to support contact do birth relatives and adoptive parents report using?
4. What are adoptive parents' and birth relatives' experiences of using contact support services?
5. How much do support services for direct contact cost?

- To answer these research questions we worked with eight different support providers: six local authorities, one consortium of local authorities and one adoption support agency. We used a mixed methodology, employing both qualitative and quantitative methods.
- We collected data both from adoptive parents and from birth relatives at two points in time approximately 16 months apart. These families were all involved in having direct face-to-face contact after adoption, and all of these contact arrangements involved an ongoing role for the agency. A total of 94 people took part (55 adoptive parents and 39 birth relatives) and the retention of people in the study at the second wave of interviews was over 90 per cent.
- Qualitative interview data were used to understand people's experiences of contact and of contact support services. In order to understand how contact was working out and the impact of support services on contact, we took account of the strengths and risks of adoptive parents, birth relatives and adopted children – the personal characteristics they bring to bear upon the contact situation.
- From the reports of adoptive parents and birth relatives we developed four different categories of contact support.
- The economic analysis element of the project generated individual costs for the support services received by the individuals participating in the study, and generated costs for the different support models.

3 The adoptive parent sample

This chapter describes our sample of adoptive families and outlines their contact arrangements. It explores the demographic characteristics of the adoptive parents and the adopted children.

The parents

A total of 55 parents participated in the study. Fifty-one were adoptive parents and four were foster carers; in most subsequent sections of this report both of these groups are referred to as "adoptive parents". The foster carers were included because their fostered child was having contact with one of the adopted children in the study. One adoptive mother was interviewed twice because she had two adopted children from different birth families, both of whom were having direct contact and both of whose birth relatives took part in the study.

The gender of parents

Because we were doing most interviews by telephone, we could only speak to one parent. We interviewed 51 mothers and four fathers.

The marital status of parents

Seven interviewees (13%) were single parents. The rest were part of a couple: 45 parents were part of a married couple, one mother was cohabiting with her male partner and two mothers had female partners.

The ethnicity of parents

Ninety-one per cent of our interviewees described themselves as white, in most cases white British. Three people were white Irish and one person was Australian. Of the remaining five people, two were black Caribbean, two of dual heritage and one was Indian.

Employment

Almost half of the parents (n = 27, 49%) were working full time or part time outside of the home at the time of the first interview. Nineteen people described themselves as full-time stay-at-home parents (34.5%) and eight people (14.5%) were employed as foster carers (this includes four adoptive parents as well as the four foster carers). One adoptive parent was retired.

Of the 27 parents who were employed, most people were working in professional or managerial roles. Over half (n = 16) were working as education, social work or healthcare professionals, including two adoptive parents who were doctors. Seven people worked as accountants, or finance or IT managers. One person was an engineer and one was a church minister. One parent was a kitchen assistant and another was a massage therapist.

Of those 19 adoptive parents (in almost all cases adoptive mothers) who were full-time parents, the range of their professional backgrounds/work experience seemed quite similar to that of the parents who were currently employed. Four people had worked in education or social work, two were scientists, four had been in administration/management, one was a town planner and one person had worked in the fashion industry. Three people had formerly been full-time foster carers and two had worked in unskilled jobs (cleaner, catering assistant). Information about the employment history of two parents was missing.

Housing

Almost all adoptive parents (n = 51, 93%) lived in owner-occupied accommodation. Only four people lived in rented accommodation (7%).

Age

The age of parents at the time of the first interview ranged from 31 to 62, the average age being 45 (sd = 6.1).

The type of adoption and motivation to adopt

Of the 51 adoptive parents, six (12%) had adopted a child they had previously fostered, two (4%) had adopted a child from within their birth family (one aunt, one grandmother) and three people (6%) had adopted a child already known to them. In over three-quarters of cases (78% n = 42) the child was previously unknown to the adoptive parents.

Of the four foster carers who took part in the study, two had begun to foster the child on a short-term basis and the placement had become long term. One foster family had specifically applied to foster a child they already knew, and this was the only child they fostered. One foster family had begun fostering the child on the understanding that they would be offering her a permanent placement.

Adoptive parents (n = 51) were asked to say why they wanted to adopt the child. Obviously, what all the parents had in common in answering this question was the desire to become a parent or to parent an additional child or children. In terms of the reasons for choosing *adoption* as the way to become a parent, responses were coded into four categories that were not mutually exclusive:

- *Infertility* (n = 32, 63%): Most of these parents had never had a birth child. Three adoptive couples had a birth child but were unable to have any further children. In two more couples, the adoptive father had children from a previous relationship. People's descriptions of their pathways from infertility to adoption were varied, suggesting it is important not to assume that all adoptive parents with infertility motivations are the same. Some people described extensive attempts at fertility treatment, considering adoption only when all hope of achieving a successful outcome was extinguished. This was usually linked to a strong desire to have a birth child and a period of adjustment to the idea that this was not to be. As one adoptive mother explained, she and her husband:

  > *needed to try all the options to have our baby . . . I needed to go through that in order to accept that this wasn't going to be for us. So it was definitely a second choice to adopt and it did take a number of years of talking about it.*

Other people moved much more quickly to adoption without trying all (or any) of the infertility treatment options. One adoptive mother explained that she chose adoption instead of attempting in vitro fertilisation because it 'seemed to be more of a certainty and I was quite happy to go along with that'. Often this was connected to a higher level of comfort with the idea of raising a child that they were not biologically related to; as one adoptive mother explained, 'I like children and we are used to other people's children so that didn't really bother me.' In other cases, people mentioned that adopting a child was something they had considered even before they realised they had fertility problems, and so the decision to adopt was easily made.

- *Family design* (n = 3, 6%): The three adoptive parents in this group all described wanting to adopt a child as a companion for an existing child in the family. One couple explained that their teenage grandson, whom they had adopted, really wanted a sibling but they were too old to have a birth child.

- *Wanting to help a child in need of a family* (n = 30, 59%): The majority of adoptive parents who mentioned this altruistic motive made general references to the situations of children in care, such as understanding that 'there were lots of children needing homes' and feeling that they had something to offer such children. Some parents' feelings of wanting to help were directed at particular children (e.g. a child they were fostering) or children with particular types of needs (e.g. related to ethnicity or disability). Almost all parents who mentioned altruistic motives mentioned other motivations too. The exception was one adoptive mother who had two children already. She could have had more birth children but preferred to help a child in need of a family.

- *Having an established relationship with the child* (n = 11, 22%): In this group were six adoptive parents who had adopted a child they had previously fostered. These parents all mentioned their bond with, and concern for, the child as a reason for applying to adopt. Two parents had adopted a child to whom they were related. Three parents put themselves forward to adopt a child they knew, but whom they had not looked after before. One adoptive mother, who also mentioned infertility as a motivation, applied to adopt a child who had been in her class (she was a special needs teacher).

The categories above are not mutually exclusive and most adoptive parents mentioned more than one motive for adopting. A minority of parents (n = 16, 31%) mentioned only infertility as a motive. Sixteen adoptive parents (31%) mentioned infertility and at least one other motive; in most cases the additional motive was the desire to help a child in need of a family. One adoptive mother explained how she saw her own unfulfilled need for a child as an opportunity to help children in need:

> We felt that we had a lot to offer, and it would be good . . . we would feel a complete family in a special way . . . we still had this hole which we felt we could put children into and would be able to offer them something.

Family size

The families in this study had an average number of 2.4 children (including adopted children, birth children, foster children and stepchildren). Almost three-quarters of parents had one or two children (one child – n = 11, 20%; two children – n = 29, 53%). Five families had three children and the same number had four children. Two families had five children. There were three families who each had either six, seven or eight children. Just over two-thirds of the families (n = 38, 69%) did not have any birth children (including one family whose birth child had died). Of the families who did have birth children (n = 17, 31%), these did not necessarily all still live in the family home; in some cases they had grown up and moved away.

Characteristics of the children

This section includes details of the 55 "index" children: 51 adopted children and four foster children. Unless otherwise specified, where we refer to the children or the adopted children this includes the four foster children.

Gender

Twenty-seven of the index children were boys (49%) and 28 were girls (51%).

Age

At the time of the first interview with adoptive parents, the children/ young people ranged in age from one to 19 years, and their mean age was 9.2 years (sd = 4.03). Sixteen per cent (n = 9) were age one to five, almost half (n = 26, 47%) were between six and ten years old, 27 per cent (n = 13) were between 11 and 14 and 9 per cent (n = 5) were over 14. The "child" who was 19 was the sibling of an adopted child. This young man had a learning disability and had remained living with his foster carers, who were now caring for him as an adult placement.

Children's ethnicity

Three-quarters of the children were white (75%, n = 41), either white British (n = 38) or white Irish (n = 3). One quarter (25%, n = 14) were from minority ethnic groups. Among them, nine were mixed Caribbean/ white, one was black Caribbean, one was Indian and three were other mixed ethnicity.

Age at which the child left the care of the birth family

Seven children (13%) left their birth families at birth. Of those who spent some time in their birth family, their average age at final removal was 2.98 years (sd = 2.34), ranging from some months to ten years.

Age at placement for adoption

The 51 adopted children were placed at an average age of 3.7 years (sd = 2.56), ranging from below one to ten years. Just over one-quarter of the sample were placed under the age of two (27%, n = 14), one-third were placed when aged two, three or four (33%, n = 17) and the remaining 39% (n = 20) were age five or older. Of the four children in long-term foster care, the mean age at placement with their current family was 10.8 years (sd = 2.8).

Number of significant carers before being permanently placed

All children experienced at least one change of main caregiver before being adopted (or placed with a long-term foster family); one child experienced up to ten changes of main caregiver (mean = 3.17, sd = 2.09). In just over half the cases (54%, n = 29), the child had a maximum of two placements prior to adoption. Fifteen children (28%) had three or four changes of caregiver and ten children (19%) had five or more changes. Information about previous placements was missing for one child. It is worth mentioning that adoptive parents were sometimes uncertain of their child's number of placements/carers, and only the number they were sure of was taken into account. Therefore, some children may have experienced more changes than is suggested by these figures.

Reasons for adoption

Adoptive parents were asked the reasons why their child had needed to be adopted (or placed in long-term foster care). Only two of the 55 children were placed for adoption at the request of their birth parents; one was a child with Down's syndrome, the other was relinquished by her teenage mother at birth.

The vast majority of children (96%) had been placed from the care system. Five of these children had been removed from their birth family at birth. In order to meet the legal threshold for a care order, the court must be satisfied that a child has suffered, or is likely to suffer, significant harm (Children Act 1989, s.31). The majority of children (84%, n = 46) had a history of abuse or neglect; only nine children (16%) did not experience any type of abuse or neglect before adoption.

In almost all cases, adoptive parents mentioned multiple problems within the birth family that necessitated the child's adoption. These problems frequently included substance misuse, domestic violence, parental mental health problems and/or learning difficulties, and problems in the birth parents' upbringing. As a result of these problems, the children experienced various types of abuse and neglect. There was some variation in how adoptive parents defined abuse and neglect and in the amount of detailed information they had about their child's history. Hence, we felt that any attempt to classify in any more detail the types or severity of abuse or neglect that children had suffered would lack accuracy. The duration of time that children spent living in their birth family is therefore a key indicator of adversity in the children's backgrounds. However, the following case studies give an indication of the problems in the birth families and their impact on the children.

Case study 1 – Robert

Robert's birth mother and father both had learning difficulties and his father spent some time in foster care as a child. Robert was taken into hospital at eight months old suffering from dehydration, and subsequently placed in foster care due to physical neglect. There was an attempt to help the birth parents with parenting skills and a prolonged period of assessment. Robert remained with the same foster carer throughout his time in the care system and was finally placed for adoption at age three. Robert has face-to-face contact with his birth mother.

Case study 2 – Janie

Janie's birth mother came from a difficult family background and had some psychological difficulties, possibly a personality disorder. Janie was taken into care aged two-and-a-half, after her mother punched her in the face, leaving heavy bruises. Janie's mother immediately called emergency services. Janie was placed in foster care while attempts were made to rehabilitate her with her mother. Janie's birth father had started a new relationship by that point and did not put himself forward as a carer for Janie. Janie was placed for adoption aged four. She has face-to-face contact with her birth mother and birth father separately.

Case study 3 – Peter

Peter's birth mother spent time in foster care as an adolescent. She became pregnant at 14 and had Peter's older brother, Joe. Joe's grandmother became his main carer when he was aged two. Peter's mother was addicted to heroin by the time she became pregnant with Peter and he was born with opiates in his bloodstream. Peter's birth father was also a drug user. His mother did not inform him of the pregnancy as she thought he posed a risk. Peter experienced neglectful care, including being abandoned in a shop, until he was left in the care of his grandmother at the age of three months. His grandmother was still looking after Joe and her own young children. Peter suffered further neglect and lack of stimulation while in his grandmother's care. When Peter was two, his grandmother took him to social services, feeling unable to continue taking care of him. Peter's brother, Joe, was removed from the grandmother's care at age six, when he was pushed down the stairs and sustained heavy bruising. Peter had two foster care placements before being placed for adoption with Joe. Contact is with the grandmother and a maternal aunt.

Length of time in placement

An average of nearly five years (mean = 4.82, sd = 3.04) had passed since children were placed with their adoptive families. Thirteen (24%) had been living with their adoptive parents for under three years, 21 (38%) for three to six years and 21 (38%) for seven or more years.

Placement with siblings

As reported by adoptive parents, almost all (n = 51, 93%) of the children in the sample had birth siblings; just four children were an only child. Thirty-nine of the 55 (71%) placements were of a single child; this includes the four children who had no siblings. Thirty-five children therefore (64%) were separated from all their siblings. Just under a quarter of children (n = 13, 24%) were placed with one sibling, two were placed with two siblings and one was placed with three siblings. Almost all of the 16 children placed for adoption with one or more siblings had more siblings living elsewhere.

The contact arrangements

This section describes the details of the target contact arrangements for each of the 55 children.

Who were the children having contact with?

There were three key types of contact arrangements: adult only (n = 27, 49%); sibling only (n = 17, 31%); and adult and sibling combined contact (n = 11, 20%). Table 3.1 gives further details of the contact arrangements within these three broad groupings. This shows that of the children having adult-only birth relative contact, almost two-thirds (17 of 27, 63%) were seeing just their birth mother. One child was having contact meetings with their birth mother, maternal aunt and maternal grandparents. Of the children who were having sibling-only contact, the largest category (12 of 17, 70%) was of children meeting with a group of siblings living in more

Table 3.1
Which birth family members were involved in contact meetings?

Broad type of contact		Frequency	%
Adult	Birth mother	17	63.0
	Birth father	5	18.5
	Birth parents	1	3.7
	Maternal grandparent/s	1	3.7
	Paternal grandparent/s	2	7.4
	Adult relative group	1	3.7
	Total	**27**	**100.0**
Sibling	Adopted sibling/s	2	11.8
	In care sibling/s	2	11.8
	Adult sibling/s	1	5.9
	Sibling group (siblings from more than one other setting)	12	70.6
	Total	**17**	**100.1**
Combined	Birth mother and sibling/s	4	36.4
	Birth parents and sibling/s	2	18.2
	Maternal grandparents and sibling/s	2	18.2
	Paternal uncle and siblings	1	9.1
	Adult relative group and sibling/s	2	18.2
	Total	**11**	**100.1**

than one other location/placement. In some cases, all of the children in the group were in care or adopted; in other cases, the group included adult siblings. There were only two children in the study whose index contact was with a sibling in another adoptive placement. This is interesting because previous research has suggested that this is the most frequent type of sibling contact (Neil, 1999). This type of sibling contact may be under-represented in the current study because in many cases adoptive families managed this contact between themselves without the need for agency intervention. Finally, one-fifth of children in the sample were having contact with siblings and adult birth relatives. In all of these cases, the siblings were living with the adult birth relatives in question, for example, where the birth mother had been able to keep a new baby or when the grandmother had taken on the parenting of a sibling.

Frequency of contact meetings

Most contact meetings occurred infrequently; the average number of meetings per year was 2.04 (sd = 1.8). As can be seen from Table 3.2, contact was once or twice a year in 84 per cent of cases. In only two cases did contact happen more than four times a year, and in each of these there were fairly unusual circumstances. One of these was a foster carer who had adopted. She had established a good relationship with the birth mother and lived in the same town as her. Although the formal contact arrangement was once a year, she frequently bumped into the birth mother informally when she was in town with the child, and they often went for coffee together. The other child who had high-frequency contact (eight times a year) was seeing her grandparents who had been her main caregivers for two years prior to adoption.

Table 3.2
The frequency of contact meetings at Time 1

	n	*%*
Once a year	23	42
Twice a year	23	42
3 times a year	5	9
4 times a year	2	4
8 times a year	1	2
12 times a year	1	2
Total	**55**	**101.0**

Duration of contact meetings

Information about the length of contact meetings was missing in three cases. The duration of contact in the other 52 cases is given in Table 3.3, which shows that almost half of the meetings lasted up to two hours, with most of the remainder lasting between two and five hours.

Table 3.3
The duration of contact meetings

	n	%
Short – 2 hours or less	25	48
Medium – over 2 hours, under 5 hours	21	40
Long – over 5 hours, up to one day	5	10
Duration of meetings varies	1	2
Total	**52**	**100**

Where do contact meetings take place?

Table 3.4 shows that most contact was taking place either at public venues such as restaurants, parks or beaches, museums, zoos or other leisure venues, or at formal venues such as contact centres or family centres. Only in six cases (11.5%) did contact meetings ever take place at the homes of adoptive parents or (less commonly) birth family members.

Table 3.4
The venues used for contact meetings

	n	%
Public venue	25	45.0
Formal venue	19	34.5
Both formal and public venues used	5	9.0
Adoptive or birth family home	6	11.5
Total	**55**	**100.0**

Are contact meetings attended by adoptive parents and professionals?

Table 3.5 shows whether adoptive parents went to contact meetings and/or whether the meeting was attended by a professional, such as contact worker or social worker. Unsurprisingly, as we were focusing on agency-mediated complex arrangements, there were no cases in the sample where children saw birth relatives by themselves (although some did so for part of the meeting). The most usual arrangement (56% of cases) was that both adoptive parents and a professional worker were at the meeting; the next most common was where adoptive parents were present but not a professional. In only three cases did the child meet their birth relatives with a worker but without adoptive parents.

Table 3.5
The presence of adoptive parents and professionals at meetings

	n	*%*
Adoptive parent/s only	20	36
Adoptive parent/s and a worker	31	56
Worker only	3	6
Mixed – some meetings with worker and adopters, some adopters only	1	2
Total	**55**	**100**

What exchange of addresses and phone numbers had taken place?

Most of the contact arrangements maintained the confidentiality of the adoptive home. In 76 per cent of cases (n = 42) there had been no exchange of address or phone number between the adoptive family and the other contact party. Seven people (13%) had exchanged all identifying details, in five cases phone numbers but not addresses had been exchanged, and in one case addresses but not phone numbers had been swapped.

How did the arrangements for contact vary by type of contact?

Table 3.6 shows how the three broad types of contact (sibling only, adults and siblings, and adult only) varied in terms of frequency, duration, venue, supervision and exchange of identifying details. Compared to contact between siblings, contact meetings that included adult birth relatives were generally shorter and more likely to be supervised at a formal venue with no exchange of identifying details. The combined adult and sibling contact arrangements seemed much more similar to adult contact arrangements than sibling-only contact arrangements. Chi square analyses (and Fisher's exact test where cell counts were small) were performed to see if there were any significant associations between broad contact type and whether meetings were infrequent (defined as once or twice a year), short (defined as two hours or less), supervised (by a worker), or held at a formal venue (contact centre or family centre), or whether they involved full or partial disclosure of identifying information (some or all details had been exchanged). These analyses showed that with the exception of frequency of meetings, all the other variables were significantly associated with contact type.

Table 3.6
Contact arrangements by type of contact

	Meetings held twice a year or less		Meetings last 2 hours or less		Worker attends meetings		Formal venue is used		Identifying details have been exchanged	
	n	*%*	*n*	*%*	*n*	*%*	*n*	*%*	*n*	*%*
Adult	23	85	16	59	22	82	13	48	4	15
Sibling	13	76	1	6	5	29	0	0	9	53
Combined	10	91	8	73	8	73	6	55	0	0
Statistics	Fisher's exact = 1.1, df = 2, ns		$\chi2 = 16.1$, df = 2, p<.001		$\chi2 = 12.7$, df = 2, p<.001		$\chi2 = 13.1$, df = 2, p<.001		Fisher's exact = 11.5, df = 2, p<.01	

For how long had contact meetings been taking place?

In all cases except two, the target contact arrangement had been planned at the start (or in one case very soon after the start) of the adoptive placement, although in several cases arrangements had changed in their precise nature over time. Hence, for most families the longevity of contact arrangements was the same as the time since placement. In two cases, when the child was placed for adoption there was no plan for direct contact with birth relatives, but the placement had been opened up at a later stage. Both of these were children placed as babies, and both had indirect contact with birth relatives for several years. One child began seeing her grandparents when she was seven and the other started indirect contact with her birth mother when aged 14.

How many contact arrangements were active at Time 1?

In six of the 55 cases the contact was not taking place at Time 1. In one case this was because the child had been placed recently and the first contact had not yet happened. In three cases contact had been stopped because of concerns about its negative impact on the child. In one case contact had been paused, again because of concerns about the impact on the child, but the decision had not definitely been taken to stop the meetings. In the final case no decision had been made to stop contact, but meetings had not taken place for two years, largely, it seems, because no one had arranged them.

Summary

This chapter has provided details of the 51 adoptive parents and four foster carers who took part in the study, and information about the nature of contact arrangements has been described. With each adoptive parent we identified an index child and target contact arrangements. Key points are as follows:

- Fifty-one interviews were with mothers and four with fathers.
- The majority of parents interviewed (82%) were married, 13 per cent were single parents and 5 per cent were cohabiting with their partner.
- Ninety-one per cent of parents interviewed were white and 9 per cent were from minority ethnic groups.
- The information parents gave us about their current employment or employment history and about their housing suggests that the vast majority of families had at least adequate, and in the majority of cases well above average, socio-economic circumstances.
- All except two of the children had been in public care before being adopted. The majority had experienced high levels of adversity in their early lives, and 84 per cent had a history of abuse and neglect.
- On average, the children in the sample were 3.7 years old at place-

ment, nine years old at the time of this study, and the average length of time since they had been placed was 4.8 years.

- One-quarter (25%) of the index children were from minority ethnic groups (this includes children of dual heritage).
- Among the 51 adoptive parents, the most frequent motive for parents to adopt was infertility; this motive was cited by 63 per cent of the sample. Most people identified a mixture of motives to adopt.
- The majority of parents (78%) had adopted a child not previously known to them. Six people had adopted their foster child, two had adopted a child from within their birth family, and three had adopted a child known to them in some other way.
- Three main types of contact were identified: adult only (49%), sibling only including adult siblings (31%), and adult and sibling (20%).
- Most contact was not very frequent (once or twice a year) and of brief or medium duration (up to five hours). In over three-quarters of cases there had been no exchange of identifying information between birth family members and adoptive families – the contact was mediated entirely by the agency.
- Contact that involved an adult birth relative (including those where siblings also attended) tended to be shorter, more likely to be held at a formal venue, more likely to be supervised and less likely to involve any exchange of identifying information than contact involving only siblings.
- Most contact arrangements had been in place from the start of the placement; only in two cases had the adoption been opened up from indirect to direct contact at a later stage. Six contact arrangements were not active at the time of the first interview.

4 The strengths and risks that affect the experience of contact for adoptive families

In their synthesis of research findings from a number of studies into contact for children in adoption and permanent foster care, Neil and Howe (2004, pp 231–4) summarised the characteristics of children, adoptive parents and birth relatives that are associated with beneficial contact and the characteristics that seem to be associated with more difficult or detrimental contact arrangements. We have drawn on this synthesis in our analysis of the strengths and risks that may affect contact for adoptive families. We describe the individual strengths and risks that we measured and outline how we constructed a combined measure that took account of all of these.

The strengths and risks for the adopted children

Neil and Howe (2004) argued that contact is likely to be more straight-forward for adopted children who are placed very young, who are secure in their relationship with their adoptive parents, whose emotional and behavioural development is progressing positively and who have good social cognition or emotional intelligence. These factors are likely to be highly correlated because early placement usually means the child has experienced fewer risks, such as multiple changes in caregiver or abuse and neglect. Children who have experienced fewer such risks have a better chance of forming new relationships and developing positively. In the current study we looked at the following factors in order to understand and quantify the strengths and risks that adopted children bring to the contact situation:

- children's emotional and behavioural problems;
- the child's feelings about adoption (based on adoptive parent reports);
- the child's age at placement.

Children's emotional and behavioural problems

We assessed children's emotional and behavioural problems using the Child Behaviour Checklist (CBCL) and adoptive parent interviews. Adoptive parent interviews were used when a completed CBCL was not available, as described below.

Child Behaviour Checklist

Adoptive or foster parents were sent the CBCL twice over the 16-month study period and the first CBCL that the parent returned was used for the following analysis. Of the 55 children in the study, 46 were the appropriate age for this measure (i.e. six to 18 years). We obtained at least one CBCL for 40 (87%) of eligible children. Of these 40 children, 21 were boys (52.5%) and 19 were girls (47.5%). The children ranged in age from six to 18 years; their mean age was 10.10 years (sd = 3.07).

In addition to individual syndrome scales, the CBCL questionnaire provides two broad grouping of syndromes: Internalising and Externalising, and a Total Problems score. The Total Problems score is the sum of the scores for all the syndromes and other problems that are not on any of the syndromes. Table 4.1 shows the percentage of children placed in the normal range for Internalising (72.5%), Externalising (50%) and Total Problems (55%) scales. Using the Total Problems scale, 17 (42.5%) children were in the borderline or clinical range.

Table 4.1
Children scoring in the clinical, borderline and normal range in the CBCL scales

	Normal		Borderline		Clinical		Missing*	
	n	%	n	%	n	%	n	%
Internalising	29	72.5	3	7.5	7	17.5	1	2.5
Externalising	20	50.0	6	15.0	13	32.5	1	2.5
Total Problems	22	55.0	4	10.0	13	32.5	1	2.5

*Not all items were completed and so these broad scales could not be scored.

Adoptive parent interview report

Adoptive parent interviews were used to assess children's emotional or behavioural problems when CBCL Total Problem scores were not available. A child was coded as having significant emotional or behavioural problems if parents identified current issues that they felt were particularly problematic and for which they had sought help. For example, Shay (aged 12) was described by his mother as having significant behavioural problems at school, where he was disruptive and uncontrollable and often ran out of class. He had an educational statement and had used the school counselling service. He had been diagnosed as having severe ADHD and was on medication for this.

Number of children with emotional and behavioural problems

By using CBCL scores and adoptive parent or foster parent reports, we were able to code all children (n = 55) in terms of whether they had significant emotional or behavioural problems. Twenty-four children (44%) were coded as having emotional or behavioural problems and 31 (56%) were coded as not having such problems. The children who had emotional and behavioural problems were significantly older at Time 1 than the children without such problems (t = 4.6, df = 53, p<0.001). This may be because emotional and behavioural problems were emerging as children became older, especially as they entered adolescence. Children with emotional and behavioural problems had also been significantly older when they were removed from their birth families (t = 3.0, df = 46, p<0.01) and when they were placed with their adoptive parents (t = 3.9, df = 53, p<0.001). These results fit with previous research which suggests that the duration of adverse care before adoption is related to subsequent development, and if children are removed from adverse environments when they are very young they have a better chance of developing normally (Howe, 1998).

Adoptive parents' perceptions of their child's feelings about adoption

Brodzinsky argues that it is normal for adopted children to have complex feelings about being adopted because adoption is inherently associated with issues of loss and stigma (1990). These feelings may not emerge until the child's cognitive capacity to understand some of the meaning of adoption has developed, usually around the age of about seven (Brodzinsky *et al*, 1984). For children with learning difficulties this may take longer or the child may never reach the point where they can understand adoption. When children are adopted from care, the answers to the question "why was I adopted?" (or "why am I in foster care?") are often difficult to understand. In order to understand why they were adopted, children need to make sense of information about their birth parents' problems and, in many cases, about their own experience of neglect or abuse. Incorporating this type of information into an understanding of adoption is likely to give rise to complex feelings for many children.

In our interviews with parents, we asked them to describe their child's feelings about being adopted. We asked very similar questions of foster carers – about the child's feelings about being fostered and about their birth family. We used the same coding system for both fostered and adopted children. We asked parents to give examples to illustrate their answers.

Using these data we took account of what parents said about how the child felt about being a member of the adoptive (or foster) family, the feelings they expressed about their birth family and their history, and the feelings they expressed about their status as an adopted (or fostered) child. Using these key themes, we looked for patterns in the data and we identified five different groups, which are described below.

Group 1 – Too young/lacking capacity to understand These were children who, by virtue of either young age or learning difficulties, were not yet able to understand the fact that they were adopted and express any reactions to this. There were eight children in this group (14.5%), almost all of whom were aged four or younger. One child was 12 but had profound learning disabilities, which impeded her ability to understand adoption.

Group 2 – Largely uncomplicated and/or positive feelings This group contained 19 children (34.5%). Some were reported by their parents as either being fairly disinterested in issues relating to the adoption or expressing only positive feelings, e.g. feeling proud or special. Other children in this group were reported to express some negative feelings or anxieties but these seemed quite low key or infrequent and seemed far less indicative of the child's overall view than their positive/uncomplicated feelings.

Case example:

Claire (age 11) was described by her mother as not being preoccupied with issues related to adoption or having particularly strong feelings:

I don't think it crosses her mind half the time . . . she doesn't get distressed about it, she is more interested . . . it has never come across to me as I don't want to talk about it . . . she asks relevant questions at relevant times . . . I think she feels she is part of this family. I don't think she has any anxieties that she shouldn't be here.

Group 3 – Complicated/birth family idealising These are children who had strong feelings about adoption. The feelings that seemed to dominate were feelings of loyalty towards or idealisation of their birth family. There were six children in this group (11%).

Case example:

Ashley (age 11) was described by his mother as being quite concerned about the reasons why he could not stay with his birth mother. She said that Ashley was:

. . . trying to make sense of his mum's bad decisions and he's struggling with it because at the end of the day he doesn't want to think badly of his mum . . . he's very protective of his mum . . . He said, 'I thought I was adopted because mean social workers took me away . . . they stole me from my birth mum.'

When talking about Ashley's overall feelings about being adopted his mother said:

If he's had a good day, then he's quite happy about it. If he's fallen out with me or somebody at school, then he thinks the world has come to an end and he should be with his birth mum and he would have been fine if he was there and it's all our fault.

Group 4 – Complicated/given up on birth family These six children (11%) had strong feelings about adoption but the dominant feeling seemed to be one of having given up on or rejected by their birth family and 'thrown their lot in' with their adoptive family.

Case example:

Jason (age 8), according to his mother, showed very little interest in talking about his birth mother. She felt that his memories of his mother were negative, explaining that 'If he mentions her he is most likely to say, "I was scared of Mummy Jane" or "She shouted at me a lot."' Talking about Jason's overall feelings about being adopted, his mother said:

I think he's quite pleased about being adopted . . . he does need to be reassured that he is always going to be part of this family . . . He constantly tells us that he loves us . . . He just needs to be reassured that we love him and that we are his family for ever . . . He does tell us that he loves us a lot more than birth children do.

Group 5 – Complicated/mixed feelings These children had strong feelings about being adopted but these feelings were very mixed. Especially in relation to their birth family, both positive and negative feelings were expressed. There were 16 children in this group (29%).

Case example:

Robin (aged 12) expressed a whole range of mixed and sometimes contradictory feelings about being adopted. His mother said that on the one hand he sometimes said 'I wish I had come out of your tummy', but on the other hand she described him as always having been loyal to his birth family. Robin sometimes expressed angry feelings about his birth mother and feelings of being replaced by her subsequent child; at the same time, he was worried whether his mother was looking after this child properly. Robin expressed feelings of anger with social workers saying, 'I think if they had helped more, maybe Mummy and Daddy would have managed better.' Although Robin's mum said she felt he was happy to have been adopted and knew his life was better than it would have been, she felt that overall his main feeling about being adopted was sad.

For children in Group 1 who did not really understand (yet) that they were adopted, we saw this position as neither a risk factor nor a strength. Where children had positive and uncomplicated feelings about adoption we saw this as a strength. For children in the other three groups (Groups 3, 4 and 5), the child's complicated feelings about adoption were considered to be a risk. Children whose feelings about adoption were positive or uncomplicated (Group 2) were significantly younger at placement (mean = 2.6 years, sd = 2.1) compared to those children in groups 3, 4 and 5 who had complicated feelings (mean = 6.2, sd = 2.8) (t = 4.9, df = 45, p<.0001).

The age of children at placement

In outlining their transactional model for thinking about contact, Neil and Howe (2004) argue that when children are placed for adoption under the age of two the dynamics of contact and openness can be easier for a number of reasons. To begin with, older children are likely to have a 'relevant relationship history with their birth family' that can 'play powerfully in the minds of new carers, children and birth relatives' (Neil and Howe, 2004, p 237). In contrast, children placed in infancy are unlikely to have established a significant relationship with birth family members. Furthermore, compared to the older placed child the younger placed child has an advantage in terms of establishing a secure attachment to new parents, largely because their exposure to pre-placement risks is likely to be less. Thus, the younger placed child is likely to grow in resilience over time, in the main because of loving relationships formed with their adoptive parents (Neil and Howe, 2004, p 242). The absence of an established relationship with birth relatives and the increased likelihood of the child being securely attached and developing healthily are factors likely to reduce the complexity of the contact experience for adoptive parents. If parents feel secure in their relationship with their child, thinking about and communicating with birth family members may be less threatening. Similarly, when children are developing well parents are likely to be less anxious about the potential impact of contact on them. We therefore identified as a strength within the adoptive family if the child had been placed with that family under the age of two years old, and a risk if the child was placed over the age of two. Three-quarters of children were placed over the age of two (n = 41, 74.5%) and one-quarter were placed under the age of two (n = 14, 25.5%).

The child's relationship with the adoptive parents

Where an adopted child has been able to form a positive relationship with their adoptive parents, this is a factor likely to enhance a child's development and build their resilience, enabling them to cope with the complexities of life. A good parent–child relationship can both build the child's personal resources and give them access to parental support in times of stress. If a parent feels their relationship with their child is secure, this is also likely to increase the satisfaction and confidence of parents, strengthening their resources as well. Hence, when adoptive parents reported an unproblematic positive relationship with their adopted child, this was coded as a strength.

In the interviews, adoptive parents were asked to talk generally about their relationship with their child and specifically about how close they felt to their adopted child and how attached they thought their child was to them. From these data, we coded two groups. The first of these, the "positive and unproblematic relationship" group, was where the parent reported positive reciprocated feelings and closeness between parents and child, and an absence of any *current* significant problems in relating to each other. Some parents felt their relationship with their child had always been excellent, and may even have been "instant" – one mother described her daughter's attachment to her as 'love at first sight and it just got stronger every day'. In terms of her own feelings about the child she said, 'I thought she was mine from the first second I saw her.' Other adoptive parents described a gradual process of establishing security and closeness; one mother felt it took a while for her daughter to trust their relationship:

> The bonding . . . we are quite solid as a family unit, no attachment problems at all; we are a solid family group . . . She has always been very loving and very cuddly . . . It's just that awareness that we were always going to be there . . . it took her about a year.

All other cases were coded as having "ongoing relationship issues". In this group, many parents felt fully bonded with and committed to their child, but felt their child was not yet securely attached to them. One mother said she felt 'very close' to her child and that he had 'settled well' and made significant progress in building an attachment with her. Yet she felt her son's attachment was anxious and insecure, characterised by his intense expressions of love and anger, underpinned by fears of rejection:

> ... he's directing his anger against me, so it's then difficult for me to help him. If I do speak to him, he says I'm making things up. If I don't speak to him, he says, 'See I told you, you don't care'. ... I think sometimes he's so attached, he's scared of it. I think he's scared it's going to be taken away from him again.

In other cases, parents reported that their own feelings of closeness towards their adopted child were less than entirely positive. They usually explained this as a reaction to the child's responses to them – either holding back or being testing, angry or rejecting, as one mother explained:

> He is complex and I think he doubts it (our relationship) and he still tests it ... I feel it is more difficult to feel close to him (than our other child). I feel pretty close to him but he does throw it back in your face a lot and we have issues with it and it makes it more difficult.

In a small number of cases parents reported high levels of problems, both in terms of their child's attachment to them and their bond with the child. One mother when asked how close she felt to her daughter, now living in residential care, said 'hardly at all, which I find very sad'. She explained this in terms of her daughter's severe problems in forming attachments:

> ... She has always been challenging, angry and provocative towards me ... I've never felt that I have had a close physical relationship with her. When she was younger, yes I could bath her and cuddle her and kiss her, and I tell her frequently that I love her, because I think it's important, but I don't know how much she actually takes in ... I

think she has massive attachment problems and difficulties acknowledging feelings and difficulties getting too close.

The number of children with a positive relationship with adoptive parents

Of the 55 families in the study, in 39 cases (71%) the parent–child relationship was coded as positive and unproblematic and in 16 cases (29%) as having ongoing relationship issues. The children who had positive and unproblematic parent–child relationships were significantly younger at the time they were placed with their adoptive parents compared to the children who had ongoing relationship issues (t = –3.2, df = 53, p<0.01).

Potential risks coming from the history of the child's relationship with the contact relative

According to Neil and Howe (2004), the nature of the relationship between the child and the contact relative is an important dimension to consider. They argue that where children do not have an established relationship with the birth relative, the contact is less emotionally charged and can be easier to handle. When children have a good relationship with birth relatives this of course helps the contact to be experienced positively, but meetings may in some cases be quite emotional, especially in terms of the child's feelings of sadness at the end of contact meetings. The most difficult scenario is likely to be when the child has contact with a birth relative with whom they have experienced a troubled or insecure, neglecting or abusive relationship. If a child has contact with a birth parent with whom they had an insecure attachment, the child may experience a range of feelings on seeing this parent again, and the impact of this history and relationship on contact is likely to be more problematic. For example, they might feel excited and pleased to see their parent but at the same time feel worried or fearful, sad or angry, or they may wish to see their birth parent out of a sense of responsibility or guilt. In some cases, contact might trigger memories or flashbacks of frightening experiences. We therefore considered that where contact involved a relative who had been a significant carer for the child in the past, and where this relative had been implicated in the neglect or abuse of the child, then this was a risk.

In 28 cases, the target contact meetings included a birth relative who had lived with the child and been one of their carers (or the only carer) and where that person had neglected or abused the child (51%). In 27 of these cases, the child was having contact with a birth parent who had neglected or abused them. One child was having contact with their grandmother. The grandmother had been the child's main carer, but the child had been removed from her because of concerns about neglect. Although all of these 28 children were seeing a birth relative who had been involved in their abuse or neglect, many of the children were not seeing one or more other people who had been involved in the abusive treatment, and often they were not seeing the person who had been responsible for the most severe ill treatment. In particular, there were a number of cases where the child had been abused (usually physically) by a male figure, often the mother's new partner, and the contact arrangements did not include this person.

Within this group of 28 children having contact with a birth relative who had been involved in their past maltreatment, the nature, duration and severity of abuse and neglect that the child had experienced varied, as we have illustrated in the previous chapter. Three cases stand out in terms of both the duration and the severity of past maltreatment the children had experienced from the birth relative with whom they were having contact. One child who had lived at home until the age of seven had witnessed several extremely violent incidents between the birth parents. The birth parents were involved in drug dealing and prostitution and the child was described as having been physically abused, sexually abused and neglected, and frequently had been left home alone. This child was having direct contact with the birth mother. Another child had been scapegoated by her mother and had been on the receiving end of particularly harsh punishments, and direct contact was with the birth mother. Another child's birth mother, with whom she had direct contact, had been involved in the sexual abuse of this child. In all of these cases, contact was supervised and, in terms of their physical protection, children were safe during contact. But given the history these children had with the birth relative they remained in contact with, it is possible they would not have felt safe psychologically (Howe and Steele, 2004).

In 25 cases (49%), the target contact did not include a relative who had cared for the child and abused or neglected them. Two children in this group were seeing a birth relative who had been a carer, in one case a grandparent and in the other an adult sibling. This group included four children who were seeing birth parents: one child who was relinquished at birth, one child who was removed from her parents at birth and two children having contact with birth fathers who had been non-resident. However, these carers had never abused or neglected the children. The remaining children in this group were seeing siblings, grandparents or other adult relatives who had never been main carer.

Risks to contact related to birth relative relationship history: summary

In summary, of the 55 children, 28 were seeing a birth relative who had been their main carer and who had been involved in their abuse or neglect. It was considered that this history of abuse and neglect posed a potential risk to the child, and so in the combined strengths/risks measure (below) these cases were assigned a score of −2. There were two children who were seeing a birth relative who had been their main carer but where there was no history of abuse or neglect from this birth relative. In these two cases, the risks were considered to be lower than in the first group, and a score of −1 was assigned. Finally, there were 25 children who were seeing a birth relative who had not been their main carer. This fact was considered to be neither a risk nor a strength and so in the combined measure, a score of zero was assigned.

The adoption communication openness of the adoptive parents

Neil and Howe (2004) argue that one of the fundamental dimensions related to the quality of contact arrangements is the psychological and communicative openness on the part of the permanent carers. Brodzinsky (2005, p 151) defines communicative openness as, 'the creation of an open, honest, non-defensive, and emotionally attuned family dialogue, not only about adoption related issues', and a willingness of individuals:

> to consider the meaning of adoption in their lives, to share that meaning with others, to explore adoption related issues in the context of family life, to acknowledge and support the child's dual connection to two families, and perhaps to facilitate contact between these two family systems in one form or another.

This section discusses how we rated the adoption communication openness of the adoptive parents in the study and the results of this analysis.

Rating adoption communication openness

A measure based on Brodzinsky's definition and developed by Neil and colleagues (2006) was used to rate adoptive parent interviews (see Neil, 2007b for a fuller description of the development of this measure). Brodzinsky's construct of communicative openness was broken down into five constituent dimensions. The five dimensions included are outlined below, with brief excerpts from the codebook included for illustration.

Communication with the adopted child about adoption

This is about the adoptive parent's willingness to talk about adoption related issues with their child and the extent to which they promote a climate of openness within the adoptive family about adoption related issues. It takes into account the extent to which the parent is emotionally attuned to the child as an individual who has his or her own feelings about communication about adoption.

Comfort with, and promotion of, dual connection

This scale has three elements: the adoptive parent's personal comfort with the reality that the child is also connected to another family (the birth family); the value or importance they attach to the child's connection with birth family; and the extent to which they take steps to encourage or promote the child's connection to birth family.

Empathy for the adopted child

This is about the extent to which the adoptive parent is willing to consider and is comfortable with the full range of the child's feelings (or potential to have feelings) about being adopted, e.g. feelings of loss, rejection, love, loyalty, fear, anxiety, identity confusion, including being able to tolerate feelings in the child that are experienced as negative or threatening to the parent.

Communication with the birth family

This dimension looks at the adoptive parent's attitude towards communication/contact with the birth family (regardless of whether any such communication occurs), and, in situations where there is communication, how the adoptive parent behaves and feels about this.

Empathy for the birth family

This dimension is about the adoptive parent's capacity to take the perspective of the birth relative. This relates to thinking about the reasons why the child needed to be adopted as well as thinking about the birth relative's current position and their behaviour in relation to contact.

The procedure for rating adoption communication openness was as follows. First, at the stage of coding the whole transcript using Nvivo, nodes relating to the five dimensions, or subscales, above were created and all data relevant to each node were coded. At the stage of writing the case summary, the adoption communication openness of the parent was rated using the codebook and reviewing all relevant data in each of the five nodes. The coder assigned the rating for each subscale and summarised the key points in the data that justified this rating. Each interview was rated by one of two people (Neil or Young, both of whom were involved in the development of this rating scale and both of whom were experienced in applying the scale on the previous project). The coding was then checked by the other person and any areas of disagreement were discussed and ratings agreed by consensus. In the cases of the four foster parents, because each of the foster children was permanently placed in the foster family we felt that the adoption communication openness rating scale could also be used.

The adoption communication openness scores of adoptive parents

Table 4.2 displays the mean scores for adoptive parents on each of the five subscales and on the combined scale ($\alpha = .92$). This shows that, in general, adoptive parents in our sample were showing high levels of adoption communication openness across all domains.

Table 4.2
The adoption communication openness scores on the five subscales and the total score

	Mean (n = 55)	sd
Communication with child	4.2	.99
Dual connection	4.1	1.1
Empathy with child	4.0	1.0
Communication with birth family	3.9	.90
Empathy for birth family	3.8	1.3
Total score (possible scores 5–25 – the sum of scores from all 5 subscales)	**20.2**	**4.6**

Neil (2009) found that adoptive parents who were high on adoption communication openness were usually able to make contact work, even when birth relatives had difficulties in accepting the child's adoption. When adoptive parents were moderately communicatively open, contact could work well if birth relatives showed positive acceptance of the adoption, although in such cases adoptive parents would only be comfortable with contact within certain limits. When birth relatives showed a lack of acceptance of the adoption, this tended to undermine the confidence of moderately communicatively open parents, often resulting in a diminution or cessation of contact. When adoptive parents were low in adoption communication openness, contact arrangements rarely worked well, stopping over time or carrying on at only a very minimal level. We therefore considered that if the adoptive parent scored highly (4 or 5) on any one of the five dimensions, this was a strength they were bringing to the contact situation. Conversely, if they scored low on any dimension (1 or 2) then this was a risk. Where adoptive parents scored in the middle of the scale (3) this was seen as neither a strength nor a risk. Table 4.3 shows how many adoptive parents fell into each of these three bands for the five dimensions.

Table 4.3
Adoption communication openness scores as high, moderate or low on the five dimensions

	High (4–5)		*Moderate (3)*		*Low (1–2)*	
	n	%	n	%	n	%
Communication with the child about adoption	43	78	7	13	5	9
Promotion of dual connection	42	76	7	13	6	11
Empathy for child	37	67	14	26	4	7
Communication with birth family	38	69	14	26	3	6
Empathy for birth family	34	62	11	20	10	18

The fact that most parents scored very high on adoption communication openness is unsurprising given that all parents in the study were involved in direct contact arrangements. This type of post-adoption contact is not the norm, and there is evidence from previous research that adoptive parents who agree to or initiate it do so because they are more communicatively open, and/or that this type of direct contact can help adoptive parents to become more communicatively open (Neil, 2007b). It may also be that the agencies involved had taken account of these kinds of characteristics in selecting and preparing the adoptive parents.

Measuring strengths and risks: summary

The approach used to look at the strengths and risks of children and parents is based on prior research and theory about factors that are likely to impact on contact and we have attempted to be rigorous in our coding/ use of measures. We do, however, acknowledge some limitations to our methods. To begin with, these strengths and risks constitute only part of the picture in relation to factors that could influence contact; in particular, no account is taken of the characteristics of the birth relatives involved. We will examine the strengths and risks of birth relatives in Chapter 6. The scoring of children's feelings about adoption is limited because it is based only on parent report. The veracity of this coding is dependent on the parent's ability to accurately perceive and understand their child's feelings, and so to some extent what we have measured here may say more about the parents than the children. However, to try and surmount this issue, we asked parents to give us examples to illustrate what they felt their child's feelings to be.

Our examination of emotional and behavioural problems (the CBCL) does not capture all aspects of children's emotional and behavioural development; for instance, it does not look at attachment. We have attempted to examine children's relationships with their adoptive parents via parent report. The simple coding system used does not capture all aspects of children's ability to form relationships – e.g. it does not take account of peer problems or differentiate between different types of insecurity in making relationships.

A further limitation of the coding of strengths/risks is that it is based only on one point in time. Almost all the strengths/risks that we measured (except for the child's age at placement and who the contact was with) are not fixed factors but may change over time and in relation to experience. We acknowledge that these same factors are likely to alter in relation to people's experiences of contact. In other words, the relationship between the strengths/risks of adoptive parents and children and the outcomes of contact is bi-directional.

Creating a combined strengths and risks score for adoptive families engaging in contact with a birth relative

In order to quantify the combined strengths and risks for adoptive families engaging in contact, we used all the variables described above. In most cases, where a factor was considered to be a risk a score of –1 was given. Where a factor was considered to be a strength a score of +1 was given. If a factor was considered to be neither a strength nor a risk a score of zero was given. In relation to the nature of the child's relationship with the birth relative, a risk score of –1 was given if the birth relative had been the main carer but had not abused or neglected the child. A risk score of –2 was assigned when the birth relative had been the main carer and had been involved in abusing or neglecting the child. Table 4.4 summarises how we calculated the combined strengths/risks score for adoptive families.

Of the ten factors that this measure takes into account, five relate to the adoptive parents (their adoption communication openness scores), three relate to the child (emotional and behavioural development, child's complex feelings about adoption, age at placement), one factor (the parent–child relationship) relates to both the parent and child, and one factor (history of child's relationship with the birth relative) relates to potential risks posed by the birth relative. Although the composite risk scores cannot indicate what the pattern of strengths and risks are in any one case (with the exception of cases scoring at the extreme ends of the scale), the composite score is a useful way of distinguishing between families who are high strength and low risk, families who are low strength and high risk, and families experiencing a mix of strengths and risks in the contact situation. In practice, a method of summarising strengths and risks may be a useful guide in targeting support services appropriately.

Scores were summed. The range of possible scores was –11 to 9. If a contact situation had every possible risk and no possible strengths, the score would be –11. A contact situation with every possible strength and no risks would have a score of +9.

Table 4.4
Variables used to create the combined risks/strengths score

	Risk (score −2)	Risk (score −1)	Neutral (score 0)	Strength (score 1)
Child's emotional and behavioural problems		Clinical or borderline on CBCL or parent report or significant problems	n/a	Child is in normal range on CBCL or parent reports no significant problems
Parent–child relationship		Ongoing relationship problems	n/a	Positive and unproblematic relationships
Child's feelings about adoption		Groups 3 to 5	Group 1	Group 2
Age at placement		Child aged two or over at placement	n/a	Child less than aged two at placement
Contact with main carer	Contact is with birth relative who was a main carer and abused or neglected child	Contact with birth relative who was a main carer but had not abused/neglected child	Contact relative was never a main carer	n/a
Communication with child about adoption		Low (1–2)	Moderate (3)	High (4–5)
Comfort with dual connection		Low (1–2)	Moderate (3)	High (4–5)
Empathy for adopted child		Low (1–2)	Moderate (3)	High (4–5)
Communication with birth family		Low (1–2)	Moderate (3)	High (4–5)
Empathy for birth family		Low (1–2)	Moderate (3)	High (4–5)

The adoptive family combined strengths/risks: results

The adoptive family combined strengths/risks of engaging in contact scores (n = 55) ranged from –10 to 9 (m = 1.9, sd = 4.9). No family had the lowest possible score of –11. The median score was 3, indicating that in most cases the risks in the contact situation were outweighed by strengths. Six families (11%) had scores between –10 and –5, suggesting many more risks than strengths, 21 families (38%) had scores between –4 and 2 suggesting a mix of strengths and risks, and 28 families (51%) had scores between 3 and 9 indicating more strengths than risks. Families where both children and adoptive parents bring a number of strengths to the contact situation may be those families who can manage aspects of post-adoption contact with minimal intervention from support agencies. In contrast, families where children have a number of problems, where adoptive parents are low on adoption communication openness and where contact is likely to be complicated by the inclusion of the birth relative who has abused or neglected the child, then contact arrangements will require the most intensive support services and the closest monitoring.

Summary

This chapter examines the characteristics of children and adoptive/foster parents which are likely to impact on the management and outcomes of post-adoption contact arrangements. Key findings are as follows:

- Unsurprisingly, given that the majority of children in our sample had experienced adverse circumstances before being placed for adoption, 44 per cent of children had emotional or behavioural problems.
- Despite this, the majority of adoptive parents (71%) reported that they and their child had developed a positive and unproblematic relationship.
- Based on adoptive parent reports, over half of children (51%) had very complicated feelings about their birth family and about their status as an adopted person.
- Three-quarters of children were aged two years or older when placed with their adoptive parents.
- Over half of children (51%) were having direct contact with a birth

relative who had played a significant role as a carer and who had neglected or abused them. Contact in such circumstances is arguably more emotionally complex for children than seeing a birth relative without this relationship history.

- Overall, it can be seen that many children in the study were continuing to struggle with the impact of their early histories. They had ongoing psychological issues or developmental problems that made them vulnerable in terms of handling complex contact situations.

- The adoption communication openness of adoptive parents was measured in five dimensions from the interview data: communication with the child about adoption; comfort with, and promotion of, dual connection; empathy for the adopted child; communication with the birth family; and empathy for the birth family.

- Adoptive parents' mean scores on the above measure indicate that the majority of parents in the sample were high on adoption communicative openness, suggesting they bring a number of resources to the contact situation.

- A combined strengths/risks score was computed to quantify the risks that both parents and children bring to the contact situation. A minority of families had many more risks than strengths (11%), two in five families (38%) had a mix of strengths and risks, and just over half of the families had many more strengths than risks (51%).

5   The birth relative sample

This chapter describes the key characteristics of the 39 birth relatives who took part in the interviews in the study. It also details the characteristics of the adopted child from their birth family and the contact arrangements they were having with the child.

The birth relatives

This section summarises the key characteristics of the birth relatives.

The relationship of birth relatives to the adopted child

Just over half of birth relatives in the study (n = 21, 54%) were birth parents: two birth fathers and 19 birth mothers. The next largest group were grandparents, these making up 23 per cent of the sample (n = 9). We interviewed seven grandmothers (two paternal and five maternal) and two grandfathers (one maternal and one paternal). Seven adult siblings were interviewed (18%) – three brothers and four sisters. All of the siblings had the same birth mother as the adopted child, and all had different birth fathers. Of the remaining two relatives, one was a maternal aunt and the other a maternal great-aunt. Overall, therefore, most (n = 34, 87%) of the relatives were from the adopted child's maternal birth family. Four birth relatives did not take part in the second round of interviews. Three of these were birth mothers and one was an adult sister.

Just over half of the birth relatives (n = 22, 56%) had at some point lived with the child and been their main carer or one of their main carers. This group consisted of 17 birth mothers, one birth father, two grand-mothers and two sisters.

Gender

Thirty-two of the birth relatives were female (82%) and seven were male.

Ethnicity

Eighty-five per cent of birth relatives were white British (n = 33). All the remaining birth relatives were of mixed ethnicity (four people were black Caribbean/white, one person was Indian/white and one was Turkish/Caribbean/white).

Age

The youngest person we interviewed was 17 and the oldest was 78 at the time of the first interview. We interviewed three generations of birth relatives: the mean age of the parent generation (birth parents and aunt) was 38 years (range = 23 to 57); the mean age of the grandparent generation (including a great-aunt) was 62 years (range = 43 to 78); and the siblings' mean age was 21 years (range = 17 to 28).

Employment

Only a minority of birth relatives were in employment (n = 8, 20.5%; this includes five people in full-time work and three people in part-time work). One birth father was an engineer. Three people worked in social care, two worked in shops and one was a catering assistant (information about the nature of employment was missing for one person). As Table 5.1 shows, the same proportion of people (n = 8, 20.5%) were employed, unemployed or unable to work because of health issues. Fifteen per cent

Table 5.1
The employment of birth relatives at Time 1

	n	*%*
Employed full time	5	12.8
Employed part time	3	7.7
Unable to work (health or disability)	8	20.5
Carer/parenting	6	15.4
Unemployed	8	20.5
Retired	4	10.3
Student	5	12.8
Total	**39**	**100**

of people were full-time parents or carers and some birth relatives were retired or in full-time education.

Marital status of birth relatives

Just under a quarter of birth relatives (n = 9, 23%) were married at the time of the first interview. A larger proportion (n = 15, 39%) were co-habiting with their partner. Twelve people were single or divorced (31%) and three were in a relationship but not living with their partner (8%).

Other children of the birth relatives

For about one-quarter of the birth parents in the study (five of 21) the index adopted child was their only child. Six birth parents had two or three children, and the remaining birth parents (ten of 21) had four or more children. The mean number of children that birth parents in the study had was 3.2 (sd = 1.9, range 1 to 8). Three-quarters of birth parents (16 of 21) were not currently parenting any of their children; all of their children had been adopted or were in foster care or the care of other birth family members. Of the five parents who did have children at home with them, in three cases the siblings were older than the adopted child and in two cases they had been born after the index child's adoption.

Two of the adult siblings were currently parenting their own child or children. A third sibling had a child who was in foster care and waiting to be adopted. Three of the grandparents in the study were the permanent carers of one of the adopted child's siblings. Altogether, therefore, about a quarter of the birth relatives in the study (ten of 39) were parenting a child who was either the sibling or the niece or nephew of the index adopted child.

The adopted children of the birth relatives

This section describes the characteristics of the adopted children of the birth relatives. Where birth relatives had more than one child adopted from their family or had experience of more than one contact arrange-ment, interviews focused on an index child and target contact arrange-ment, these being defined as the child/contact arrangement that they felt was most complex.

The reason for the child's adoption and birth relatives' agreement with the adoption plan

All except one of the adopted children had been adopted from the care system. The exception was the grandchild of one of the interviewees who had been placed for adoption by her birth parents who felt unable to manage her disability. In most cases, birth parents and other relatives described a broad range of problems that brought about the care proceedings and compulsory adoption. These reasons were very similar to those described by adoptive parents and they seem typical of the circumstances of children adopted from the care system (e.g. birth relatives described problems of parental incapacity related to drug and alcohol misuse, mental health problems and/or learning disability, relationship problems between birth parents including domestic violence, and social and economic problems). Although almost all children had been adopted from the care system, this did not mean that all the birth relatives we interviewed disagreed with the adoption plan.

Looking first at the 21 birth parents in the study, over four-fifths (n = 17) said they were not in agreement with the plan for their child (we are referring here to subjective feelings of agreement as opposed to actually signing the adoption papers or not). Some birth parents disputed the grounds of the adoption and argued that the problems were not as bad as social services had portrayed. Other birth parents argued that they were given insufficient support to keep their child. A few birth parents said they signed their consent for the adoption even though they did not agree with the plan. In some cases this was because they felt the adoption would go ahead whether they gave their consent or not. One birth mother explained that she signed consent for the adoption when she was in hospital after having had a nervous breakdown. She said, 'If I was straight in my mind I would never have signed it.' Four birth parents said that although their child had been adopted from the care system, they had been in agreement with this plan at the time. These four included the two birth fathers in the study, both of whom felt that the children were not getting good care with their mother, but they felt unable to look after the children themselves. Both of the birth mothers who were in agreement with the adoption plan had been addicted to drugs. Each of these mothers explained that they recognised at the time that they could not look after the child adequately and so they asked social services to pursue an adoption plan.

The picture in relation to grandparents, siblings and other birth relatives was more varied. Of these 17 other relatives, over half (five of the grandparents, two of the siblings and the great-aunt) believed at the time of the adoption that this was the right plan for the child. What each of these had in common was a recognition of the birth parents' problems and an acceptance (often painfully reached) that they themselves were not in a good position to offer the child a permanent home. One person said:

> If I'd have been younger and my husband hadn't been disabled I would have taken the baby on myself, but it wasn't realistic . . . it's not fair to him [the child]. I felt quite sad that he was going to go . . . but then I thought it would be best for him.

One of the siblings explained how she wanted her younger brother:

> . . . to have the chance that we never ever had, a chance of being settled in a normal family environment and do normal family things and be happy . . . not to be stuck with my family.

Four of the other relatives (one grandmother, two siblings and an aunt) did not agree with the adoption plan at the time the child was placed. For example, one grandmother felt that the birth mother had been given insufficient help to care for her child and placement within the birth family would have been preferable to adoption. Of the two siblings, one had wanted to care for the child themselves but had not been allowed to do so. Another sibling had not wanted the child to be adopted because he did not recognise the problems with his mother's parenting and did not want to be separated from his brothers and sisters. The other six relatives had very mixed feelings about the child's adoption. For example, one older sister was very upset and angry that adoption was going to split up her large family and that they would become 'scattered all over the place'. But she did accept the reasons why the children were removed from the parents' care and she wanted her younger siblings to find happiness and be cared for. In another case, a grandparent accepted the reasons why the child could not stay with the birth mother but was desperately upset that circumstances prevented the grandparents from looking after the child themselves.

The age of the index child at placement for adoption and at the time of interview, and time since placement

As is typical of children adopted from care, the children of the birth relatives in this study were almost all removed from the birth family when they were under five years old. As Table 5.2 shows, one in five children was removed before their first birthday; several of these were removed at birth.

Table 5.2
The age of the index child when they left the birth family

	Age when child left birth family	
	n	*%*
0	8	21
1	6	16
2	3	8
3	7	18
4	7	18
5 or older	7	18
Mean	2.7 years	
Sd	2.1	
Range	0–7	
N	38*	

*Data were missing on one child

At the time of the first interview, the majority (25 of 39, 64%) of the index adopted children of the birth relatives were aged between seven and 12 years. As Table 5.3 shows, the mean age of the index children at the time of the first interview was nearly nine years. An average of four-and-a-half years had elapsed since the children had been placed with their adoptive family, but the range here was wide, from nought to 12 years (see Table 5.3).

Table 5.3
The age of the index children at Time 1 and time since placement for adoption

Years	Age of the child at Time 1		Time since placement for adoption	
	n	*%*	*n*	*%*
0–3	7	18	15	39
4–6	2	5	13	34
7–9	13	33	7	18
10–12	12	31	3	8
13 or older	5	13	0	0
Mean		8.8		4.6
Sd		3.9		3
Range		0–17		0–12
N		39		38*

*Data were missing on one child

Gender and ethnicity of the adopted child

Nineteen of the index children were girls and 20 were boys. Thirty-two of the children (82%) were white British; all the other children were of mixed parentage (five were white/black Caribbean, one was white/Turkish and one was white/Indian/Saudi Arabian).

The contact arrangements

This section explores the nature of the contact that the birth relatives were having with the child who had been adopted from their family.

Who was involved in the contact meetings?

Twenty-eight of the target contact arrangements involved only adults from the birth family; none of the adopted child's siblings were included. Seventeen birth relatives (two birth fathers, one grandparents and 13 birth mothers) were the only member of the birth family involved in the target contact arrangement. Eleven birth relatives (five grandparents, four birth mothers, an aunt and a great-aunt) were involved in contact arrangements that included one or more other adult birth relatives (for example, birth parents sometimes had contact jointly with the other birth parent and/or with their own parent).

Seven of the target contact arrangements involved *only siblings* from the birth family. Three adult siblings were seeing one younger brother or sister, and one sister was seeing a pair of younger siblings placed together. The other three adult siblings were involved in sibling group contacts where they met with a number of brothers and sisters living in different places. Two of the adult siblings also brought their own child (the adopted child's niece/nephew) to the contact meetings.

Finally, four of the birth relatives were involved in combined adult and sibling contact meetings. This included three grandparents and one birth mother, all of whom went to contact bringing along the adopted child's sibling, who lived with them.

The frequency of contact meetings

As we found in the adoptive parent sample, almost all contact was fairly infrequent. As Table 5.4 shows, over 90 per cent of target contact meetings happened less than four times a year, the most common frequency being twice a year.

Table 5.4
The frequency of contact meetings at Time 1

	n	*%*
Once a year	14	36
Twice a year	17	44
3 times a year	5	13
4 to 6 times a year	2	5
Stopped/suspended	1	3
Total	**39**	**101**

The duration of contact meetings

Almost half of contact meetings were less than two hours long (n = 19, 49%). Eighteen contact meetings lasted between two and five hours (46%). Two contact arrangements involved meetings that lasted longer than five hours (5%).

The venues used for contact meetings

In two-thirds of cases (n = 26, 67%) the target contact meetings were held at a neutral venue, such as a café, park, museum or zoo. A quarter of contact meetings took place at a formal venue such as a contact centre or family centre (n = 10, 26%). In two cases (5%), the venue for contact had alternated between neutral and formal venues. There was only one case where contact meetings had been held at the adoptive parent's home and the birth relative's home.

Were contact meetings attended by adoptive parents and professionals?

Only two birth relatives spent time alone (i.e. without either the adoptive parents or a professional being present) with the adopted child during contact meetings. In both cases this had been a recent development and adoptive parents remained involved at the beginning and end of meetings. One birth mother saw her child at a contact centre supervised by the social worker. The adoptive parents brought the child there and collected them at the end but did not stay during the meeting. In all other cases (n = 36, 92%) the adoptive parents were present for the whole of the contact meeting. In 25 cases (64%) the contact was also attended by a worker in a supervisory/facilitator role.

What exchange of identifying information had taken place?

In over two-thirds of cases there had been no exchange of identifying information between birth relatives and adoptive parents (n = 27, 69%). Five relatives said they had exchanged phone numbers and addresses with adoptive parents (13%), and the same number said they had exchanged phone numbers but not addresses. There were two cases (5%) where birth relatives and adoptive parents had exchanged addresses but not phone numbers.

How did contact arrangements vary by broad contact groupings?

Using the three same broad contact groupings as were used in Chapter 3 (adult birth relatives only, sibling only, combined adult and sibling contact), we looked at how key aspects of the contact arrangements varied across these groups. Because the numbers of people in the sibling-only and combined adult and sibling contact groups were small, we did not attempt to undertake any statistical analysis; because of the small numbers in these groups, the percentages presented below should be viewed with caution. Table 5.5 shows how contact arrangements varied in relation to frequency, supervision, duration, venue and exchange of identifying details. Generally, the results look similar to those reported in the adoptive parent chapter, in that the sibling-only contact arrangements were more likely to be longer in duration, held outside of formal venues and less likely to be supervised by a worker. In the adoptive parent sample, adult–sibling contact looked much like the adult-only contact, but in this sample the results are less clear, probably because this group is so small (n = 4).

Table 5.5
The variations in arrangements for contact by broad contact groupings

	Meetings held twice a year or less		*Meetings last 2 hours or less*		*Worker attends meetings*		*Formal venue is used*		*Identifying details have been exchanged*	
	n	*%*	*n*	*%*	*n*	*%*	*n*	*%*	*n*	*%*
Adult	24	89	17	61	18	67	10	36	7	25
Sibling	4	57	0	0	2	29	0	0	3	42
Combined adult and sibling	3	75	2	50	3	75	0	0	2	50

How long had contact arrangements lasted?

In all but one case, the direct contact arrangements had been in place from the start of the placement. One grandparent had only begun to have direct contact seven years after the grandchild was adopted. At the time of the first interview, all contact arrangements except two were active. In one case the first contact meeting had not yet taken place, and in the other case contact had been recently suspended because of concerns about the child's reactions.

Summary

This chapter has described the characteristics of the 39 birth relatives who took part in the study, and has outlined the nature of the contact they were having with the child. Key points are as follows:

- The sample consisted of 21 birth parents, nine grandparents, seven adult siblings and two aunts.
- The majority of these birth relatives (87%) were from the adopted child's maternal family.
- Just over half of birth relatives had been the child's main carer prior to adoption.
- Although almost all of the adoptions were non-voluntary, the extent to which birth relatives agreed with the adoption plan at the time varied. The majority (81%) of birth *parents* were not in agreement with the adoption plan; in fact, most were strongly opposed to it. About half of the other birth relatives (grandparents, siblings and aunts) indicated that they had been in support of the adoption from the start.
- Fifteen per cent of birth relatives were from minority ethnic groups; the remainder were white British.
- The ages of interviewees ranged from 17 to 78.
- Only 21 per cent of birth relatives were in employment.
- Twenty-three per cent of birth relatives were married, 39 per cent were cohabiting with their partner, 31 per cent were single or divorced and 8 per cent were in a relationship but not living with their partner.
- The adopted children with whom these birth relatives were having contact had all been removed from the birth family under the age of eight, with the mean age at removal being 2.7 years.
- Four out of five contact arrangements happened only once or twice a year and meetings lasted between one and five hours in almost all cases. In the majority of cases contact took place in neutral or formal venues and adoptive parents and a supervisor were present. Just under one-third of birth relatives had exchanged some identifying details with adoptive parents.

6 The strengths and risks that birth relatives bring to contact

In their summary of birth relatives' characteristics that are related to the success (or otherwise) of post-adoption contact, Neil and Howe (2004, pp 233–4) emphasised three types of factor. The first relates to the birth relative's attitude to the child's placement with adoptive parents. What is likely to be helpful to the adopted child is if their birth relatives show acceptance and approval of the child's position in the adoptive family. Contact is likely to be difficult for children and adoptive parents if birth relatives do not accept or support the placement, or where they seek to undermine it. The second type of characteristic is the nature of the relationship between the birth relative and the child; a history of maltreatment, ongoing rejection or the unwillingness to relinquish the role of primary carer are risk factors. The third type is the birth relative's own level of functioning, in that factors such as mental health problems, drug misuse, etc. may make it difficult for birth relatives to maintain contact consistently and helpfully over time.

In this chapter we report the results of our analysis of birth relative characteristics that are potentially relevant to the outcome of contact. In particular, we focus on their mental health, their coping with adoption and their relationship with the child. We developed a combined score to quantify strengths and risks in the same way that we did for the adoptive families.

The mental health of birth relatives

The mental ill-health of birth parents is often part of the picture of why children are taken into care and subsequently adopted. Children often enter the care system at a time of crisis, and the compulsory removal of the child from the family is frequently experienced as a highly stressful event that can further destabilise a birth relative's psychological equilibrium (Neil *et al*, 2010). The loss of a child to adoption has often been likened to a bereavement and has been associated with subsequent problems of anxiety and depression. Because of these factors, it is reasonable to assume that the birth relatives of children adopted from care will have much higher than average levels of psychological distress. In order to examine this assumption, we asked relatives to complete the Brief Symptom Inventory (BSI) (Derogatis, 1993).

The BSI consists of 53 items, each of which is rated by the individual on a 5-point scale of distress from 0 (not at all) to 4 (extremely) in relation to symptoms experienced in the last seven days. The results of the test can be examined at the level of individual items, the nine symptom dimensions and three global indices.

On the BSI, the nine primary symptom dimensions are:

1. somatisation;
2. obsessive compulsive;
3. interpersonal sensitivity;
4. depression;
5. anxiety;
6. hostility;
7. phobic anxiety;
8. paranoid ideation;
9. psychoticism.

The three global indices are:

- GSI: global severity index (takes into account the number of symptoms and intensity of distress);
- PSDI: positive symptom distress index (an intensity measure corrected for number of symptoms; indicates average level of distress);
- PST: positive symptom total (number of symptoms reported).

The BSI can also be used to identify which individuals are "case positive" in terms of their psychological distress.

Results of the Brief Symptom Inventory

Twenty-seven people completed the BSI at Time 1 and 21 did so at Time 2. Eighteen people completed the measure at both points in time. To maximise our sample size we used the first BSI that each birth relative had completed, and this gave us a sample of 31 (79.5%). These were 17 birth mothers, two birth fathers, eight grandparents (the great-aunt is included in this group) and four adult siblings. Twenty-six were female and five were male.

Table 6.1 shows the mean raw scores of birth relatives on the nine symptom dimensions and the three global indices of the BSI. Birth relatives' scores were much higher than those of the adult non-patient comparison sample norms and much closer to the adult psychiatric outpatient comparison sample norms (Derogalis, 1993). The standard

Table 6.1
Scores of birth relatives on the BSI

	Mean – adult non-patients	Mean – adult psychiatric	Mean and sd – birth relatives in our sample	
			mean (n = 31)	sd
Somatisation	.29	.83	.73	.87
Obsessive compulsive	.43	1.57	1.26	1.19
Interpersonal sensitivity	.32	1.58	1.27	1.30
Depression	.28	1.80	1.15	1.29
Anxiety	.35	1.70	1.05	1.12
Hostility	.35	1.16	.77	.92
Phobic anxiety	.17	.86	1.11	1.41
Paranoid ideation	.34	1.14	1.28	1.14
Psychoticism	.15	1.19	1.00	1.29
GSI	.30	1.32	1.07	1.05
PDSI	1.29	2.14	1.94	.83
PST	11.45	30.80	23.68	16.74

deviations of the scores are generally quite large, indicating that scores within our sample were very widely spread.

Individuals are "case positive" on the BSI (suggesting a clinically significant level of psychiatric symptomatology) if their GSI T-score is greater than or equal to 63, or if any two primary dimension T-scores are greater than or equal to 63. Over half of the birth relatives (n = 17, 55%) had case positive scores (scores within a clinical range), including over half of the birth parents (n = 11), two of the four siblings and four of the eight grandparents. Where birth relatives were case positive on the BSI, this was considered as posing a potential risk to contact. Where scores were within the normal range, this was considered as being as strength in a contact situation.

Coping with adoption

The "coping with adoption" measure consists of three subscales:

- accepting dual connection;
- feelings about the outcomes of adoption for the child;
- dealing with the impact of adoption on self.

We wanted to examine adoption-specific outcomes, both outcomes that indicate something of the birth relatives' well-being and also aspects of coping with adoption likely to be relevant to the adopted child's welfare. We also looked at how birth relatives coped with the adoption in our parallel study "Helping birth families" (Neil *et al*, 2010), in which we interviewed 73 birth relatives. We developed our "coping with adoption" coding scheme using data from both studies in order to take advantage of variation in the two samples. The birth relatives in the parallel study differed from the birth relatives in the current study in two ways: first, the adoptions of the children in the other study were much more recent; and second, hardly any relatives in the other study were having direct contact with their child. Time since placement and the type of post-adoption contact available to the birth relative may affect their ability to cope with adoption. Using data from both studies allowed us to develop a coding scheme that applies to examples of coping right across the expected range of variation in the population of birth relatives. The process of elaborating this coding scheme is described below.

Developing the "coping with adoption" coding scheme

To attempt to understand and measure differences in how birth relatives cope with the challenges of adoption immediately begs questions about what is a "good" outcome. We rejected the idea that a good outcome would be indicated only by positive indicators of people's broad psycho-social functioning, because the majority of birth relatives in our sample had long-standing difficulties that predated the adoption. We also knew from previous work with birth parents in adoption, and the bereavement literature generally, that good outcomes were unlikely to mean a cessation of negative emotion or disconnection from thoughts and feelings about the child: the notion of "getting over" the experience was inappropriate. Neither did the term "accepting" adoption seem entirely right, as many people we had spoken to (both interviewees and people in our service user reference groups) rejected this term, arguing that when the adoption had not been planned or agreed by the birth relative, the notion that they should accept this was inappropriate. Previous qualitative analysis on a sample of contemporary birth relatives identified three different patterns of feelings about the adoption seven years after the event: positive accept-ance; resignation; and anger and resistance (Neil, 2007a). This previous research informed our coding of "coping with adoption", but we decided to start our analysis afresh with the two current samples working through a number of stages, summarised below.

1. Exploring the meaning of "coping with adoption" with our reference groups of birth relatives: Briefly, this involved selecting four interviews felt by the research team to represent a range of ways of dealing with adoption. These interviews were edited to form four 10-minute scripts, which were read by actors and recorded. These recordings were then played to our two groups of birth relative consultants and people were asked to assess how well each person was coping with adoption (assigning a number) and to give reasons for their answers. We asked people to consider aspects of coping with

adoption that were positive for the birth relative and aspects of dealing with the experience that were likely to be "good" for the adopted child. Key messages about understanding the notion of "coping with" adoption were summarised at the end of this process and taken forward for consideration at the next stage.

2. Using feedback from the birth relative groups, insights from previous research and consideration of our own data, the research team identified three dimensions of dealing with adoption: accepting dual connection; feelings about the outcomes of adoption for the child; and dealing with the impact of adoption on self. Descriptions of each of these were drafted and applied to a sample of five interview transcripts; the coding team rated cases as high, medium or low and noted reasons. Using feedback from this, definitions were then refined and it was decided to use a 5-point scale for the first dimension and three points for the second two dimensions. Descriptions and examples of each point on the scale were written into the coding handbook as more cases were examined.

3. The coding team applied this rating scale to all birth relative interview transcripts collected as part of both the "Helping birth families" and the "Supporting contact" studies, using the coding handbook. Complex or difficult cases were referred to another coder for discussion before codes were assigned. Cases were coded using the case summary for each case, plus an examination of the relevant nodes in Nvivo. In the current study, the coding of birth relatives' coping with adoption was undertaken using the Time 1 interviews. All coding was then checked by one coder (the director of the study) to ensure consistency of coding.

On the following pages we present a definition and case examples for each of the three "coping with adoption" subscales: accepting dual connection, feelings about the outcomes of adoption for the child, and dealing with the impact of adoption on self. Results for each subscale and for the composite multidimensional "coping with adoption" scale are provided at the end of the coping with adoption section.

Accepting dual connection

Adopted children are members of two families. This creates certain challenges for them: to establish a coherent sense of identity; to make sense of where they belong; to understand the different roles of their two sets of parents; and to be aware of why they were adopted. The child's dual connection also challenges birth relatives to negotiate a major "psycho-social transition", a term borrowed from the bereavement literature (Parkes, 2001): to understand their change in role from being the legal parent to having no legal relationship with the child; from being or expecting to be a psychological parent to having someone else take over this role; from being the child's only mum or dad to understanding that another person is to be known by this name; to work out what being a birth parent, sibling or grandparent actually means. As much as the child has to make sense of their identity, these issues challenge birth relatives to think about "Who and what am I to my child (grandchild/sibling) now?" Brodzinsky (2005) argues that it is healthiest for the child if both adoptive parents and birth parents can recognise and support the child's membership of both families.

This dimension was rated on a 5-point scale, 5 being high (almost all positive indicators applied) and 1 being low (almost no positive indicators applied). A score of 4 was allocated for cases with more positives than negatives, 3 where there was no clear predominance of positive or nega-tives, and 2 for cases with more negatives than positives. In rating this dimension, we drew heavily on what birth relatives thought about the child's place in the adoptive family. Below, we summarise the positive and negative indicators of this dimension from the codebook, and we include case examples to illustrate people coded at different levels.

Positive indicators of acceptance of dual connection:

- The birth relative shows that they both **recognise and support the child's membership of both families** (as opposed to claiming an exclusive role as the real family).
- There is recognition that they **no longer have any status as the child's legal parent** and that this change is permanent (e.g. recognising that reclaiming the child is not possible, hoping the child may come and find them but realising this is the child's decision).

- There is **empathic understanding of the child's** (and perhaps the adoptive parent's) **point of view** – such as awareness of the attachment that will or has developed between them and of the child's need and ability to settle into the new family and feel secure in their permanent placement there. There is awareness that the children will also have feelings, thoughts and questions about their birth family, which will depend on the child's age and individual circumstances. There may be awareness that the adopters would feel loss if the child were to leave them.
- The birth relative is able to put their feelings aside and **consider what is best for the child**. They are happy to see the child settled with the adoptive parents.
- The birth relative may feel that the adoptive family and birth family are all family together and that **both families must work together** to get the best for the child.
- The birth relative **accepts and works within reasonable boundaries and limitations of contact** (but may take steps to make changes in contact if it is not working).
- They show recognition that contact might be helpful to adopted children in dealing with issues related to identity, separation and loss. They recognise the child's needs in contact and they can **see contact from the child's point of view**.
- They show **willingness to work with adoptive parents**, e.g. to meet with them, contribute to life story work, respond to letterbox contact or go to direct contact, persist with contact even when difficulties occur.
- If contact is occurring, the birth relative is able to: **respond as required and convey their acceptance of the placement to the child and adoptive parents, convey their positive feelings for the child and pass on information as required**.
- The birth relative is **realistic about their role** in relation to the child, both now and in the future. They recognise, for example, that reclaiming the child is not possible, realise that it is up to the child whether they seek out the birth relative in the future and what type of relationship they will have with them, or hope to move from indirect

to some face-to-face contact but understand this may only be limited and only happen if the adoptive parents and child want it.

Negative indicators of acceptance of dual connection:

- The birth relative may **overplay their connection to the child**. Although the birth relative might be realistic in understanding that adoptive parents now have the legal authority, they will **assert their superior status as the *birth* relative** and may claim this gives them superiority as a psychological parent/relative. They may unrealistically see the young placed child as having an ongoing bond with them that is stronger and will never be replaced by their bond with the adoptive parents.
- There is **limited empathy for the child's position**, such as an understanding of how they need to be/will have settled and bonded with their adoptive parents.
- Some people may admit to a **desire to get the child back** – and see it as their right that they could get the child back, **feeling that the child is "theirs"**. They show little or no understanding of the child as an individual and lack empathy for how this might affect them. The birth relative may not necessarily express the desire to reclaim the child or disturb the placement, but this is based on their view that it is not possible rather than that it would not be good for the child. They may express the view that the child would be better off with them than with the adoptive family.
- **Resentment of the adoptive parents** may be present to a greater or lesser extent. Feelings about the adoptive parents may not necessarily be totally negative – they may see them as nice people and carers but just not like parents or a "proper" family. They may not show any interest in the adoptive parent (either as a parent of their child or as a person) or their other children, or may seek to avoid thinking about them because it is too painful to acknowledge their existence.
- In some cases the parent might have **unrealistic hopes regarding the future** (e.g. that the child should have regular staying contact or come back and live with them when older).
- Alternatively, the birth relative may **deny the nature of their**

connection to the child. They may not show any understanding that the child might need to maintain a connection, or that the birth family might be important to them.

- The birth relative may **not turn up for contact or refuse to reply** to letters (or not get around to doing so), refuse to meet adoptive parents, etc.
- They might **maintain contact, but in an unhelpful way**, for example by being unable to contain their own feelings of anger or loss and not showing signs of thinking how this might negatively affect the child or adoptive parents, such as saying things that may disturb the placement.
- The person might **take steps to track down the child**.

In applying these indicators the following guidance was followed:

- Still feeling connected to, or having a bond with the child, or seeing that child as a part of their family does not preclude a high rating of accepting dual connection, providing it is combined with acceptance of adoptive parents and realistic expectations.
- Feelings of hurt, pain and discomfort over the loss of the child does not preclude a high rating of accepting dual connection.
- Thinking that the child should not have been removed or that adoption was unfair does not preclude a high rating of acceptance of dual connection, providing it is combined with acceptance of adoptive parents and realistic expectations.
- There may be different words used to refer to the two types of parents: e.g. step, surrogate, foster, etc. for the adoptive parents. People may even use the term "real" when describing the birth family. It is important to look at the context in which birth relatives use the terms, their understanding and the role they consider both types of parents to have, rather than focusing on word choices out of context.
- For siblings, grandparents and other relatives, comfort and promotion of dual connection also involves recognising and supporting the adoptive parents, siblings and grandparents as the legal and psychological relatives of the child.

Case example: High acceptance of dual connection (score 5)

Mary Jane is the birth mother of four children, three of whom were in foster care and one (Gregory, aged seven) who was adopted. Mary Jane said that she was 'devastated' when she realised that Gregory was going to be adopted, and that she still had 'a pain in my heart' when she thought about him. However, she showed a good understanding of Gregory's connection both to her family and to his adoptive family. She described his adoptive parents as his real parents, but added, 'He'll always be my son . . . I'm just his birth mum, and his real mummy is the one that will bring him up.' Although she enjoyed being called "Mummy Mary Jane" during contact she said:

I'm probably more like an auntie . . . I'm sad about it, but we're doing what's for Gregory's best interests . . . helping him move on . . . I think to Gregory [the adopters] are his mum and dad now.

Looking towards the future, Mary Jane said she did not think Gregory would want to come back and live with her but she hoped he might come and visit and she would be able to explain more clearly why things happened as they did. She showed empathy for Gregory's feelings as an adopted person, recognising his need to understand why he was adopted and to know that 'none of it is his fault'. She recognised that one reason why contact might be important to Gregory was because 'he remembers his brothers and sister' and contact with her was a way for him to find out about them. She was happy to stick to the boundaries of contact. Even though she wished meetings could be more frequent, she said that she would not 'push it'.

Case example: Low acceptance of dual connection (score 1)

Birth mother Deirdre's son Jay (now aged 11) was taken into care when he was two and adopted at age four. Deirdre described her role in relation to Jay as follows:

I am not just the birth mother, I am his mum . . . I don't care what anybody says, I am his mum . . . I said [to the adopters] 'Well, you didn't carry him for nine months . . . so how can you say you are his parents – you will never be.'

Even though Deirdre had not parented Jay for over nine years, she emphasised what she saw as the close nature of their relationship, saying 'Jay and I were really bonded and they can't break our bond: that's unconditional love.' She believed she got on much better with Jay compared to how he got on with his adoptive parents, saying that during contact meetings (where the adoptive parents were present) she and Jay entered their 'own little world'. On hearing that Jay was reportedly disturbed following contact meetings with her, she expressed the view that 'He is telling [the adopters] that he doesn't really want to be with them.'

Feelings about the outcomes of adoption for the child

In a previous examination of birth relatives' feelings about adoption by Neil (2007b), an important theme that emerged was how people felt about the outcome of the adoption for the child. Feeling confident that the child was happy and loved in the adoptive family seemed a very important part of managing the difficult feelings that often surrounded the adoption. A hope or confidence that the child was having a good life appeared to mitigate some of the pain of adoption; some birth parents expressed this as, 'something good has come out of something bad'. A feeling that things had worked out for the child seemed related to people's ability to move on in other areas – in some cases to let go of anger, blame or guilt. A sense of assurance of the child's welfare seemed to be both an indicator of positive aspects of adjustment for the birth relative and a predictor of other positive outcomes, e.g. accepting dual connection.

We rated people's feelings about the outcomes of adoption for the child as follows: score 5 was positive (there was a clear predominance of positive indicators applying); score 3 was mixed (there was no clear predominance of positives or negatives); and score 1 was negative (there was a clear predominance of negative indicators applying). The positive and negative indicators of this dimension are described below and case examples are given.

Positive indicators of feelings about the outcomes of adoption for the child

• The birth relative has **peace of mind** that the child is OK; they feel the child is developing well and is happy (though they may have occasional non-specific worries, or the type of anxieties that any birth relative might have about a child).

- They feel **reassured** that the child is being cared for properly and is loved by the adopters.
- They feel the adopters are **good parents**; they trust their parenting decisions and feel confident they will do the best for the child and will not let them come to harm (emotionally and physically).
- They see a **loving attachment** between the child and their adoptive parents.
- The birth relative shows **positive feelings/happiness** for the child (thinking about the child often or having an ongoing sense of loss in relation to them is not seen as a contra-indicator).

Negative indicators of feelings about the outcomes of adoption for the child

- There is **no confidence** that all will be OK for the child.
- The birth relative refers to **fears** that the child may be being abused or is unhappy.
- There are **worries** about the child's health, development or happiness.
- The birth relative may **express much negativity** around simply not knowing about their child's life and/or the adoptive parents – feelings of anxiety, being preoccupied with thoughts or anxieties about the child.
- There is **no (or very minimal) reference to positive factors** about the child's life.

Case example: Positive feelings about the outcomes of adoption for the child (score 5)

The following birth mother had written down her reflections on her daughter's adoption and read these out in her interview. This quotation is taken from these reflections:

> *I'll never forget Kelly, I'll never stop being concerned about her as I carried her for nine months – it is a natural instinct . . . [but] I am very grateful that my lovely daughter has gone to two*

wonderful parents and I wouldn't destroy the relationship that they have got together . . . she has grown into a bright, intelligent, beautiful girl. I do miss certain things like sports days, school activities and school plays, but life has to go on. I know she is very happy where she is and I'm glad she's happy, as that obviously makes me happy. She is my pride and joy.

Case example: Negative feelings about the outcomes of adoption for the child (score 1)

One birth mother was very worried that her child (age six) was 'not settling' with her adoptive parents. She felt that this child, the oldest of her five children, all of whom were in care or adopted, was 'unhappy' and she said she worried about this child more than any of her other children. She was concerned about her daughter's behavioural development, saying she had 'started to play up at school'. She was worried that her child had not wanted to be adopted, that she wanted to come home and that she was worried her birth mother didn't love her any more and that she had 'got rid' of her.

It is clear from the case examples above that in forming a view about the welfare of their child after adoption, birth relatives draw on the information available to them through their contact with the child and the adoptive parents. Many people referred to the positive impact of having contact after adoption, so the dimension of coping with adoption is heavily influenced *by* contact as well as being an influence *on* contact.

Dealing with the impact of adoption on self

Having a child or grandchild adopted almost always precipitates negative emotions for the parent or grandparents; these include a sense of loss and bereavement, feelings of guilt, shame or stigma, and anger. For some people these negative emotions bring about a deterioration in their ability to function socially and psychologically at their normal level. Our birth relative consultants drew our attention particularly to the need to consider how well relatives cope with managing negative emotional states, including feelings about themselves and the practical and social challenges of trying to carry on with life after such a difficult experience. Thus, we attempted to examine and measure how well the birth parent/relative was dealing with the impact of the adoption on their lives. Key areas we considered were:

- how people think about themselves in relation to the adoption;
- dealing with negative emotions;
- getting on with life;
- the ability to take positive actions to help themselves.

We rated "dealing with the impact of adoption on self" as follows: score 5 was positive (there was a clear predominance of positive indicators applying); score 3 was mixed (there was no clear predominance of positives or negatives); and score 1 was negative (there was a clear predominance of negative indicators applying). The positive and negative indicators that we used in our coding are described below.

Positive indicators of dealing with the impact of adoption on self:

- The birth relative can voice reasons why the adoption may have been necessary, including how they may have failed as a parent (if applicable). They can **take a realistic view of their parenting and the adoption**.
- They **show signs of self-worth**, e.g. by understanding that they may be important to child or they still have something to offer to the child and adoptive parents.
- They are likely to be **able to make efforts to work towards improving the situation for themselves** and the child, or for others (or wish to take up support if it is offered and they are practically able to).
- Although they are very likely to feel that the adoption has been a negative experience, **the negative impact has not completely penetrated all/most aspects of their personality and life experience**. They may see some positive effects or be able to focus on positive outcomes of the adoption. Positive feelings are expressed or there are positive signs about the way they are living with the adoption.
- The **adoption experience does not prohibit them from engaging**

115

positively in wider life activities (although they may be limited by ongoing psychological/learning difficulties that were present prior to the adoption).

Negative indicators of dealing with the impact of adoption on self:

* They are **overtaken by guilt, worthlessness or shame**, and think the child might be better off without them. Conversely, they might **see themselves as entirely blameless**, even in the face of significant evidence to the contrary.
* **Negative feelings and thoughts are dominant**, e.g. there are overriding, all-encompassing feelings of loss or anger.
* They find it **difficult to engage positively in wider life activities** because of the adoption experience (rather than because of psychological/learning difficulties that were present prior to the adoption).
* They may feel they do not deserve any help or support because they are bad. Or they express strong feelings of powerlessness. **They are unable to take positive actions to improve things for themselves.**

Case example: Dealing with the impact of adoption on self – high (score 5)

One birth mother had her baby removed when he was 18 months old. She said she was 'hurt inside' by the loss of her son and that this brought on a bout of depression. At the time, she felt her son's removal was unfair but in the interview she said, 'Looking back on it now I think they might have been right.' Although she recognised her limitations as a parent, she did see herself as loving and being able to help her son in the future by telling him about his background. She took great comfort from being able to continue to see her son, saying that contact made her 'heart feel warmer'. She still found it painful that he calls his adoptive mother 'Mum', but she said this hurt much less than it used to. She had recovered from her depression and said she had friends she could turn to in times of need. She said she was happy with her life now, she had a partner and a part-time job and that when she thought of her son she felt happy. Her sense of loss had not entirely gone away, however, and she explained, 'I think there is still something missing – that is why I got the cat – she's my little baby now.'

Case example: Dealing with the impact of adoption on self – low (score 1)

One birth mother showed a lot of signs of intense and ongoing feelings of grief because of the loss of her child to adoption. She had problems sleeping and would often cry in the night. She had kept all her child's toys and other things and had even continued to buy more toys, feeling that her daughter was going to come home, even though she knew she would not. She said:

> I'm stuck in the house all the time, thinking of [my daughter] and it's really hard . . . sometimes I just feel like packing up all my stuff and moving, just moving away from here, leaving everything that reminds me of [my daughter].

She felt that the adoption was affecting her in a number of ways: 'Before, I used to go out with my friends all the time. I used to go out with [my partner]. Now we just sit in the house. We hardly go out.' She found it hard to be in the company of people with babies and avoided such situations if possible. She did not recognise the validity of the reasons why the child was taken into care. Although she wanted to have contact with her child, she found meetings extremely painful because it brought home the reality of the child's connection to the adoptive family.

Results for the three "coping with adoption" subscales

Results are presented for each of the three "coping with adoption" subscales:

- accepting dual connection;
- feelings about the outcomes of adoption for the child;
- dealing with the impact of adoption on self.

Table 6.2 shows the results of the coding of acceptance of dual connection at Time 1. The scores on this dimension were clustered towards the higher end of the scale, suggesting that even though most of these adoptions had been non-voluntary, many birth relatives could nevertheless offer support to the adoptive parents and the child. There were some relatives, however, who remained resistant to accepting the child's connection to the adoptive family and in these cases the feelings of birth relatives could pose difficulties for both children and adoptive parents.

The fact that the majority of birth relatives supported the child's dual connection is likely to be linked to the fact that all these birth relatives had ongoing contact with the child. In Neil's previous research (Neil, 2007c), birth relatives who had direct contact with the child after adoption were significantly more likely to show positive acceptance of the adoption than those who did not have such contact. Neil argued that the relationship between acceptance of adoption and contact plans is likely to be bi-directional: relatives who initially accept the adoption may in some cases be allowed a higher level of contact, but also high levels of contact can lead to a greater acceptance of the adoption. This is also likely to be true in the current study, where, generally speaking, children had been adopted several years previously. Birth relatives who could not accept the child's membership of the birth family may not have been allowed to have direct contact or their contact may have been stopped at an earlier stage.

Table 6.3 shows how birth relatives were coded on feelings about the outcomes of adoption for the child at Time 1. Three-quarters felt very positive about their child's welfare and their life in the adoptive family.

Table 6.2
Ratings of acceptance of dual connection at Time 1

	n	%
1. Very low	2	5.0
2. Low	2	5.0
3. Mixed	7	18.5
4. Mainly high	9	24.0
5. Very high	18	47.5
Total	**38***	**100**

* One person could not be coded on this dimension because the child was not yet placed for adoption

Only one person had very negative feelings and the remaining birth relatives (n = 9, 24%) had a mix of positive and negative feelings. All the relatives in the sample had repeated opportunities to meet with adoptive parents, to see what they were like, to observe the child's progress and to experience first hand the difference in their role compared to that of the adoptive parents. Many relatives emphasised the positive impact of these opportunities on them.

Table 6.3
Feelings about the outcomes of adoption for the child

	n	%
1. Negative	1	3
2. Mixed	9	24
5. Positive	28	74
Total	**38***	**101****

* One person could not be coded because the child was not placed for adoption
** The total percentage equals 101 because of rounding

Table 6.4 contains the data about how birth relatives were rated on dealing with the impact of adoption on self. Compared to the other two dimensions, birth relatives' scores here are less positive: almost half were coded in the "mixed" category, and 40 per cent were coded as positive. Like many of the adopted children, many birth relatives enter the contact scenario carrying a lot of pain from the past and many ongoing problems in their day-to-day functioning.

Table 6.4
Dealing with the impact of adoption on self

	n	%
1. Negative	5	13
3. Mixed	18	47
5. Positive	15	40
Total	**38***	**100**

*One case could not be coded because interview answers were too brief

119

Results for a multidimensional "coping with adoption" scale

The correlations between scores on each of the three different dimensions of coping with adoption were significant (p<.01) and positive, but not so high as to suggest that they were measuring identical factors (correlations varied between 0.528 and 0.624). Scores from each of the three dimensions were summed and averaged to form one overall "coping with adoption" scale ($\alpha = .82$). To receive a score, at least two of the three subscales had to be rated. Table 6.5 shows the mean scores for the whole sample, and broken down by birth relative type. Higher scores indicate better coping. The range of scores for the whole sample was 1 to 5. The mean score was highest for adult siblings and was lowest for grand-parents/other relatives. However, because only six siblings and 11 grand-parents/other relatives are included, caution should be taken in interpreting these results.

Table 6.5
Mean scores on the coping with adoption combined scale for the whole sample and broken down by birth relative type

	Mean	*n*	*sd*
Whole sample	3.99	38	1.03
Birth parents	4.05	21	1.02
Adult siblings	4.39	6	.95
Grandparents/other relatives	3.67	11	1.07

The nature of the birth relatives' relationship with the child

As we reported in Chapter 5, over half of the birth relatives had at some point been the main carer (or one of the main carers) for the adopted child. This was true for most of the birth parents but also the case for a minority of grandparents and adult siblings. Where birth relatives had been the child's main carer in the past, this might complicate the experience of contact for the relatives themselves, as the loss of the child to adoption requires the need to relinquish this role to the adoptive parents. Where relationships have been characterised by dependency of one person on the other, this has been identified as a risk factor that can complicate resolution of bereavement (Parkes, 2001). If the relative having contact had been a main carer this might also make contact more complex for the child and adoptive parents (as we argued in Chapter 4). This is especially likely to be true when the relative having contact had been involved in the abuse or neglect of the child. Hence, in thinking about this in terms of risk, it was decided to distinguish between birth relatives who had not been involved in any abuse or neglect, and those whose child had been removed because of such concerns.

Of the 22 birth relatives who had at some point been the child's main carer, the 18 birth parents (17 birth mothers and one birth father) had all had their child removed. Although in the interviews some birth parents disputed that they had neglected or abused their child, all these children had been adopted from the care system and the threshold criteria of section 31 of the Children Act 1989 must have applied for this to have happened (i.e. the child had been, or was likely to be, significantly harmed and that this was attributable to the care given by the parents). Cases such as these were considered to present the most potential risks/challenges to contact. Two grandmothers and two adult siblings had acted as the main carer for the adopted child, but the child had not been neglected or abused by them. These four cases were considered to present more risks/challenges compared to cases when the birth relative had never been the main carer, but the level of risk was considered to be lower than in the 18 cases involving abuse or neglect.

Therefore, as Table 6.6 outlines, if the birth relative had been the main carer and the child had been removed from their care because of concerns of abuse or neglect, then a risk score of –2 was assigned. If the relative had been the main carer but had not been involved in any abuse or neglect a risk score of –1 was assigned. If the relative had never been the child's main carer (as was true in 17 cases), this was considered to be neutral.

Creating a combined strengths and risks score for birth relatives engaging in a contact situation

In order to quantify the combined strengths and risks that birth relatives were bringing to the contact situation we used all the three variables described above (mental health, coping with adoption scores, and whether or not the relatives had been the child's main carer). Table 6.6 summarises how we calculated the combined strengths/risks score for birth relatives.

Using this methodology, if a birth relative had every risk, the lowest score on this scale (indicating the highest risk) would be –5. If a relative had none of the risk factors and all the highest possible strength factors,

Table 6.6
Factors used to calculate birth family strengths and risks combined score

	−2 risk	−1 risk	0 neutral	+1 strength	+2 strength
Birth relatives' mental health problems	n/a	In clinical range	n/a	Not in clinical range	n/a
Birth relative has been caregiver for child	Has been main carer and child removed from their carer	Yes – has been main carer but not involved in neglect or abuse	Not main carer	n/a	n/a
Birth relatives coping with adoption	Very low (1–2)	Quite low (2.1–3)	Mixed (3.1–4)	Quite high (4.1–4.9)	Very high (5)

Table 6.7
Birth relatives' scores on the combined strengths/risks scale

	n	*%*
–5	1	3.2
–4	2	6.5
–3	3	9.7
–2	7	22.6
–1	2	6.5
0	3	9.7
1	10	32.3
2	1	3.2
3	2	6.5
Total	**31**	**100.2**

Percentages do not equal 100 because of rounding

then the highest score on this scale (indicating highest strength/lowest risk) would be +3. The scale therefore had nine points from –5 to +3. There were eight cases where the combined scale could not be computed because BSI data were missing. The mean score on the scale was –.6 and the standard deviation was 2.1. The median was 0 and the mode 1.

Table 6.7 shows the number of birth relatives scoring at each point of the total risks and strengths scale. This shows that just under one in five birth relatives (n = 6, 19%) had scores in the bottom third of the range, indicating they had many more risks than strengths. Twelve (39%) had scores in the middle of the range, indicating some strengths and some risks. The largest proportion of birth relatives (n = 13, 42%) had scores in the top third of the range, indicating more strengths than risks. This composite risk score cannot by itself indicate all the strengths and risks of contact situation. In practice, it will be important also to take account of the strengths and risks affecting the adoptive family.

Of the 31 birth relatives for whom we could compute the combined score, 19 were birth parents, four were siblings and eight were grandparents. The mean score for birth parents was –1.2 (range –5 to +1), for siblings it was .5 (range –2 to +2) and for grandparents 0 (range –4 to +3). Because numbers of siblings and grandparents are so small, care should be taken in interpreting this data.

Summary

This chapter has focused on the strengths and risks of birth relatives that are likely to impact on the outcomes of contact for all parties. Key points are as follows.

- The mental health of birth relatives was measured using the Brief Symptom Inventory. Over half of birth relatives (55%) had scores on this measure within the clinical range.
- In order to assess more adoption-specific outcomes, the interview data from birth relatives were used to develop a three-dimensional measure looking at how people were coping with adoption. The three dimensions were "acceptance of dual connection", "feelings about the outcomes of adoption for the child" and "living with the impact of adoption on self".
- In terms of acceptance of the child's dual connection, over 70 per cent of birth relatives scored mainly high or very high on this measure, indicating they can support the child as a member of the adoptive family. A minority of birth relatives remained resistant to accepting the adoptive placement, and in these cases contact may be difficult for the child or adoptive parents.
- The second dimension of coping with adoption explored how confident birth relatives felt about the child's welfare. Three-quarters felt very positive about how the adoption had worked out for the child and many commented on how the experience of having contact had helped them to reach this position.
- The third dimension of coping with adoption related to how well birth relatives were dealing with the impact of adoption on themselves. In comparison with the other two dimensions, fewer birth relatives scored in a positive range on this dimension: 60 per cent still had some or quite significant problems in managing the negative consequences of adoption, e.g. dealing with difficult feelings and re-engaging with wider life activities. It is clear that for many birth relatives the loss of

the child from their family presents long-term challenges that are not easily overcome.

- The third factor we looked at in this chapter was whether the birth relative had or had not been the main carer of the child before adoption, and whether they had been involved in the neglect or abuse of the child. Four relatives had been a carer for the child but had not been involved in neglect or abuse. Eighteen birth parents had been the main carer and the child had been removed from their care because of concerns of neglect or abuse. Seventeen birth relatives had never been the main carer for the child.

- Using coding from all three dimensions (mental health, coping with adoption, previous history of being the child's main carer) combined strengths/risks scores were calculated for birth relatives. Scores on this measure were spread across the range, with 42 per cent (n = 13) of people having scores in the top third of the range, indicating more strengths than risks.

7 Evaluations of contact from the adoptive parents, and the role of adoptive family strengths and risks

This chapter presents data relating to the 51 adoptive parents and four long-term foster parents who participated in interviews, and for the sake of brevity all 55 parents will be referred to as adoptive parents.

The chapter will present findings from the quantitative data – adoptive parents' scores in relation to their comfort with contact, perception of the child's comfort with contact and satisfaction with their relationship with the birth relative, plus their scores on the "adoptive parent views of contact" Likert scale. These quantitative data were used to help distinguish between cases where contact was "working very well" and cases where there were "unresolved issues", and these two categories will be described. We then examine if and how adoptive parents' evaluations of contact are influenced by adoptive family strengths and risks. Qualitative data illustrating adoptive parents' experiences of contact will be described in the following chapter.

Adoptive parents' comfort with contact

Adoptive parents (n = 47 at Time 1 and n = 46 at Time 2) gave a mark from 1 to 10 to report their current levels of comfort with contact (that is, with contact in the last year), 1 being "extremely uncomfortable" to 10 "extremely comfortable". At Time 1, eight scores were missing because contact had stopped (n = 5), contact had not started (n = 1) or responses were not codable (n = 2). Results, therefore, do not represent the views of adoptive parents in cases where contact had stopped. Generally speaking, adoptive parents reported high levels of comfort with contact. At Time 1, the mean score was 7.45 (sd = 2.2), the median was 8, and the mode (most common response) was 10. A small proportion of adoptive parents (n = 6, 13%) chose numbers under 5, indicating they were uncomfortable with contact at Time 1. At Time 2, adoptive parents' scores were similarly high:

the mean was 7.85 (sd = 2.25) and the median and mode were 8 and 10 respectively. Four adoptive parents (9%) gave scores of less than 5 at Time 2. At Time 2, nine scores were missing – six because contact had stopped, two because the adoptive parents dropped out of the study and one because the response was not codable.

Adoptive parents' satisfaction with their relationship with the birth relative

Adoptive parents were asked to give a mark from 1 to 10 to indicate how satisfied they were with their relationship with birth relatives with whom their child was having contact, 1 being extremely dissatisfied and 10 being extremely satisfied. The mean scores at both points in time were relatively high (Time 1: mean = 7.9, sd = 2.1, n = 47; Time 2: mean = 7.2, sd = 2.6, n = 41). At Time 1, the median was 8.75, and the mode 10, and at Time 2 the median and the mode were 8 and 10 respectively. A small proportion of adoptive parents gave scores of less than 5, indicating they were relatively dissatisfied with their relationship with the birth relative (n = 5, 10% at Time 1, and n = 9, 22% at Time 2). Eight scores were missing at Time 1 (five because contact had stopped, one because it had not started and two cases were uncodable). At Time 2, 14 scores were missing (six because contact had stopped, two because parents did not take part and six cases were uncodable).

Adoptive parents' ratings of the child's comfort with contact

Adoptive parents were asked to give a mark from 1 to 10 to indicate how comfortable they believed their child had been with the contact arrangements during the past year, with 1 being extremely uncomfortable and 10 being extremely comfortable. At Time 1, the mean, median and mode were all 8 (sd = 1.7, n = 46), and at Time 2 they were 8.1 (sd = 1.9, n = 46), 8.5 and 10 respectively. At Time 1, two parents gave a score of less than 5 (4%), as did four parents at Time 2 (9%). Managing children's reactions to contact was a significant theme in adoptive parents' discussion of the complexities of contact, and this is discussed in more detail in the following chapter. Nine scores were missing at Time 1 (five because contact had stopped, one because it had not started and three cases were uncodable). At Time 2, nine scores were missing (six because contact had stopped, two because parents did not take part and one case was uncodable).

Adoptive parents' ratings of contact – summary

On the three questions where adoptive parents were asked to give a mark out of 10 to describe various aspects of contact (the child's comfort, their own comfort and their own satisfaction with their relationship with the birth relative), mean scores were high for all three questions, and the highest mean scores were for the child's comfort with contact. With the exception of a few cases, parents usually gave similar scores to all three questions; if their child was comfortable with contact they tended to be comfortable with contact, and they also tended to be satisfied with their relationship with the birth relative; if the child was considered to be uncomfortable with contact, the adoptive parent, unsurprisingly, was often uncomfortable with it. In considering these ratings of contact, it is important to remember that mean scores do not reflect the parents' views in cases where contact had stopped, and the perception of these parents is likely to be more negative than in cases where contact was ongoing. Also, while most adoptive parents are likely to understand their child's feelings very well, the ratings of the child's comfort with contact are from the parents' perspective and not the child's.

The "adoptive parent views of contact" measure

The "adoptive parent views of contact" measure is a Likert scale with 16 items ($\alpha = .91$). The scale contained a mix of positively and negatively worded items, each rated on a 6-point scale as follows: 6 = strongly agree, 5 = mainly agree, 4 = slightly agree, 3 = slightly disagree, 2 = mainly disagree and 1 = strongly disagree. Negatively worded items were reverse scored so that higher scores indicate a more positive view of contact. Items on the scale relate to ongoing contact arrangements, so adoptive parents did not complete the scale if contact had stopped. A mean score was computed when parents completed at least 13 of the 16 items (81%). At Time 1, 33 of the 50 (66%) parents with ongoing contact completed the scale. The mean scores ranged from 1.4 to 5.9, with an overall mean of 4.27 (sd = 1.10). Twenty-nine cases (88%) had mean scores of three or above, indicating that most parents with ongoing contact had positive views of it.

At Time 2, 37 adoptive parents completed the measure. The range of mean scores was 1.6 to 6, the overall mean was 4.35 (sd = 1.20, minimum = 1.63). Eighty-four per cent had a mean score of three or higher, indicating that most parents with ongoing contact had positive views of it.

Table 7.1 shows how many adoptive parents agreed (strongly agreed, mainly agreed or slightly agreed) with each of the 16 statements at Time 1 and Time 2. Most adoptive parents agreed with the positively worded items, such as 'I think my child is better off because he/she has this contact with the birth family.' While between 24 and 42 per cent, depending on the item, agreed with the negatively worded items, such as 'I worry that this contact may be doing my child more harm than good.' A few items stand out. For example, only about half of adopters agreed that 'the face-to-face contact we have with our child's birth relatives supports me as a parent', and the majority agreed with the statement that 'having face-to-face contact puts more pressure on adoptive families than not having such contact'. Adoptive parents' answers to these two questions may indicate that although some may value many aspects of contact, the experience may not always be easy and may add demands to their parenting role. It is also interesting to note that almost four out of five adoptive parents agreed with the statement 'I think my child is better off because he/she has this contact with the birth family', whereas only about three out of five agreed with the statement 'seeing my child's birth family is helpful to me'. This suggests that in some cases parents may be facilitating contact for the sake of their child while perceiving no or few benefits for themselves.

Table 7.1

Adoptive parent views of contact measure – overall agreement with the items

	Time 1 (n = 33)		Time 2 (n = 37)	
	n agree	%	n agree	%
I think my child is better off because he/she has this contact with the birth family	27	82	28	78
I worry that this contact may be doing my child more harm than good	12	36	9	24
Seeing his/her birth family upsets my child	14	42	14	38
Seeing his/her birth family comforts my child	22 of 32	69	22	59
My child feels comfortable with this face-to-face contact	25 of 32	78	28 of 36	78
My child enjoys this face-to-face contact	27 of 32	84	28 of 36	78
Having face-to-face contact with his/her birth family causes my child to worry more about them	8	27	8 of 32	22
I feel comfortable with the face-to-face contact I have with my child's birth family	22	66	26	70
I worry about these birth relatives intruding in my family's life	12	36	13	35
Seeing my child's birth family makes it harder for me to really feel like my child's parent	8	24	9	25
Seeing my child's birth family is helpful to me	20 of 32	63	25	68
Having face-to-face contact puts more pressure on adoptive families than not having such contact	20	61	24 of 36	67
The face-to-face contact we have with our child's birth relatives supports me as a parent	14	42	20	54
I feel I have the right amount of control over decisions about this face-to-face contact	28	85	29	78
I regret having this face-to-face contact with the birth family	11	33	10	27
If I had a magic wand I would stop this face-to-face contact today	8	24	2	22

How many contact arrangements were "working very well"?

Adoptive parents' contact arrangements were categorised into two groups: working very well (for brevity, sometimes referred to as "working well") and unresolved issues.

Membership in the "working very well" group required meeting all three of the following criteria:

- Contact had to be ongoing. In other words, all cases where contact had stopped were automatically in the unresolved issues group.
- The mean score on the "Adoptive parent views of contact" measure was greater than or equal to three.
- The sum of scores on three measures – adoptive parents' comfort with contact, adoptive parents' satisfaction with their relationship with the birth relative, and adoptive parents' ratings of the child's comfort with contact – was 24 or above and the child's comfort was rated 8 or higher.

In addition, even those cases meeting the criteria described above were assigned to the "unresolved issues" group if the qualitative data revealed that adoptive parents had raised issues that indicated contact was not really working well.

Finally, if quantitative data were not available, a researcher reviewed interviews and the criteria for inclusion in the "working very well" group included:

- the child's reactions to contact were reported by adoptive parents to be unproblematic;
- the adoptive parents were positive about contact;
- the adoptive parents reported no significant problems with contact.

In summary, contact arrangements in the "working very well" group were uniform in there being an absence of any significant problems.

At Time 1, 43 per cent of cases (n = 23) were classified as "working very well" and 57 per cent of cases (n = 32) were classified as having some "unresolved issues" (based on 54 cases; one case not included as contact had not started). At Time 2, 45% (n = 24) were coded as "working very well" and 55 per cent (n = 29) had "unresolved issues" (based on 53 cases; two cases were missing because parents did not take part).

Although the percentages in each group were very similar at each time point, there had been significant change in over one-quarter of cases (based on the 52 cases where we rated the contact at both time points): 16 cases (31%) were working very well at both points in time, 22 cases had unresolved issues at both points in time (42%), seven cases (13.5%) had improved from having unresolved issues at Time 1 to working very well at Time 2, and the same number (n = 7, 13.5%) had deteriorated from working well to having unresolved issues. This illustrates the dynamic nature of contact arrangements and suggests that people's needs for support may fluctuate over time.

Case example: Working very well

Harry, age eight, had contact with his birth father twice a year, meeting him in the park in summer and at a museum in the winter. The whole adoptive family came along, as did a social worker. These arrangements had been stable for the three years of the placement and no particular difficulties had ever arisen. Harry's adoptive mother felt he enjoyed the meetings and was always pleased to see his father – she rated his comfort as 9 out of 10 and her own comfort as 10 out of 10. She said that she liked the birth father and appreciated the respect he showed for the rules and boundaries of contact; she rated her satisfaction with her relationship with the birth father as 8 out of 10. The adoptive mother's mean score on the "views of contact" Likert scale was 5.2. In her interview she evidenced a high level of satisfaction with contact, feeling it was straightforward and beneficial for her and for Harry.

The "unresolved issues" group was diverse in the nature and extent of problems that complicated contact. The majority of cases in this group could be described as on balance positive but with some concerns (see Case example 1 below). There were issues associated with the contact that were less than satisfactory, but overall adoptive parents were persisting with the arrangement because they felt the benefits outweighed the drawbacks. But the "unresolved issues" group also included cases where contact had stopped completely because it was working so poorly or where it was carrying on but with major problems (see Case example 2).

Case example 1: Unresolved issues

Michaela, age six, met with her two older sisters (both adopted in separate placements) once a year, the three adoptive families getting together for a day out at a leisure park. The girls were always really pleased to see each other and they got on well. The adoptive mother felt that seeing her sisters had helped Michaela to settle. She rated Michaela's comfort with the contact as 7 out of 10, saying that although Michaela was really happy during the meetings, she could be 'a bit more cross' for a few days afterwards, possibly because the meeting stirred up memories. The unresolved issues in this case included the behaviour of one of the sisters during contact, problems in co-ordinating the arrangements between the three families and difficulties related to the instability of the placement of one of the sisters.

Case example 2: Unresolved issues

Rio, age 13, was adopted at the age of seven. Contact with his birth mother was once a year. The problems with contact were numerous. Rio's birth mother denied problems in the past and refused to answer his questions about difficult experiences that he remembered. She also talked inappropriately to Rio and about how he would be coming back to live with her. She brought along her much younger children who were very demanding during the meeting. The contact meetings seemed to bring out very mixed feelings in Rio, who swung between wanting to see his mother and feeling angry with her and wanting not to see her. Rio's adoptive mother was very unhappy with contact, worrying about the impact on Rio's feelings and behaviour, and on her relationship with him. Over the years, contact had stopped and started a number of times as Rio's feelings changed about whether he did or did not want to see his birth mother.

It is important to remember that these two categorisations of how well contact was working are based on adoptive parents' perceptions. The impact of contact on the child is taken account of via adoptive parent reports and is central to how these categories work, in that contact is only described as working very well when adoptive parents perceived their children to be very comfortable with it. It is possible, however, that in some cases where parents perceived the contact to be working well the child may actually be experiencing problems or anxieties about it. In other cases, parents' perceptions of contact may be the source of unresolved issues, e.g. if they find contact personally difficult, but from the child's point of view the contact is working well.

The role of adoptive family strengths and risks in determining adoptive parents' experiences of contact

It would be useful for practitioners to know when contact has a good chance of working and which risk factors may get in the way of contact working well. Understanding how the strengths and risks of adoptive families may impact on contact would also help to determine the right type and level of contact support. In this section, we report our exploratory analyses that assessed whether the strengths and risks within the adoptive family were associated with placement in one of the two categories, "working very well" or "unresolved issues".

Five chi-square tests were performed to examine whether each of five categorical variables representing strengths and risks were associated with contact working well. The five variables included whether:

- the child had emotional or behavioural problems;
- adoptive parents reported problems in their relationship with the child;
- adoptive parent reports indicated that their child had complicated feelings about adoption;
- the child was over age two at the time of placement with the adoptive family;
- the child was having contact with a relative who had been the main carer and who had neglected or abused them.

Results are reported below.

The child's emotional and behavioural problems

Significantly more children who had emotional or behavioural problems were in the "unresolved issues" group than would be expected by chance ($\chi 2 = 4.6$, df = 1, p<.05). Overall, 24 children (44%) had emotional or behavioural problems. However, in cases where contact was working very well (n = 25) only seven children (28%) had such problems, while 18 children (72%) had no emotional or behavioural difficulties. In contrast, where contact had unresolved issues (n = 30), over half of the children (n = 17, 57%) had emotional or behavioural problems. This provides additional evidence (see the argument put forward in Chapter 4) that contact is more likely to run into difficulties when children have emotional or behavioural problems. Such children have fewer resources to cope with stresses inherent in contact.

The relationship between the adoptive parent and the child

The association between the parent–child relationship (positive and unproblematic versus ongoing problems) and contact working well was not statistically significant ($\chi 2 = 3.8$, df = 1, p = .051), but results were very close to being significant.

In 39 cases (71%) adoptive parents described a relationship with their child that was coded as "positive and unproblematic". In cases where contact was working well, 84 per cent (n = 21) of adoptive parent–child relationships were positive and only 16 per cent (n = 4) had ongoing problems. In contrast, where contact had unresolved issues, a smaller proportion (n = 18, 60%) of children had a positive and unproblematic relationship with their adoptive parents and in 40 per cent of cases (n = 12) the parent–child relationship had some ongoing difficulties. Where the parent–child relationship was not entirely positive, only one in four contact arrangements were working well.

It would be a mistake to conclude from this non-significant result that the relationship between the adoptive parent and child is irrelevant to the workings of birth family contact. Further research is critical in this area. A good parent–child relationship is likely to be a resource that children can draw on to manage contact, and a difficult parent–child relationship may make it harder for contact to be successful.

135

The child's feelings about adoption

The chi-square test looking at the association between the child's feelings about adoption and contact working well was not statistically significant ($\chi2 = .87$, $df = 1$, $p = .35$). Children were coded into two groups representing their feelings about adoption:

a) children described by adoptive parents as having complicated feelings (complicated/birth family idealising, complicated/given up on birth family, complicated/mixed feelings);

b) children described by parents as having either uncomplicated positive feelings or being neutral because they were unable to understand adoption.

See Chapter 4 for a detailed description of each of these groups.

Just over half of children were in group (a) (n = 28, 51%) and just under half were in group (b) (n = 27, 49%). It was argued in Chapter 4 that children's complex feelings about adoption could make the experience of birth family contact more difficult for them. In cases where contact was working well, 44 per cent of children (n = 11) were in group (a) and 56 per cent (n = 14) were not. In cases where the contact had unresolved issues, the proportions were reversed: 57 per cent of children (n = 17) had problematic feelings and 43 per cent (n = 13) did not.

It may be that no clear relationship was found because of the diversity within the group of children who had problematic feelings. For example, some children in this group idealised their birth family, while other children appeared to have given up on them. It could also be that using adoptive parent reports is an insufficiently sensitive measure of children's feelings.

The child's age at placement

Children were classified into two groups: if the child had been placed for adoption under the age of two (n = 14) this was considered to be a positive factor, likely to make birth family contact easier (see Chapter 4); if the child had been placed over the age of two (n = 41) the opposite was proposed, i.e. that this posed a risk for contact.

The results of the chi-square test support an association between age of placement and contact working well. More of the under-twos than would be expected by chance were in the working well contact group ($\chi 2 = 5.1$, df = 1, p<.05). In the contact working well group, 40 per cent of children were under age two at placement (n = 10) and 60 per cent were over age two (n = 15). In the group where contact had unresolved issues, 87 per cent of children were over age two (n = 26) and only 13 per cent (n = 4) under age two at placement.

The child's previous relationship with the contact relative

As described in Chapter 4, where children were having contact with a birth relative who had been their main carer and who had been implicated in neglecting or abusing them, this was considered to be a risk factor. This was the case with 28 children (51%) and in all of these cases except one the birth relative was a birth parent. Of the remaining children, most were having contact with a grandparent, sibling, other relative or birth parent who had never been their main carer, or in two cases with a grandparent or older sibling who had looked after them but who had not abused or neglected them.

The chi-square test was statistically significant, suggesting an association between the child having contact with a relative who had abused or neglected them and whether contact worked well ($\chi 2 = 6.6$, df = 1, p<.01). Where contact was working well, in just over two-thirds of cases (n = 17, 68%) contact did not involve the child seeing a person who had been their main carer who had neglected or abused them, and in about one-third of cases it did involve such a birth relative (n = 8, 32%). However, in cases where contact was not working very well (the unresolved issues group), the proportions were reversed: 20 children (67%) were having contact with a main carer who had abused or neglected them and ten children (33%) were not. These findings suggest that where children are having contact with a person who abused or neglected them, particular attention needs to be paid to the management and support of the arrangement, and any benefits of such contact will need to be weighed against potential risks.

Results of logistic regression analysis: the adoption communication openness of adoptive parents

In Chapter 4 it was argued that where adoptive parents are more communicatively open, contact is more likely to work well and vice versa. A logistic regression analysis was performed, with the two contact groupings ("working very well" and "unresolved issues") as the dependent variable and the total adoption communication openness scores of adoptive parents as the predictor variable. The full model significantly predicted group membership ($\chi2 = 5.5$, $df = 1$, p<.05). The model predicted 65 per cent of cases accurately, with 72 per cent of the "working very well" contact arrangements successfully predicted and 60 per cent of those with "unresolved issues". Table 7.2 gives the co-efficients, the Wald statistic and associated degrees of freedom and probability values for the predictor variable (adoption communication openness scores).

Table 7.2
Results of logistic regression: contact working well and adoptive parent adoption communication openness scores

	B	S.E.	Wald	DF	Sig.	Exp (B)	95.0% C.I. for Exp (B) Lower	Upper
Adoption communication openness	−.15	.07	4.7	1	.03	1.16	1.01	1.33

The odds ratio (Exp (B)) of 1.16 indicates that the odds of being in the working well group are 1.16 times greater, with a one unit increase in the adoption communication openness score of the adoptive parent. In other words, the odds of being in the working well group are increased by 16 per cent for every one more point on the adoption communication openness scale. These findings suggest that assessing and promoting the communicative openness of adoptive parents is an important consideration in contact support work. However, this variable did not predict whether or not contact was working well in a third of cases, and was less effective at predicting "unresolved issues" than "working very well" cases. This indicates that adoptive parents' adoption communication openness, while clearly being very important, is not the only relevant factor in determining the quality of contact. For example, in a case where the adoptive mother was assigned the maximum score in terms of adoption communication openness, contact was still tricky in some respects because of the severe mental illness of the birth mother, which affected her conduct during contact, and the mixed feelings of the child about seeing his birth mother.

The adoptive family combined risks/strengths scores

The adoptive family combined risks/strengths score (see Chapter 4) draws together data from all the variables discussed above. For purposes of this analysis, the scores were transformed by adding 11, so the minimum score was one and the maximum 20.

Logistic regression analysis was performed to examine whether adoptive parents' scores on this combined scale predicted whether contact was working very well or whether there were unresolved issues. This analysis showed that the risks/strengths score significantly predicted group membership ($\chi2 = 9.7$, $df = 1$, p<.01). Overall, the model predicted 67 per cent of cases accurately, with 60 per cent of cases where contact was working very well accurately predicted, and 73 per cent of unresolved issues cases correctly predicted.

Table 7.3 gives the co-efficients, the Wald statistic and associated degrees of freedom and probability values for the predictor variable (adoptive family combined risks/strengths scores).

The odds ratio (Exp (B)) of 1.22 indicates that the odds of being in the working well group are 1.22 times greater, with a one unit increase in the adoptive family combined risks/strengths score of the adoptive parent. In other words, the odds of being in the working well group are increased by 22 per cent for every one more point on this scale. Examples of what one point on this scale represents include the difference between an adoptive parent having a low score on one of the communicative openness subscales versus them having a moderate score. Two points on this scale would represent the difference between the child being under or over age

Table 7.3
Results of logistic regression: contact working well and adoptive family combined risks/strengths scores

	B	S.E.	Wald	DF	Sig.	Exp (B)	95.0% C.I. for Exp (B)	
							Lower	Upper
Combined adoptive family risks/strengths	.198	.07	7.5	1	.006	1.22	1.06	1.41

two at placement, or them having emotional or behavioural problems or not having such problems.

It is unsurprising that combined risks/strengths score predicted whether contact worked well, as most of the individual components of this score had a significant effect. It would be useful for future research to consider the relative impact of all the different factors that can have a bearing on contact. Another future step would be to evaluate whether it is the number of strengths or the number of risks that best predict whether contact goes well versus the presence of any one or two particular strengths or risks. A larger and/or a more homogeneous sample would be needed to test these research questions.

As practitioners will know, and as the analyses in this chapter demonstrate, many factors enter into the dynamics of the contact situation. Social workers would be well advised to take these various elements into consideration, particularly:

• the child's emotional or behavioural problems;
• the child's previous relationship with the birth relative;
• the age of the child at placement; and
• the adoptive parents' level of communicative openness.

Social workers who assess the level, or the presence or absence, of these factors will more likely offer better advice, training and support to everyone involved in the contact situation than social workers who do not have this information.

Summary

This chapter reported on the quantitative data collected from adoptive parents about their experiences of contact. Relationships between adoptive family strengths and risks and the outcomes of contact from adoptive parents' perspectives were then explored. Key findings are as follows:

- Adoptive parents involved in ongoing contact arrangements were asked to give marks from 1 to 10 indicating how comfortable they were with contact, how satisfied they were with their relationship with the contact birth relative and how comfortable they believed their child to be with contact. On all three dimensions, mean scores were in the region of 7–8 out of 10, and only a small minority of adoptive parents chose scores of under 5.
- Adoptive parents completed a 16-item Likert scale that sought their views about contact. Responses indicated that about two-thirds to three-quarters were in agreement with statements that were positive about contact. About one-third to one-quarter were in agreement with statements that were negative about contact. Over four out of five adoptive parents (88%) had a mean score on this scale that indicated they were more positive than negative. These findings only apply if the contact arrangement was ongoing at the time of the study.
- Contact arrangements were classified into two groups using both quantitative and qualitative data. The first group, "working very well", were cases where very few problems had been experienced and where adoptive parents were very positive about the comfort and value of contact for themselves and their child. The second group, "unresolved issues", included cases where adoptive parents had largely positive experiences but some difficulties have been experienced, through to very unsatisfactory cases where contact had stopped or was of very poor quality.
- Between 43 per cent and 45 per cent of cases were "working very well"; 55–57 per cent of cases had "unresolved issues". Whether or not contact was working well changed for just over a quarter (27%) of families over time, indicating the dynamic nature of contact.

- Contact working very well was significantly associated with the following factors:
  - the child not having emotional or behavioural problems ($p<.05$);
  - the child being under age two at placement ($p<.05$);
  - the child not having contact with a person who had been their main carer and who had abused or neglected them ($p<.01$).
- The child having a positive and unproblematic relationship with their adoptive parent was not statistically significant ($p = .051$), but future research is needed to examine this further, as it may be an important factor.
- The adoption communication openness scores of adoptive parents significantly predicted whether contact was working very well or not; the more "communicatively open" adoptive parents were, the more likely contact was to be working well ($p<.01$).
- The adoptive family risks/strengths scores significantly predicted whether contact was working well or not ($p<.01$).

8   The challenges and benefits of contact: themes from interviews with adoptive parents

This chapter uses adoptive parents' accounts of their experiences of contact to understand the factors that contribute to the success or otherwise of contact. The chapter describes the themes identified from the data that relate to the quality of contact and its benefits as perceived by adoptive parents. The factors associated with successful contact are summarised and adoptive parents' needs in relation to contact support are suggested.

Themes related to the quality of contact

Adoptive parents' accounts of their experiences of the target contact arrangements were coded, initially under three overarching themes:

- the challenges of contact;
- the benefits of contact;
- the factors associated with the success of contact.

Every adoptive parent identified at least one factor in each of these three categories, but the balance of challenges, benefits and successes varied considerably from case to case. Success factors and challenges together provide an understanding of when and how contact works or does not work – i.e. the quality of contact.

Five main themes were identified:

- the child's reactions to contact;
- relationships between adoptive parents and others involved in contact;
- the quality of interactions between the child and birth relatives during contact meetings;
- managing risk, boundaries and confidentiality;
- managing adoptive parents' own emotions.

These themes are explored in more detail below.

The child's reactions to contact

A central concern for all adoptive parents, regardless of whether contact was experienced negatively or positively, was about the impact of contact on their child. Adoptive parents were asked to describe in detail their children's reactions to contact, including the child's feelings and behaviour before, during and after contact meetings. Three main patterns emerged. Some parents felt that their child's reactions to contact were unproblematic and positive. Other parents described a more mixed response in their child and identified a range of reactions, including some level of sadness, anxiety, stress or disturbance. A third group of parents felt their child was disinterested or disengaged with contact. These three groups are discussed in more detail below.

Where children evidenced difficult feelings or behaviours, adoptive parents obviously experienced this as challenging. It was also apparent that different parents could experience the same types of reactions in their children in very different ways. An example of this was the different ways parents responded to children feeling emotionally "stirred up" or confused by contact. Some felt this was an unhelpful consequence of contact, while others felt it was normal or even potentially useful. One adoptive parent said:

It stirs up memories . . . but maybe that's healthy in itself because I think sometimes there's a danger that he could bury the memories that actually need to come to the surface for him to deal with.

Examples such as this suggest that the extent to which children's reactions challenge adoptive parents is determined by the characteristics of both child and parent.

Some adoptive parents referred to methods they had to use to help children deal with their difficult feelings or behaviours. Several parents mentioned arranging a pleasant family activity immediately after contact. Other parents referred to thinking carefully about the timing of contact meetings. Some felt it was better for their child to avoid contact coinciding with other significant events, e.g. starting a new school year. What worked in terms of helping children feel comfortable varied from case to case. Some adoptive parents felt their child was more comfortable with contact if it took place in the school holidays. Others felt that having contact during the school term helped the child cope with difficult feelings because they could get straight back into their normal routine.

Together, the data suggest that the challenges of contact are influenced by the characteristics of both the child and the adoptive parent as well as the sub-context in which contact occurs.

Parents who described their child's reaction to contact as unproblematic and positive

Twenty-five of the 55 adoptive or foster parents felt their child did not show any significant signs that contact was a worrying or upsetting experience. Seven of the 25 children (28%) were having contact with just adult birth relatives, 12 children were having sibling contact (48%) and six (24%) were having contact with adults and siblings combined.

Within this group, parents believed that contact was, for most of the children, something to look forward to. They felt their children showed no signs of distress or anxiety either before or after contact. This group included parents of very young children, who did not yet understand the significance of contact, and children with significant developmental disabilities. In such cases, parents felt that contact was unremarkable for their child. For example, the adoptive mother of a three-year-old child who had significant disabilities said that her son showed no understanding of the meaning of contact and no recognition of his birth mother. However, she felt he enjoyed contact meetings just because he liked 'going out and doing activities'.

Other parents in this group felt their child saw contact as something special and exciting. One adoptive mother described her son Bobby's reaction to seeing his older brother after a long gap as follows:

We told him that morning that he would see [his brother] that afternoon and he was so excited. Bobby called out the car window. He was out of the car and across the car park . . . he ran into [his brother's] arms and they hit it off straight away.

Another adoptive parent described how her child was 'on a real high, not silly – just really happy . . . delighted' after seeing his siblings.

Although parents in this group were not concerned about any negative impact of contact on their children, few felt that contact meetings were emotionally neutral. In some cases, parents felt their child had some mixed feelings associated with contact, for example, excitement beforehand or sadness afterwards, but did not interpret these reactions as problematic but as normal in the circumstances. One mother, for example, said that immediately after the contact meeting her daughter was like an 'excited little miniature volcano which is about ready to erupt'. However, she went on to say that after they talked about the contact for a while 'she gradually calms down and by the time we are on the train she will be talking about school or other things and it's not mentioned unless I mention it'.

Another mother described her child's reactions to contact with siblings as follows:

> She doesn't really mention it much when it's not happening, but she looks forward to it and enjoys it. [After contact] she is always OK . . . sad but not difficult. Sad, sad that she's not going to see them for a while.

For parents in this group, the fact that they believed their child to be untroubled by contact, and in most cases to really enjoy it, was something that motivated them and helped them to feel that contact was worthwhile.

Parents who felt their child showed mixed or problematic reactions to contact

There were 26 parents in this group (47% of the total). More in this group were having adult-only birth relative contact compared to the first group (n = 16, 62%). Five children (19%) were having sibling contact and five (19%) were having combined adult and sibling contact.

For parents in this group, managing some level of distress in their child's feelings or behaviour was a feature of contact. In some cases this distress was quite mild, but in others it was of more concern. The group includes five parents whose children showed very severe negative reactions to contact. The nature of children's difficulties with contact varied from case to case, but a number of themes were recurring.

One issue described by several adoptive parents related to the build-up towards contact meetings. For example, one mother described her child as 'snappy and argumentative' before the annual contact meeting with his grandparents. Another mother described how her son looked forward to contact, but at the same time, 'He goes through funny feelings. He goes through anger and he goes through excitement all in one and they can come out very aggressively.' Other people referred to poor concentration or bad dreams in the run-up to contact. Several adopters said they did not tell children about an imminent contact meeting until the day of the meeting or the preceding day in order to avoid the child's anticipation and anxiety.

Some parents felt that contact meetings could bring to the surface children's feelings about adoption and memories about their time in the birth family. One mother said, 'He wanted the contact, but it would stir up a lot of memories and not all of them good, and it was almost too much for him to cope with.' Another mother described how her daughter had said to her, 'I feel funny afterwards and it reminds me of things I don't want to be reminded of.' One parent described contact as 'opening up a wound' for the child.

Some parents described disturbances in their child's behaviour after contact – the "fallout". This could take the form of defiance towards adoptive parents. One adoptive mother said that her children became 'right lippy' after contact. Other children fought more with their siblings. This was a particular issue for one boy who felt that during the contact meeting his birth mother favoured his sibling. One adoptive mother explained that after some early contact meetings her daughter appeared withdrawn and would not eat for one or two days. In some cases, children's distress manifested itself in a number of different ways, as the following example shows. For these children, contact with the birth mother had actually stopped:

There was very big fallout. Their behaviour . . . they were very clingy, more volatile and we couldn't tell them off. They'd be very upset and [my daughter] would say, 'You don't know how it feels to be adopted.' They were very cross and angry.

Some parents perceived that their child felt sadness or loss after contact. One mother said about her son, 'If he could have anything he wants in his little world, he would want his mum and dad living together and he living with them and all being happy.' She felt that her son loved seeing his birth mother and brothers but that afterwards he felt sad that his siblings were at home with his birth mother and upset that he could only see them once a year. Another mother described how her daughter was upset at having to separate again from her older sister after contact:

> She hates goodbyes, she's had so many goodbyes . . . and of course when she has a goodbye with [her sister], especially at first, it brings all those other ones back . . . She was very upset afterwards . . . She was in tears.

The majority of adoptive parents in this group described positive as well as negative aspects of their child's reaction to contact. For example, it was clear that despite feeling sad or angry afterwards, many children valued and enjoyed meetings with their birth relatives. These reactions provided motivation for parents to continue with contact even when there were challenges.

In five cases, children's reactions to contact were sufficiently concerning that adoptive parents, sometimes on the advice of professionals, had stopped it. These tended to be cases where multiple stresses were apparent in the child's placement. These children tended to have significant emotional or behavioural problems that affected their functioning both at home and at school. One child had serious mental health difficulties as a result of her early life experiences. Another had a very troubled relationship with her adoptive parents and was currently living in residential care. These parents described their children as being ambivalent about whether they wanted contact to continue. One mother said her daughter had written to her birth mother to say she no longer wanted to see her. Another child was relieved when told by his adoptive mother that contact was stopping. In some cases, adoptive parents felt that having direct contact with birth family members had contributed to or exacerbated problems in their child's functioning or in their relationship with the adoptive parents. One mother felt that contact stopped her child 'moving on'. She felt the annual meetings with the birth mother did nothing to challenge her daughter's idealisation of her birth family.

Parents who felt their child was disinterested or disengaged with contact

Finally, there was a small group of four parents (7%) who said their child appeared to be disinterested or disengaged with contact. Two of these children were having contact with their birth mother and two with their birth father. Contact for these children was described by adoptive parents as not something that was really difficult for the child, but something that they showed little interest in. One adoptive mother said:

> *I would say that [he] wants the contact and I think he's glad when he has had the contact . . . But I think when he's doing the actual contact, mostly he just wants to go off and do something different. He is interested in a present that he might get, and he's interested in knowing that [his birth parent] is OK . . . and once he has established that in the first five minutes then pretty much he just wants to go.*

Some adoptive parents said their child reacted to going to contact meetings as if it was 'a chore' or in one case 'like going to the dentist'. Where children were disinterested or disengaged, contact appeared to continue for one of three possible reasons, that is, because of the adopter's belief in the long-term benefit of contact for the child, the adopter's commitment to meeting the needs of the birth relative or the adopter's reluctance to make the decision to stop contact.

Relationships between adoptive parents and others involved in contact

In just under half (n = 22) of the 55 cases, adoptive parents described past or current challenges in their relationship with the other people involved in contact, such as adult birth relatives or siblings, or the adoptive parents or foster carers of the adopted child's siblings. In cases where the adoptive parent was having contact with siblings who were in foster care or adopted, challenges sometimes came up when the different sets of parents wanted different types or levels of contact. In some cases, challenges in relationships were brought about because of differences in outlook or lifestyle between adoptive parents and the other people involved in contact. For example, one adoptive mother said that although her adopted child's uncle was of the same ethnic background as her, he was more religious and more embedded in that minority culture.

There were a small number of cases where relationships between adoptive parents and birth relatives were particularly difficult. Often these were situations where the adoptive parents and birth relatives had known each other before the child's placement; for example, where the child was adopted by foster carers or birth relatives, and where there was a past history of conflict between the parties. One adoptive parent who had fostered the child applied to adopt him once it was established that the birth mother was not able to have him back. A member of the birth family also expressed an interest in caring for the child and this led to an extended period of conflict and uncertainty. Even some years later, this adoptive parent described how relationships with the birth relatives continued to be marked by 'mistrust and animosity'. In two or three cases, relationships between adoptive parents and birth relatives were so poor that adoptive parents did not attend contact and meetings were supervised by a third party. As one kinship adopter described:

When it comes to me and [birth mother] getting together, I am like a red rag to a bull for her . . . So for [the child] that's his little time, so it's better that he has somebody else there that he trusts and likes to help him . . . I think one of the best things that has come out of this is that I don't have contact with [birth mother] whatsoever and that I'm very happy with.

In other cases, challenges seemed to arise largely from adoptive parents' feelings towards the birth family. For example, some adoptive parents had strong feelings of anger towards the birth family because of the harm the child had experienced. In one case the child's birth parents had separated and later the child was physically abused by the mother's new partner. The adoptive mother was angry with the birth father (with whom the child had direct contact after adoption) for not being there to protect the child:

[The child] is our son now. [His birth father] lost his rights the minute he let his son get beaten up and attacked . . . I just think he gave up his rights . . . I don't want to meet [the birth father] . . . that's his old life and this is his new life and I think this way I can sort of separate them.

In some cases, as this example illustrates, it was hard for adoptive parents to relate to birth relatives because of their difficulty accepting the child's connection to that family. In other cases, the challenges in relationships between adoptive parents and others seemed to be related to the lack of support by birth relatives for the adoptive parents. In the most worrying cases, these two factors coincided and adoptive parents described a mutual lack of acceptance between themselves and birth relatives.

Where relationships between adoptive parents and birth relatives (or the adoptive parents or foster carers of siblings) were positive, this made a significant contribution to the success of contact. In over half of our cases, adoptive parents identified such positive relationships as a success factor. The most successful relationships were characterised by mutual liking, support, trust and acceptance. It was clearly helpful when birth relatives showed their respect for adoptive parents as the legal and psychological parent of the child. One adoptive parent described how the birth mother had said, 'she doesn't want to intrude . . . so has left us completely in control'. Because of this, the adoptive mother said, 'Our confidence in her is growing. If she wants to say a bit more about what she wants I think that would be OK now.'

Relationships between adoptive parents and birth relatives were clearly improved in many cases through the active efforts of adoptive parents to include and respect birth relatives and to work through problems or tensions. There were several cases where relationships between birth relatives and adoptive parents began on shaky ground, but over time trust had been built and good relationships developed.

In some other cases, success within relationships seemed related to shared interests, or just "hitting it off". One adoptive parent said, 'We got on like we were four people out in the pub having a drink and a chat.' One adoptive mother felt that her shared culture with the birth father helped their relationship:

We are from similar cultural backgrounds . . . I think what did it was I was having a conversation and then I latched into Jamaican speak . . . I think he was quite surprised and I think that made him feel a bit more comfortable.

Some adoptive parents described how they saw birth relatives as being 'like part of the family', although this was not an essential component of successful relationships.

The quality of interactions between the child and birth relatives during contact meetings

Over half of adoptive parents (32 of 55) described challenges in relation to the quality of interactions between the child and the birth relative in contact meetings.

In several sibling contact cases, problems with interactions between siblings were often related to their different ages, situations and needs. For example, in one case the sibling group consisted of nine brothers and sisters children ranging in age from pre-school to young adults. The children were living in seven different households. Some had lived with the birth parents and with each other, while others (the younger siblings) had not.

In some cases, difficulties or issues for the birth relative in relating to the child seemed compounded by their lack of competence, such as a lack of practical childcare skills or inability to play imaginatively. A few birth relatives (this usually applied to birth parents) were described as being passive during meetings, that is, unable or unwilling to initiate a connection with the child. One adoptive mother described this as follows:

There was never anything coming back from mum. She never asked any questions. She never spoke to [the child], never touched her – there was just nothing there.

In other cases, the opposite was true; the birth relative did not allow the child to get used to them before trying to pick them up or play with them:

Sometimes mum and dad overpower her and want to pick her up and

152

want to touch her and she backs off, because she doesn't always remember who they are.

Birth relatives' inconsistency in their interactions was sometimes related to not being up to date with the child's needs and interests. For example, for birth relatives having annual contact with a child it was difficult to stay abreast of their favourite toys or games. In other cases, birth relatives were described by adoptive parents as not really tuning in appropriately to the child's age or developmental stage. One adoptive mother said:

[The birth mother] seems to find it really difficult to relate to the children. At the first contact she was asking [the child] whether he still liked the same bands and whether he'd got a new girlfriend at his school. Considering he was only seven, it was not what seven-year-olds want to talk about – they want to talk about football, not music and girlfriends.

In some cases the birth relative's mental health or emotional well-being could affect their ability to relate to the child on the day of contact. One adoptive parent described how the birth mother's mental health problems meant she could not cope with meetings that were longer than about 45 minutes. In another case, the adoptive parent described how the birth mother, who suffers from depression, seemed unable to concentrate or focus on the children:

She kind of switches off. She asks [the child] a question, he starts to tell her and then you can see that she's obviously gone off. And then she'll say something else completely different.

A lack of age-appropriate play materials or activities that children and birth relatives could share could also have a detrimental effect on interactions. In one case the adoptive mother described how the contact meeting between the child (a baby) and the birth grandmother and sibling was held in a social services meeting room with no toys and no space on the floor where the baby could safely be put down. Conversely, contact was more successful when the physical environment was right. Some families needed the safety and containment of a family centre-type environment where there was a good range of play activities. Other people found that public venues such as the zoo, park or museum could work really well, especially when people shared an interest in the activity. It was important, however, that wherever contact was held the activities available enabled people to interact. For example, one family went to an amusement park but found this did not work because they spent most of the time queuing for rides.

Some children were upset because of their birth relative's non-attendance at contact meetings. The reasons why birth relatives sometimes did not attend often related to their own problems, such as mental health issues, or placement breakdowns of siblings in foster care. In one case, there had been several occasions over a number of years when the child's birth parent had not turned up for contact meetings; the child was upset and worried, and felt rejected when this happened.

Where birth relatives showed interest in, and warm feelings towards, the child and could interact positively with him or her, this contributed to the success of contact. One adoptive mother described the birth mother's ability to relate to the child as follows:

> *She has got quite a rapport with him . . . She does come down to his level; you know she'll get down on the ground and play a game or whatever and he will enjoy that.*

The adopted child's obvious enjoyment of relationships with birth relatives motivated adoptive parents to continue with contact. In other cases, the adoptive parents had worked hard to try and promote positive interactions, for example by encouraging the child or birth relative to approach each other or suggesting the child tells the birth relative about something they had achieved or been involved in. Some adoptive parents took along games, photos or food to encourage interaction.

Managing risk, boundaries and confidentiality of information

About one-third of adoptive parents expressed concerns about the possibility that the child might be exposed to risks from birth relatives during or as a result of contact. Some adoptive parents worried   that information about their identity might become available to people within the birth family who they considered posed a risk. In several such cases, adoptive parents were not concerned about the birth relative involved in direct contact, but they were anxious that this birth relative might inappropriately disclose information to other members of the birth family. Such concerns arose in a number of sibling contact cases where some siblings had direct contact with (or information about) a birth parent and others did not. In some cases adoptive parents' fears about not being in control of the flow of information were realised; for example, an older sibling showed pictures of the birth mother to a younger sibling on his mobile phone. Some adoptive parents were worried about having contact meetings in venues that were too close to where birth relatives were living. In a small number of cases, adoptive parents had experienced birth family members who were not part of the contact plan turning up uninvited at meetings. A few adoptive parents were worried about what their child might say to birth relatives. One adoptive mother described how soon after placement she taught her child to memorise their address and phone number in case he got lost. The child then gave his birth relatives this information.

Some adoptive parents were concerned their child might be, or less commonly had been, psychologically harmed by inappropriate comments from birth relatives during contact meetings. The types of comments that worried adoptive parents were those that indicated the birth relative's lack of acceptance of the child's position within the adoptive family. One mother described how the birth father told her teenage son that if he was unhappy at home he could come and live with him. In one or two cases, adoptive parents expressed concerns that birth relatives (usually birth parents) had talked in an unhelpful way to the child about past experiences. One adoptive mother told us her daughter had prepared a number of questions about the past to ask her birth mother. This child had experienced some particularly difficult situations in her life with their birth mother, including violence, drug misuse, physical and sexual abuse, and neglect. In response to the child's questions, the birth mother denied her involvement in these issues. She also told the child a number of what the adoptive parent described as "horror stories", including stories about the child being violent and stealing money. The child was very upset and said she did not want to see her birth mother again.

It was very unusual for adoptive parents to express concerns about the possibility of children being physically or sexually at risk during a contact meeting. There was one large sibling group who had contact with each other, and in this case the adoptive parents of younger children within the group did express some fears that the much older adult siblings, more than one of whom had significant problems (e.g. drug taking, mental health issues), could pose a risk. In another case, contact with the birth mother had been stopped when she relapsed and started taking drugs again.

The issue of venues was again mentioned in relation to managing boundaries and risks. Where adoptive parents perceived there to be risks to their child during contact meetings, they were concerned that the contact venue allowed some control over these, for example an environment that was contained and where the child would remain visible at all times.

In some cases, adoptive parents felt there were few risks associated with their contact arrangements, and where this was the case people tended to feel comfortable with contact. But for most adoptive parents some level of risk, however small, was perceived. In such cases, what appeared to contribute to the success of contact was where adoptive parents felt able to control, or at least influence, potential risks and boundaries. Many adoptive parents described how helpful and reassuring it was when birth relatives showed their acceptance and respect for boundaries: one adoptive mother said about the birth father:

He is always very careful to make sure he is well behaved and he doesn't step over any lines. You know he never says anything to the children like 'I wish I could take you home.'

While the attitude and behaviour of birth relatives clearly influenced adoptive parents' feelings of being in control, it was apparent that the confidence and assertiveness of adoptive parents varied from person to person. Some adoptive parents felt confident in challenging birth relatives where this was required, or in suggesting changes to contact they felt would make their child more comfortable. For other adoptive parents it was important to feel that risks and boundaries were being managed on their behalf. In some cases, adoptive parents referred to the familiarity or predictability of contact as factors that helped them to feel in control. One adoptive mother was reassured by the fact that, 'when you go you can predict what it's going to be like . . . It's always basically the same you know . . . the same kind of set-up, the same things happen.'

One particular issue raised in a number of cases related to boundary-setting and gifts given to the child by the birth family. The exchange of presents during contact was a feature of many arrangements. The giving of presents by birth relatives was often considered to be a positive feature of contact, something that the child enjoyed, signified the affection of the birth family, built relationships or provided a focus for interaction during meetings. But in about a quarter of cases, the issue of presents was a challenging feature for adoptive parents, in particular the amount and nature of presents. In some cases, adoptive parents worried that the number of presents made the child overexcited. Others were concerned that the number of presents would give the wrong message to the child about who their "main" family were. One adoptive parent said she was worried that on Christmas Day her son would think, 'Wow – you know these people love me to bits. Look at all these presents – they have given me far more than anyone else has.' One adoptive mother objected to lots of presents because she worried that her son was more 'focused on the presents than the actual contact with his birth parent'. She wanted the contact to be about relationships, not gifts. One adoptive parent was worried about how her other adopted child, who did not have any birth family contact, would feel on seeing all the presents the other child had received from her birth family.

In some cases, it was the appropriateness of presents that concerned adoptive parents, that the gifts were not matched to the child's age, developmental level or interests; for example, buying make-up for a young girl, or that the birth family were buying the child toys they already had. In other cases, adoptive parents felt the present was too emotionally laden – a special piece of jewellery being such an example. In one case difficulties arose because the birth father offered to buy the child a bike. The adoptive mother wanted the child to work towards a bicycle, as a reward for good behaviour. Hence she was concerned that the birth father's offer made him look like 'the good guy' and her 'the bad guy'.

In a couple of cases, adoptive parents were concerned that birth relatives used presents to give inappropriate messages to the child. For example, one birth mother had written in the front of the book 'this book belongs to . . .' and had used the child's birth family name.

Managing adoptive parents' own emotions

The final theme relating to the challenges and success factors of contact relates to adoptive parents' management of their own feelings about contact. Some adoptive parents did not highlight specific issues, but described how they found contact meetings generally quite an emotional, stressful or draining experience. Other adoptive parents felt sad for birth relatives, and worried about their problems. One adoptive mother talked about the 'overwhelming sadness' she felt about the problems of her adopted child's older siblings. Some adoptive parents said that contact made them feel angry about the difficult experiences their child had been through in the past. The most common emotional reaction to contact, however, related to adoptive parents' feelings about the child's connection to the birth family. In about one-quarter of cases, adoptive parents said contact reminded them that the child had another family and had not been born to them. For some people these types of feelings were not problematic; as one adoptive mother said:

> Most of the time you forget that he is adopted and he is not ours by birth, he is just so much part of our family. And then of course you have got the contact and . . . suddenly the reality in a sense comes back . . . it doesn't make me feel any different, it just refreshes my memory that he hasn't always been here, because it feels like he has always been here.

In some cases, these feelings were more than just a reminder; they were uncomfortable. One adoptive mother said about contact: 'I get a little bit anxious about it, I don't know why – it's probably irrational, but I do. It's probably the fact that it is reiterating that I'm not his birth mum.' About one in five adoptive parents said contact made them feel that the child was "on loan" as opposed to being "theirs". These feelings could vary over time. One mother who adopted siblings when they were aged four and seven described the trajectory of her feelings:

> My feelings have kind of changed as my relationship with the children has become more secure . . . at first I would say I was very insecure in my relationship with them . . . it made us feel that we were looking after other people's children . . . as we've got more confident with the children and . . . I suppose they've become more like us . . . it's only now that I can kind of say, 'Oh well, it's OK, they can love the birth mum and they can love me.' But at first I didn't feel like that. I felt the birth mum and I . . . we were sort of standing in the same space.

Conversely, another adoptive mother described how she had found contact more difficult as her relationship with the children developed:

> As each contact's gone on, it's got harder. Because I am, in a way, closer to the children. They're more and more my children now. And it's a strange feeling to have someone else come along and interact with them.

One adoptive mother said contact made her want to 'tighten her grip' on the child. An adoptive father said contact made him feel the child had another family 'waiting in the wings'.

Not all adoptive parents found the reality of the child's birth family difficult to deal with on an emotional level. Often this was expressed in terms of confidence about their own relationship with the child. One adoptive mother said:

> We are confident about who we are in Katie's life and who she is in our life. And even if there are ups and downs or whatever in the future, you know as long as there is a kind of strong bond, you know you can love more than one person.

The benefits of contact as perceived by adoptive parents

Every adoptive parent identified at least one current or future benefit of direct contact, even in cases where the contact was very challenging. Most of the benefits that parents mentioned fell within one of three themes: maintaining relationships, helping the child with identity issues and strengthening adoptive family relationships.

Maintaining relationships

Many adoptive parents felt it was important that if the child had an established and positive connection with birth family members then contact should continue. One adoptive mother described how her son 'loves his mum, he loves [his siblings] and he just loves seeing them'. Several adoptive parents talked about the pleasure and consolation siblings took in seeing each other. For example, one adoptive mother described how her daughter appeared to find 'comfort and closure' through seeing her older brothers. Some adoptive parents felt that contact helped the child feel less worried about birth family members. One said: 'She needed the reassurance that her mum was OK.' Other parents felt the child would have been angry or upset had they not been allowed to continue important relationships, and these feeling could then have got in the way of their relationship with the child: 'He is the sort child that if you said he wasn't allowed to see his birth family at all, I think it might have made him a bit withdrawn.' Another parent said that to cut contact 'would be ripping her away from the family she loved . . . and she would never allow herself to love us if that was the case'. Some adoptive parents felt it benefited the child to see their birth family and adoptive family getting on with each other, that it gave their child a message that they were free to have feelings for both of their families.

Some adoptive parents felt that allowing the child to maintain important connections mitigated the losses of adoption and provided the child with valuable messages about relationships in general. One adoptive parent expressed the view that maintaining a relationship with the birth mother would be 'better for his relationships when he grows up. If he sees it is not losing all the time, then it is good for him.' Another person said it would help a child to know that 'these people in the photographs don't just sail out of her life . . . I think it is important that . . . her birth father hasn't disappeared out of her life.'

Helping the child deal with identity issues

Over half of adoptive parents expected that contact would help a child gain information about, and understanding of, their birth family and their personal history. They referred to children being able to 'fill in the gaps', 'put together their past', or learn about their 'roots'. Some white adopters who were parenting dual heritage children hoped that contact would help their child understand and value their ethnic heritage. Direct contact had allowed children to ask questions about what they were like as a baby or about members of the extended birth family. Adoptive parents had the opportunity to ask questions about the family medical history or gain information to tell the child in the future. Some adoptive parents expressed the view that ongoing direct contact with birth family members allowed their child to deal with identity concerns incrementally, and avoided the potential for stress and disappointment if the child were to seek out their birth relatives in the future:

> I want her to know who they are so she hasn't got to go cloak and dagger looking to see who they are and trying to find out from people where she has come from . . . she's not going to go looking for them at a later date and perhaps find something she's not prepared for. The questions can be answered when they come up rather than in one big go when she is older, which I don't think it's good for anyone.

Several adoptive parents felt direct contact helped children to understand why they were adopted. Some believed that it helped the child to understand that their birth family still loved them and cared about them, and that adoption was not a rejection or their own fault. In other cases, parents felt that direct contact had helped the child to understand the limitations of their birth parents, and hence they could make sense of why they needed to be adopted. Two adoptive parents mentioned the benefit of acquiring memories and photographs from contact meetings, as enduring resources that could be drawn on in the future even if direct contact stopped.

Strengthening adoptive family relationships

About half of the adoptive parents believed that direct contact had brought about, or would lead to, benefits in their relationship with the adopted child. This was sometimes expressed in terms of helping children avoid developing an idealised or fairytale image of their birth family. One adoptive mother felt that her children tended to 'put on rose-coloured glasses a little bit, and try and paint a picture that wasn't real'. She argued that because they were maintaining direct contact with the birth parents she could 'very gently make sure that they actually remembered it as it was'.

Some adoptive parents felt that contact helped them to realise how important they were to the child. One adoptive mother said:

> *I think it actually really makes them feel more part of our family. The contact is something extra that happens with their birth family, but this is the family they live in and are growing up in. Every contact, we come away feeling more secure really. I mean more certain that they need us as parents and that they are our children.*

Direct contact meetings provided an opportunity for adoptive parents to test out their fears about birth parents. It was reassuring when children were pleased to see their birth relatives, but quite happy to go back home with the adoptive parents. One adoptive mother, whose child did not remember his birth mother, said contact had reinforced just how attached the child was to her.

Some adoptive parents felt their child needed reassurance that their birth relatives were OK in order to settle in the adoptive family:

> *I think that every time he sees [his brothers] he's just a little bit more settled. I think you can see in him that he is happier and more content knowing his brothers are OK.*

Other people felt it could help the child to know that their birth relatives accepted and supported their membership of the adoptive family. One adoptive father said, 'They know [their birth mum] is happy for them to be where they are, and that helps them in their settling.'

Several adoptive parents talked about how maintaining birth family contact created an atmosphere of honesty and openness between themselves and the child, and that this would strengthen relationships. As one mother put it:

I think if you let them go in love and give them their freedom and trust . . . then I think you have a more honest relationship at the end of the day – it's more real.

Balancing the benefits of contact against the challenges: the needs of adoptive parents for contact support

Both challenges and benefits of contact were identified by all the adoptive parents we interviewed. In some cases the challenges far outweighed the benefits and success factors, but in other cases the reverse was true. In many cases contact was most successful when:

- relationships between adoptive parents and birth relatives (or the carers of siblings) were good;
- birth relatives supported adoptive parents;
- there were positive interactions between the child and birth family members;
- children were comfortable with contact and wanted it to continue;
- there was clarity about the risks and boundaries of contact and adoptive parents felt in control of these;
- adoptive parents could manage the emotional impact of contact;
- the structure and physical environment of meetings allowed and promoted interactions.

The reverse of these factors was associated with poorer contact experiences, and where more of these negative factors exist the need for support is greatest. Differences between adoptive parents emerged in relation to their attitudes about contact and capacities to manage its complexities. What one person considered a problem, another person might view as an opportunity. Adoptive parents were often motivated to continue with contact, sometimes even in situations where they found it very challenging. Despite the challenges, parents felt contact allowed their child to maintain important relationships and could help their identity concerns or strengthen relationships within the adoptive family.

These findings suggest that the following factors need to be taken into account when planning support for contact:

- It is clear that some adoptive parents are likely to need more support than others because the individual characteristics, skills and attitudes of parents vary widely.
- Contact is a relationship-based process. Some people are likely to need help in negotiating the nature and boundaries of these relationships, and in managing underpinning feelings.
- The venues for contact need to be considered carefully – in particular, activities that allow and encourage birth relatives and child to relate to each other need to be available.
- Contact has an emotional impact on both adoptive parents and adopted children, and support should be available for both to manage these feelings.
- Some families are likely to need help in assessing and managing risks and boundaries. The potential risks of contact need to be openly discussed and appropriate strategies put in place to manage them. This may need to include discussing seemingly trivial aspects of contact like the exchange of gifts. It is important that people not only know what is allowed, but why it is or is not allowed. Adoptive parents need to be fully involved in negotiating risk and boundaries, and some people will need help in taking control of these. An important aspect of supporting adoptive families with contact is likely to be corresponding work with birth relatives, especially work focused on helping birth relatives accept and support the placement.
- It will be important for professionals supporting contact to periodic-ally review arrangements to consider how challenges can be addressed and benefits achieved. The relative balance of challenges and benefits needs to be kept under careful review in cases where the former outweigh the latter.

Summary

This chapter presents a qualitative analysis of adoptive parents' interviews, focusing on themes that emerged in relation to the quality of contact. Key findings are as follows:

- All adoptive parents described challenges related to contact, benefits of contact and factors they felt related to its success. These were summarised in terms of five main themes relating to the quality of contact. These five themes were as follows:
    - the child's reactions to contact;
    - relationships between adoptive parents and others involved in contact;
    - the quality of interactions between the child and birth relatives during contact meetings;
    - managing risk, boundaries and confidentiality;
    - managing adoptive parents' own emotions.
- The benefits of contact, as perceived by adoptive parents, clustered around three main themes:
    - maintaining relationships;
    - helping the child with identity issues;
    - strengthening adoptive family relationships.
- Five suggestions were made about adoptive families' needs in relation to contact support:
    - different adoptive parents need different types and levels of support;
    - contact is a relationship-based process and help is often needed in negotiating the nature and boundaries of these relationships;
    - contact has an emotional impact on both adoptive parents and children and support should be available for both to manage these feelings;
    - risks and boundaries need to be openly discussed and thoughtfully managed;
    - the relative balance of challenges and benefits of contact needs to be kept under careful review, especially in cases where the former may outweigh the latter.

9   Birth relatives' satisfaction with contact

The chapter begins by looking at birth relatives' overall satisfaction with contact, categorising people into three groups related to their satisfaction and describing the characteristics of each group. We look at differences in satisfaction with contact between siblings, birth parents and grandparents. There is then discussion of the way in which birth relatives' strengths and risks related to satisfaction with contact. Further details of birth relatives' experiences of contact are elaborated in the following chapter.

Birth relatives' overall satisfaction with contact

Birth relatives' satisfaction with contact was measured using information from their interviews. We developed three categories to describe their levels of satisfaction:

- mainly satisfied – satisfied with most aspects of the contact, though may still have some suggestions for improvement;
- mixed satisfaction – some satisfaction but also some dissatisfaction that currently affects quality of contact;
- mainly dissatisfied – dissatisfied with many aspects of contact.

Table 9.1 shows how many birth relatives were in each category at Time 1 and Time 2. It indicates that: just over half of birth relatives were mainly satisfied with contact; seven birth relatives expressed both satisfaction and dissatisfaction with contact; and 11 were dissatisfied with many aspects of it. As the case examples below illustrate, despite any dissatisfaction it was notable that all birth relatives expressed their pleasure at seeing and spending time with the adopted child(ren), even where it was difficult or raised issues. In addition, all relatives, regardless of levels of satisfaction or dissatisfaction with contact as it currently operated, spoke of the importance of maintaining contact with the adopted child. Almost all birth relatives also expressed a desire to have more

Table 9.1
Levels of satisfaction with contact expressed by birth relatives

Levels of satisfaction with contact	Frequency T1	% T1	Frequency T2	% T2
LEVEL 1 Mainly satisfied	20	53	16	53
LEVEL 2 Mixed satisfaction	7	18	5	17
LEVEL 3 Mainly dissatisfied	11	29	9	30
TOTAL	**38***	**100**	**30****	**100**

*At T1 contact had not started in one of the 39 cases
** At T2 contact had been suspended in five of the 39 cases and data were unavailable in four of the 39 cases because the birth relative did not take part in the second interview

contact such as more frequent or longer meetings, or more varied types of contact. Those who were seeking more variety often wanted more informal contact between meetings and formal letterbox arrangements; for example, they would have liked occasional phone calls between themselves and the child. Birth relatives were often reluctant to make adoptive parents or professionals aware of their wishes, as they feared it would be seen as demanding and would jeopardise the contact they currently enjoyed.

The experiences of birth relatives who were mainly satisfied with contact

The first group of birth relatives expressed good overall satisfaction with contact across many areas. Particular emphasis was given to the good relationships that existed between the birth relative and the adopted child(ren) and between birth relative and adoptive parents. Although satisfaction levels were high in this group, these birth relatives still identified improvements that could be made in the arrangements, such as alternative venues and greater informality. Often this group of birth relatives would have liked more frequent contact, longer meetings and more informal arrangements, such as visits to their home, exchanges of mobile phone numbers or occasional phone calls to the child's home. The general trend within this group was towards greater contact and more informality. It was notable that in 13 of the 20 cases in this group at Time 1 (65%), contact was not supervised by a social worker and in some cases the adoptive parents were not present during contact. In the 35 per cent of cases where contact was supervised, relatives commented on their satisfaction with the discreet approach taken by workers and the subtlety of their interventions. Levels of supervision were much higher in the dissatisfied group and the group that was both satisfied and dissatisfied, at 91 per cent and 86 per cent respectively.

There were two striking characteristics of this group. First, the good relationships that had been developed between birth relatives and adoptive parents had been achieved through considerable hard work by relatives, often over several years, to prove their trustworthiness to adoptive parents. Relatives were very conscious of the need to tread carefully and not make too many demands of adoptive parents in relation to contact. Some had spent many years building relationships and trust with adoptive parents and found these efforts were rewarded with increased levels of contact or informality. Some achieved very modest rewards for their efforts, such as contact being increased by half an hour. Second, the group was characterised by an air of acceptance that "things are as they are". Some birth relatives expressed a feeling of relief or luck that contact had been granted and a feeling of gratitude towards adoptive parents for allowing contact to take place. One birth father said: 'I had to sort of think myself lucky I got [annual contact].'

Case example: Mainly satisfied with contact

Birth mother Michelle had an annual contact meeting in a restaurant with her son and was very happy with almost all aspects of this contact. She enjoyed seeing her son, although meetings did throw up mixed emotions:

> When I'm with him I feel great and everything is OK . . . but before I feel very nervous . . . I do look forward to it, it makes me happy, definitely . . . I'm happy to be there.

She felt that she had a good relationship with the adoptive parents and that the atmosphere between everyone at the meeting was good: 'It's just natural, all of us.' She felt that contact was of benefit to her because she could see her son and how well he was doing, and it was positive for her child because he could learn about his past and his birth family. The aspects of contact with which she expressed dissatisfaction were minor; for example, she said the restaurant was quite noisy and it was difficult to hear everything that was said.

The experiences of birth relatives who had mixed satisfaction with contact

The second group of birth relatives expressed satisfaction in some areas but equally noted some dissatisfaction. All the people in this group spoke of their joy at spending time with their birth child(ren). They got particular pleasure from seeing how the child was growing and developing. All had some positive things to say about their relationship with adoptive parents, which they described as friendly, fun and, sometimes, 'like family'. However, some expressed worries about their relationship with the child or their ability to sustain the relationship in the long term. Some also felt a degree of discomfort during contact or a desire for a closer relationship with adoptive parents. In two cases, birth relatives were sharing contact with several adopters or foster carers and they reported better relationships with some than others, resulting in a mixed report of satisfaction with these relationships.

Within this group the greatest satisfaction appeared to come from a positive relationship with the child. None of the birth relatives expressed any satisfaction with their ability to influence contact – all indicated dissatisfaction with this. Overall, there was a sense of birth relatives feeling powerless and fearful about the sustainability of contact long term.

Birth relatives in this group described good relationships with most contact supervisors, though some felt the supervisor did not fully understand or take account of their needs; for example, one birth mother expressed distress at the rules and restrictions placed on her at contact as she was not allowed to hug her children.

Dissatisfaction with practical arrangements included one birth relative's unhappiness with the length of the journey made for a one-hour meeting. Cost was an issue for another birth relative. In another case, parking restrictions meant that the ending of contact was always rushed.

Case example: Mixed satisfaction with contact

Denise was the carer for her five-year-old granddaughter. The younger brother of her granddaughter, who was two, had been adopted when he was six months old. Denise and her granddaughter had contact with the adopted child twice a year in meetings lasting two to three hours held at a local park or similar venue. In terms of satisfaction with contact, Denise described the contacts as 'lovely, beautiful'. In particular, she expressed happiness at seeing the connection between the two siblings, saying that seeing them together was 'amazing'. She felt there was no awkwardness in her relationship with the adoptive mother: 'I like her because she's like me – down to earth . . . We say what we've got to say . . . she is quite a good person.' Although Denise felt both she and the children benefited from contact she was unhappy with a number of aspects. In particular, she felt the meetings were too far apart and that as a consequence her young adopted grandson didn't really know her, describing how he seemed to shy away when she wanted to give him a kiss. She felt that six months between meetings was too long for both her and her granddaughter. She also felt that it affected her relationship with the adoptive parents – that they felt like strangers and consequently the contact could feel like 'a funny situation'.

The experiences of birth relatives who were dissatisfied with many aspects of contact

These birth relatives all expressed dissatisfaction with a very broad range of aspects of contact. These are discussed below.

Level of formality and ability to influence contact

The two aspects of contact with which birth relatives most frequently expressed dissatisfaction were the formality of the meeting and their lack of control over or influence on the arrangements. These aspects of contact overlapped to some extent, as highly formal arrangements often employed rules to maintain the formality and exert a degree of control over the birth relative's behaviour.

Unsatisfactory contact was characterised by birth relatives as rigid, rule ridden and unnatural, whereas they were seeking an arrangement that was more relaxed, homely or normal. Birth relatives appeared to find rigidity, unnaturalness and reliance on rules as stifling and counter-productive to the development and maintenance of relationships with their child. The formality of the venue also added to some relatives' sense of dissatisfaction. Two birth grandparents in this group felt they had been led by social services to expect a more informal and frequent arrangement than what was in place.

Birth relatives said they often were not consulted about basic practical arrangements. This sometimes led to their needs not being met. One birth mother found contact difficult because it was in a busy public place and she had a fear of crowds. Another relative had been given a date for contact by the adoption support worker without any consultation and this was the date her baby was due to be born. Some relatives felt they were able to express an opinion about contact arrangements, but felt their opinion was given less weight than the views of the adoptive parents and the support agency. It was common within this group of dissatisfied birth relatives for them to express a reluctance to give an opinion in case they were seen as "rocking the boat" or difficult. They feared that such a perception would lead to contact being reduced or stopped altogether.

The relationship with the adoptive parents, the supervising worker and the child

The aspect of contact that caused most concern to birth relatives after the formality and control of the contact was relationships with adoptive parents, supervising workers and the children. Many people in this very dissatisfied group said they were confident the adoptive parents would be able to care well for the adopted child, but a number expressed concerns about their own relationship with adoptive parents. They described a tension in the air, a feeling of mistrust and a degree of suspicion between the adults involved in contact. Birth relatives in this group were particularly sensitive to the presence of adoptive parents at contact meetings and most had previously had the expectation that adoptive parents would be marginal to the contact.

The relationship between the birth relative and supervising worker was another aspect of dissatisfaction. Many relatives in this dissatisfied group experienced supervision as controlling and unsupportive, and felt the worker did not know or understand them well. They were unhappy when workers were obtrusive, eager to enforce rules about talk and behaviour during contact, and seen to lack subtlety.

Despite significant dissatisfaction with contact, four of the 11 birth relatives in this group (at Time 1) felt that their relationship with the adopted child was good. Some, however, feared that existing or newly developing relationships were being negatively affected by the contact arrangements. Relatives were fearful of losing their relationship with the child, in terms of the child 'slipping away', or they felt like an 'observer' or 'outsider' rather than an active participant in contact. Two of the 11 birth relatives were so dissatisfied with contact and had such concerns about the effect of poor contact on the child that they were considering terminating it. They appeared to view a "clean break" as preferable for the child.

The practicalities of contact

About half of the group of dissatisfied birth relatives raised concerns about the practical arrangements of contact. Some were unhappy about making a two- or three-hour journey to meet the child for only one hour. Some raised issues about the suitability of family centres used for contact. One centre was described as uncomfortable. Another did not allow refreshments in the room where contact took place. In one centre, a small room was allocated for a contact involving ten people. The practicality of involving ten people in one meeting was also questioned. One relative felt the activities available in the centre were unsuitable for the children, leading to them being bored. One felt that her need for contact in a crowd-free environment and in a free venue had not been taken into account.

Case example: Mainly dissatisfied with contact

Birth mother Holly had contact with her children, aged seven and four, who had been placed together for adoption. Her contact with the children was once a year for one hour with supervised meetings held at a contact centre. Holly was happy that she could see her children after their adoption, saying 'It keeps me going . . . I think that if the contact wasn't there I would feel like "what's the point" . . . I think it helps.' However, she was very unhappy with many aspects of the contact plan. In general, she felt the meetings were too controlled by the agency. She described one meeting that was attended by three social workers, which she found 'a hundred per cent intimidating'. She felt the meetings were too short and infrequent: 'By the time I got in and sat down and we said hello and they were snapping photographs, it was all just too full on, too quick.' She felt the meeting room was too small and crowded and that it was 'official' rather than comfortable:

It was appalling, it was just a little office room with chairs around the outside of the room. It wasn't comfortable and it wasn't relaxing at all.

She was unhappy that she was not allowed to give presents to the children or bring personal things to show them, even things she had made for them: 'You can't do this and you can't do that, you can't mention this and you can't mention that.' She felt the frequency and duration of contact was 'disgusting', not just for her but for the two children. She argued that, at their age, 'a year is a long time to wait' and this very limited form of contact must be 'soul destroying' for them. Although she wanted to continue with the contact, she described how difficult she found the meetings, using words like 'heart rending' and saying that before one meeting she was physically sick with anxiety.

Satisfaction with contact by birth relative type

Tables 9.2 and 9.3 show how birth parents, siblings, grandparents and other relatives varied in terms of their satisfaction with contact. Looking first at birth parents, over half of birth parents at Time 1 were satisfied, with the remainder about evenly split between mixed and dissatisfied. At Time 2, just under half of birth parents were satisfied and most of the remainder were dissatisfied. In contrast with siblings, at both points in time the vast majority of siblings were satisfied with contact. No siblings were in the dissatisfied group at either point in time. Levels of dissatisfaction with contact were quite high among grandparents, especially at Time 1 where six of 11 grandparents were in the dissatisfied group, and only a minority were satisfied with contact. At Time 2, half of the grandparents were satisfied. Overall, these data suggest that adult siblings were most likely to be happy with their contact compared to either parents or grandparents, but with such small numbers no firm conclusions can be drawn.

Table 9.2
Satisfaction of birth parents, siblings, grandparents and other relatives with contact at Time 1

	Satisfied	*Mixed*	*Dissatisfied*
Birth parents	11 of 20	4 of 20	5 of 20
Siblings	5 of 7	2 of 7	0
Grandparents/ others	4 of 11	1 of 11	6 of 11

Table 9.3
Satisfaction of birth parents, siblings, grandparents and other relatives with contact at Time 2

	Satisfied	*Mixed*	*Dissatisfied*
Birth parents	6 of 14	2 of 14	6 of 14
Siblings	5 of 6	1 of 6	0
Grandparents/ others	5 of 10	2 of 10	3 of 10

How did birth relatives' strengths and risks relate to their satisfaction with contact?

In this section, birth relative satisfaction with contact is looked at in relation to the strengths and risks that were discussed in Chapter 6. Chi-squared tests were used to look at the categorical variables (caseness on the BSI, and whether the birth relative had been the main carer for the child), and binary logistic regression was used to examine whether birth relatives' "coping with adoption" scores predicted whether they were satisfied with contact. For all these analyses, the satisfaction with contact rating used was the last one obtained from the relative. In most cases this was the Time 2 rating, but Time 1 ratings were used for those relatives who dropped out of the study (n = 4) and for cases where contact was not happening at Time 2 (n = 5). Satisfaction with contact was considered using two groups; those who were satisfied with contact were the first and those who were mixed or dissatisfied with contact were the second group.

Mental health outcomes and satisfaction with contact

A chi-square test was used to look at whether a birth relative being "case positive" on the BSI (indicating a clinically significant level of distressing psychological symptoms) was associated with satisfaction with contact. The results were not significant ($\chi^2 = 1.6$, $df = 1$, p = .2). Overall, 55 per cent of birth relatives were case positive on the BSI. Two-thirds of relatives in the mixed/unsatisfied group were case positive on the BSI (ten of 15), compared to 44 per cent (seven of 16) in the satisfied with contact group.

Having been the main carer for the child and satisfaction with contact

A chi-square test was used to look at whether a birth relative having been the main carer for the child (this group including the four who had not maltreated the child) was associated with satisfaction with contact. The results were not significant ($\chi^2 = .47$, df = 1, p = .5). Overall, 55 per cent of birth relatives had been the child's main carer. Half of the relatives (10 of 20) who were satisfied with contact had been the child's main carer, as had a little over half of those in the mixed/dissatisfied group (11 of 18).

Coping with adoption and satisfaction with contact

A logistic regression analysis was performed, with the satisfaction groupings as the dependent variable ("satisfied" was one group and "mixed or dissatisfied" was the other) and the combined "coping with adoption" scores of birth relatives as the predictor variable. Thirty-seven cases were included, but data were missing for one case because coping could not be coded and for another because contact had stopped before the Time 1 interview. Since this analysis involved a small sample size, parameter estimates and standard errors were evaluated to ensure they were reasonable, providing evidence that there was a sufficient ratio of cases to variables (Tabachnick and Fidell, 2007). The full model significantly predicted membership of the satisfied with contact group ($\chi^2 = 8.7$, $df = 1$, p<.01). The model predicted 73 per cent of cases accurately overall, with 84 per cent of the satisfied contact group successfully predicted and 61 per cent of the mixed/dissatisfied group correctly predicted. Table 9.4 gives the co-efficients, the Wald statistic and associated degrees of freedom and probability values for the predictor variable ("coping with adoption" scores).

Table 9.4
Results of logistic regression: satisfaction with contact and birth relatives' coping with adoption scores

	B	S.E.	Wald	DF	Sig.	Exp (B)	95.0% C.I. for Exp (B)	
							Lower	Upper
Birth relatives coping with adoption Combined scores	1.12	.44	6.4	1	.011	3.07	1.29	7.30

The odds ratio (Exp(B)) of 3.07 indicates that the odds of being in the satisfied group are three times greater with a one-unit increase in the coping score of the birth relative. In other words, the odds of being in the satisfied group are increased by 300 per cent for every one more point on the mean "coping with adoption" measure.

Although these findings indicate a relationship between birth relatives' coping with adoption and their satisfaction with contact, it cannot identify the direction of effect. Coping with adoption is likely to influence relatives' perception of contact and the dynamics of contact. Additionally, the quality of their contact experience is likely to have an effect on all three dimensions of coping with adoption.

Strengths and risks of birth relatives and their satisfaction with contact

Neither the birth relatives' mental health status on the BSI nor whether or not they had been a main carer who had abused and neglected the child were significantly associated with birth relatives' satisfaction with contact. Therefore, we decided not to use the birth relatives' combined strengths and risks measure in a logistic regression. However, in order to explore whether the combination of birth relatives' mental health and having been a main carer might contribute to their satisfaction with contact independent of their coping with adoption, a logistic regression was performed. It examined whether the risks/strengths scores for these two variables added together predicted satisfaction with contact. The results were not significant. Overall, therefore, it appears that of the three factors we looked at, the main factor associated with whether or not relatives were satisfied with contact is their coping with adoption. Although we cannot know the direction effect here, as noted above, it is likely to be important to bolster relatives' capacity to cope with adoption in order to achieve better contact outcomes. Birth relatives' satisfaction with contact is obviously a benefit to them, but it may also benefit adoptive parents and the child. In future research, an important question to evaluate would be the extent to which birth relatives' coping with adoption and their satisfaction with contact impact on the experience of contact for the adopted child and adoptive parents. It would also be useful to explore the impact of this factor relative to the strengths and risks of the adoptive family.

Summary

In this chapter we discussed birth relatives' levels of satisfaction with contact arrangements, and these have been looked at in relation to the strengths and risks of birth relatives that were described in Chapter 6. Key findings are as follows:

- Just over half of birth relatives were mainly satisfied with contact, approximately two in every ten expressed mixed feelings of satisfaction and dissatisfaction, and about three in ten were dissatisfied with many or most aspects of contact.

- Although levels of satisfaction varied, almost all birth relatives expressed great pleasure at being able to see the adopted child.

- Almost all birth relatives would have liked to have more contact, though in many cases they were reluctant to express this wish in case it was perceived negatively by others.

- Among those birth relatives who were dissatisfied with many aspects of contact, many were unhappy with the formality of contact arrangements and their lack of ability to influence these. Relatives also cited poor relationships with the adoptive parents, supervising worker and child, and dissatisfaction with the practicalities of contact.

- Adult siblings were mainly very satisfied with contact arrangements. In comparison, the satisfaction of birth parents and grandparents was more varied.

- Whether or not birth relatives were scoring in the clinical range on the mental health measure (the BSI) was not significantly associated with their satisfaction with contact.

- Having been the main carer for the child was not significantly associated with satisfaction with contact.

- Results of a logistic regression analysis indicated that birth relatives' scores on the "coping with adoption" measure significantly predicted whether or not they were satisfied with contact. Birth relatives who were coping better with adoption were more likely to be satisfied with contact than those who were coping less well.

10 The challenges and benefits of contact: themes from interviews with birth relatives

This chapter presents the qualitative analysis of birth relatives' interview data. It focuses first on what birth relatives considered to be the challenges of maintaining contact. Next, the themes related to the success of contact for birth relatives are outlined and their perceptions of the benefits of contact are described. The importance of the adoptive parents' role in contact meetings are then discussed, and the experiences of birth relatives in cases where contact had stopped are described.

Themes related to the challenges of contact for birth relatives

For many birth relatives, although contact was highly valued, there were aspects of the experience that were often quite challenging. The key themes relating to these challenges are elaborated below.

Loss of power: the need to manage the relationship with adoptive parents

For some birth relatives, their experience of contact was of being restricted and controlled. This was the case even where there was no direct supervision of contact. Relatives often felt they did not have a say in such aspects as the amount of contact, timing of contact, activities or venue used, the presence of spouses or the acceptability of hugs and kisses. They felt that adoptive parents, supported by social workers or social work guidance, were in control. Birth relatives also expressed a sense of inevitability and acceptance of their powerlessness in such situations. One birth mother explained, 'Well I have to get on with [the adopters] for my kid's sake really, because if I was difficult they could stop contact.'

It was common for birth relatives to fear that adoptive parents would choose to reduce or end direct contact and they were anxious to avoid any actions that might precipitate such a decision. This was a particular anxiety where the relationship between birth relatives and adoptive parents was troubled. A birth mother said:

I thought, you've got to make an effort, because if you don't and you start slagging them off, they have got [your birth child], they can make the rules, and if they choose to not let me see [my daughter], that is down to them.

Some relatives felt they were very much at the mercy of the adoptive parents. One birth relative said:

They are clearly really not wanting to do [contact] and . . . have tried persistently to evade having it. You know, there's been a date set and then they've changed it, then they've changed it again . . .

Birth relatives were deeply aware of the need to reassure adoptive parents if they appeared to feel threatened by contact. The same birth relative reported:

We just hope that in time, trust can be built up. I mean all we can do is try and abide by all the rules and regulations and not do anything that will frighten them or upset them and hope that in due course things could relax a bit.

Loss of role: the change of birth relatives' roles in the lives of adopted children

Post-adoption contact inevitably involves a change in role for the birth relative. This change is not easily defined and must to some extent be negotiated through the process of contact. A birth mother explained that during one contact meeting her birth daughter had an accident on her bicycle. Her instinct was to go to her, pick her up and comfort her but she had to reassess this as the child's adoptive mother took charge of the situation and took the child to the toilets to get cleaned up. Two birth mothers felt they were probably now more like aunties than mothers to their adopted children.

For some birth relatives, the role demarcated for them at contact was heavily at odds with their expectations of an ongoing role in the life of the child. One grandmother described her disappointment and deep regret that her relationship with her adopted grandchildren had not progressed in the way she had hoped. She had not expected the relationship to carry on as it had been, but instead had expected it to be similar to a relationship with grandchildren who had moved to another part of the country or emigrated. Rather than meeting the children once a year for an hour-and-a-half in a venue 50 or 60 miles from her home, she would have preferred to see them three times a year, take them to her home, arrange for them to play with her other grandchildren and have sleepovers, have a weekly phone call and exchange presents and letters. She viewed all these activities as part of the grandparent role, yet they were all outside of the contact agreement. This appears to have confirmed to the grandmother her ambiguous and "unnatural" role in the children's lives.

A birth father's expectations were equally mismatched with reality when he asked to see copies of his birth son's school reports but these were not forthcoming.

An adult sibling who had contact with her two younger siblings expressed concern about her new role in their lives. She had been the main carer and mother figure for the two preschool-age children before the adoption. The arrangement was for her to see her siblings three times a year, yet there was some uncertainty about when these meetings would happen. This uncertainty was unsettling for the older sibling, who would have preferred more contact and a more definite arrangement that acknowledged the importance of her previous role and continuing strong relationship with the children.

Some birth relatives expressed concern about the uncertainty caused for all by the presence of two mothers or two fathers in the room together. This was often discussed in relation to the titles given to birth parents; for example, in some cases children called both birth and adoptive mother "Mum". In other cases birth mothers were called by their first name, which could be a source of sadness for them. Names and labels had a deep significance for birth relatives, as they indicated the maintenance or loss of birth parents' status in the child's life. Even where relationships between all parties were good and contact was positive, the loss of title was indicative of a loss of status. These issues were also not confined to the language used in relation to birth parents; one birth grandfather who was not called "granddad", despite this being his wish, explained the sadness that this brought. He said, 'One day, if she calls us granddad and nanny it will probably bring a tear to my eye.'

This suggests that more careful and active negotiation is needed among all parties to ensure that language used is acceptable to everyone or, if that is not possible, that the consequences of a lack of fit are acknowledged and supported.

Fear of loss of relationship with the child

Some birth relatives reported feeling marginalised in contact meetings, out of their depth and fearing a loss of closeness and relationship with the children over time. One birth mother explained:

> *Basically, the contact is so ... we don't lose touch with the children ... but I feel as if I'm losing them ... you know ... they're growing up ... I never see them growing up and I feel as if I'm losing them more and more to the adoptive parents.*

A birth mother with learning difficulties expressed her distress as she struggled to play and care for her children during contact. The adoptive parents were not present and the birth mother would have liked them to support her during contact. A birth sibling voiced her concern that her adopted sister might 'outgrow' her or vice versa.

Where contact was very infrequent and short in duration, the loss of relationship was seen as a particular threat. Several birth relatives were concerned about contact visits that were only one hour long. They felt they had no sooner settled in and relaxed with each other than it was time to leave. One birth mother acknowledged the limited place she could have in her young adopted child's life when direct contact was infrequent. She said:

> *He's only 18 months now ... he's going to be with his new mum and dad [all the time]. I only see him once a year, so ... really he*

isn't going to have [as] much feeling towards me as I have [for] him.

Another birth mother revealed the great pressure that infrequent contact places on her to ensure that the precious time she has with her birth children is positive. She said:

I get so tense, enormously tense, and frightened to death that something will go wrong on the contact. I think what it is, is the expectation that I want everything to be so perfect for the girls on the contact . . . I want it to be so perfect because it is only once every six months that we get to see one another.

Even if contact meetings were longer, relatives still perceived infrequent contact as inadequate. One birth father who had annual contact for two or three hours said:

You're looking forward to it . . . then all of a sudden it's all [over]. If it was somebody you bumped into on a regular basis it probably wouldn't be quite so bad, but, er, that short amount of time just once a year, it's not, not too much, is it really?

The perception of birth relatives as a source of ongoing risk

Many birth relatives who found contact meetings difficult often felt unwelcome, mistrusted or even demonised by adoptive parents or supervising workers. One maternal grandmother speculated that the adoptive mother assumed, wrongly, she believes, that she shared, or even caused, the birth mother's problems. This has resulted in the birth grand-mother feeling that the adoptive mother treats her with contempt. Another birth grandmother was bemused by an adoptive mother's request that Christmas presents bought for the children should be vetted by the child's social worker and handed over by the adoptive parents rather than given directly by the birth grandmother to each child. One birth mother said she had decided to take some fruit to contact for the children. She had thought carefully about this, as one of her birth children has a health condition that requires him to eat a restricted diet. Her preference was to ask an acquaintance who owns a fruit and vegetable stall to make up a large basket of various fruits. However, this was not allowed by social services and instead she had to buy fruit from the local supermarket with the worker present. When asked by the researcher about the rationale for this, the birth mother replied with irony: 'I presume they think I'm going to poison them.' This example suggests that in some cases, birth relatives' actions are interpreted as potentially risky rather than beneficial for the children without evidence to support such an assumption.

Themes related to the success of contact

A number of themes emerged from the accounts of birth relatives that were thought to contribute to a positive contact experience. These are discussed in more detail below.

A continuing connection with the child

A major theme that emerged in positive accounts of contact was the ability of many birth relatives to maintain a constructive and rewarding relationship with the child, sometimes despite the great emotional and practical challenges of contact. The majority of relatives were extremely happy to spend time with the adopted child(ren). They were very pleased to see how children were growing and developing and were greatly reassured by seeing how well they had settled into their new family.

Birth relatives described the joy they experienced from being greeted warmly by children on arrival and the enjoyment they got from chatting to them and sharing activities. One birth mother said:

> *I do love spending time with them and it is a real lift to see them and be able to chat away to them and listen to what they've done . . . It can be a bit of a downer having to come away from the visits, of course, knowing that I'm not going to see them again for a long time, but . . . it's always good to be with them.*

A birth father stated: 'They come running up to me and cuddle me . . . I just enjoy every moment, every time I see them . . . I love having contact.'

Ability to manage the strong emotions raised by contact

For many birth relatives, contact raised strong emotions. They described a mixture of intense feelings, including excitement at seeing the adopted child but also a deep sense of fear about how the contact would go. One birth mother described herself as 'drained at the end of it . . . drained and upset'.

Some contacts were also filled with tension. One birth grandmother described how the adoptive father paced the room during contact, making the atmosphere very tense and the contact stressful. Some relatives described the great pain they experienced when having to leave children at the end of each contact meeting. One birth mother explained: 'The only thing that's bad . . . about contact with any of them is the leaving . . . the end. It's just leaving them and going off.'

Contact often raised complex emotions for birth relatives even if it was going well. For example, one birth mother expressed her happiness that her children were settled with their new family. She said: 'The boys have looked up to [their adoptive parents] and called them Mum and Dad, and been really happy around them. So that's great.' But she also acknowledged the hurt she felt seeing them together: 'It's lovely to see them together as well, although I feel a bit jealous [laughs] when I see them all together.'

Contact with the adopted child led some birth relatives to revisit painful or traumatic memories. One birth grandmother, whose daughter had died, spoke of her intense sadness each time she met her daughter's child at contact as the child resembled his birth mother so much. She also described her emotional reaction to referring to the adoptive parents as "Mummy and Daddy". She explained:

> *The first contact we had, it was like trying to swallow a big bullet to say 'your Mummy and your Daddy'. But now it is how I think of them, even inside my head.*

This extract demonstrates, however, the capacity of some relatives to make the adjustment. A birth sibling said that after contact he was very upset. He explained: 'Sometimes I cry. I miss them, I do.' But he also said that spending time with his siblings made him happy.

One of the ways relatives dealt with feelings of loss was to acknowledge the benefits for the child of being cared for in their new family. In the words of one birth mother:

I'm glad I did it, because I know the kids are really happy and they love it where they are, and I still get to see them. I still feel bad about letting them go and I'm worried they are going to hold it against me but I know it's for the best.

While contact was highly distressing for some birth relatives, for others it was less so. This is not to suggest that adoption and contact were unproblematic for these relatives but that they had found ways, over an extended period of time, to manage their feelings. They were able, to some degree, to integrate the loss of the child into their life and accept the child's new life with their adoptive family. They managed to cope with life between contacts and made the most of the time they had with the child. They found contact both enjoyable and rewarding. One birth mother whose experience of contact was largely positive explained:

I do feel a bit emotional but it's only to be expected . . . I do have tears, tears of joy, not sadness, because I know she is in good hands.

In some cases, contact between the child and birth relative was arranged so that the difficult feelings associated with saying goodbye could be alleviated to some extent. For example, one sibling sends a text to her younger sister on her way home after contact to let her know how much she enjoyed seeing her.

These examples are testament to the ability of some birth relatives to manage the severe stress and emotional turmoil caused by contact in order to maintain a positive relationship with the adopted child.

Developing trust within the relationship between adoptive parents and birth relatives

Some birth relatives had managed to develop very good relationships with adoptive parents, which made the contact experience much more pleasant, enjoyable and relaxed. Typically, these relationships had taken many years to develop and deepen, but in a small number of cases birth relatives described an instant connection between them and the adoptive parents. One birth mother described her first impression of the couple who adopted her birth children, saying:

> *They were absolutely lovely people, really nice, and I got on really well with them . . . They seemed like really, really steady, dependable kind of people. They did seem the kind of people that would be very loving to anybody that was in close contact with them . . . I was quite happy about the idea of the boys going to them.*

Where relationships were good, it appears that adoptive parents did not view birth relatives as a risk to their child or a threat to their identity as a family, and the same was true vice versa. Relatives also often spoke of adoptive parents as being 'friends' or 'like family'. One birth mother with learning difficulties had been able to develop a very good relationship with the adoptive parents of her two children, describing them as 'just like a brother and sister to me'. These positive relationships led to a more relaxed atmosphere during contact and some birth relatives talked of 'having a laugh' with adoptive parents.

Agreeing to increase the openness of a contact arrangement appeared to be one tangible way in which adoptive parents could demonstrate their trust in the birth relative. In a few cases, a trusting relationship had developed to the point where adopters and birth relatives had exchanged telephone numbers and were visiting each other's home. One or two relatives were meeting adopted teenagers without the adoptive parents or a social worker present. Some previously supervised contacts had become unsupervised. Some more modest adjustments were also reported, such as annual contact being increased to twice a year, contact duration being extended, more use of informal venues and a birth relative being allowed to spend part of the meeting alone with a child. These relatively modest adjustments were highly valued by birth relatives.

At the same time, birth relatives were very aware of the power imbalance within the relationship and were careful to ensure they did not make adoptive parents feel uncomfortable or pressurised. One birth mother said:

> *I've noticed each contact does get a little bit longer . . . [but] I don't want to push it, because I have built up this relationship and I don't want to undo it.*

Visits to the adoptive home by birth relatives had a special significance for them. One birth mother described being invited to see her adopted teenage son's bedroom. She said that she and her son took great pleasure in her 'going into his world'.

The perception of caring as a shared agenda and the role of reciprocity in relationships

The accounts of some birth relatives indicated that they acknowledged the dual connection of their adopted child with both the birth family and the adoptive family (see also Chapter 6). One birth mother said, 'She is part of me and part of them. That's how I see it . . . [she is] our daughter . . . it's like sharing her.'

As well as this suggestion of dual connection or belonging, birth relatives' accounts also indicated a sense of a shared agenda with adoptive parents or being 'on the same side' rather than 'adversaries'. This did not necessarily mean they had equal status or took equal roles in the life of the child but that there was an acknowledgement that they both cared equally for the child and were working in his or her best interests.

Sometimes this shared agenda involved small examples of what could be described as shared parenting. In one case an adoptive parent asked a birth mother how she would like her birth daughter's hair. However, more commonly the shared agenda was confirmed through acts of reciprocity. For example, one birth mother demonstrated her gratitude to the adoptive parents for caring for her children by giving them gifts. They, in turn, gave her gifts and were happy for the birth mother to give presents to the children too. There was a sense within this arrangement of adoptive parents trying to overcome the inequities within the situation and the birth mother feeling there was a genuine attempt to share the relationship with the child. A sense of shared agenda was also supported in very simple ways through, for instance, swapping photographs at the end of contact.

Where there was a sense of a shared agenda, contact was also more likely to be treated as part of an ongoing relationship rather than a series of one-off meetings. Adoptive parents and birth relatives would chat about how the children were doing and what they had been up to.

Feeling valued and included in decision making

Birth relatives who reported more positive experiences of contact also gave examples of the ways in which adoptive families included them in decisions about contact. These were usually quite modest decisions, such as the date or venue for meetings, but were appreciated by birth relatives. These small gestures made relatives feel respected and indicated to them that their feelings were important. Where relatives were consulted, the contact arrangements tended to be more informal and there was room for flexibility. In addition, where there was some dissatisfaction with contact, the parties could also negotiate adjustments to the arrangements.

Demonstrations of empathy between adoptive parents and birth relatives

Birth relatives gave a number of examples of occasions when adoptive parents had showed great empathy towards them and their circumstances. For example, one birth mother described the sensitivity the adoptive mother had shown in understanding the birth mother's feelings and anxieties:

> . . . I asked her to kiss them and cuddle them every night for me and she said she would. She did say to me that there would always be photographs there and they would not shut us out of their life and they know I am the mum and things like that.

Another birth mother reported that she was told emphatically by an adoptive mother that she would never consider stopping contact. An adoptive mother made it clear to another birth mother that she would always have a place in the children's life and that her adopted children would call her 'mummy [name]'. The birth mother explained: 'They said they would never take that away from me.'

Other birth relatives were reassured that the adoptive family would talk about the birth family at home and always speak respectfully about them. These gestures were greatly valued.

Birth relatives also showed empathy for adoptive parents. One birth mother spoke of her discomfort when her child called her "Mum" during contact and her awareness of the adoptive mother's distress.

Birth relatives' perceptions of the benefits of contact

Given the very challenging nature of direct contact, we wanted to explore in more depth the benefits of, or motivation for, contact as perceived by birth relatives. Birth relatives often felt strongly that it was in the child's best interests as well as their own to maintain a relationship after adoption. Some had fought hard to persuade the courts of the value of contact and had managed to secure direct contact where the previous plan had been for indirect contact only. The main benefit of direct contact mentioned by relatives was the reassurance that it could offer to both child and birth relative about the other's well-being. A birth mother reported that seeing her children well cared for by their adoptive parents 'puts my own mind at ease'.

One birth grandmother explained that after her son's death, her grandson was anxious that she might die too. Direct contact, therefore, reassured him that his grandmother was well. Contact was also seen as offering reassurance about the continuing love that the birth family has for the child. Another birth grandmother explained:

> ... the children need this contact ... it's actually for their benefit primarily, to help them adjust to what has happened in their lives. Because they must be very confused about how it has all come about, and we feel that they just need the reassurance of knowing that their birth family is still there and cares about them.

This quote suggests yet another benefit of contact, namely the opportunity it brings to birth relatives to be directly involved in helping a child to make sense of the adoption story. The grandmother wanted to be able to help her adopted grandchildren understand the circumstances leading to their adoption and their birth mother's mental health issues and provide support to deal with this. Many relatives were keen to ensure that children's questions were answered and curiosity alleviated through contact. One birth mother said, 'He won't be so worried about who's his mum when he's older.'

Several birth relatives expressed the anxieties they had about the care the children would receive when they were first placed with adoptive parents. They worried about the children's physical well-being, such as whether they would be fed well or warm enough, as well as their emotional well-being and whether they would be loved and cherished. Direct contact, therefore, offered them an opportunity to judge first hand whether the care being offered by adoptive parents was good enough and the ways in which the children were benefiting from this care. Relatives identified a further benefit of contact, which was the great pleasure they took from seeing children grow and flourish. A birth mother put it like this:

> . . . *seeing them grow, seeing how they are changing, how they are mentally progressing in their life, how they are turning into young women, knowing their opinions on everyday things in life, just growing with them.*

Many of the benefits of contact to which birth relatives referred suggest that they feel a strong sense of ongoing responsibility for the child, even though their legal responsibility has been removed. A further benefit of contact, therefore, appears to be that it allows relatives to actively express this sense of ongoing responsibility for the child through spending time with them. Some also saw contact as an important acknowledgement of the continuing connection between the child and birth family and a tangible acknowledgement of the existence of the birth family. A fear was expressed that, without contact, this connection would be lost and children might forget birth relatives. Some birth mothers went further, describing the continuing connection as almost a physical bond. Where this was the case, a loss of contact was unthinkable even if the experience of contact was very painful or upsetting. One birth mother stated that 'It would have been terrible . . . to not see them or hear them.' This physical experience of seeing and hearing the other person somehow seemed to reinforce the validity of the relationship.

A further benefit of direct contact identified by birth relatives was the opportunity it provided for children to see adults getting on with each other. This would not be achieved easily through indirect contact. Relatives reported that there would perhaps be hugs and kisses between the adoptive parents and birth relatives, even where these relationships were at times strained. Finally, one birth sibling suggested that contact with his little sister was a benefit to him, as it was a motivation to stay out of trouble with the police.

Few birth relatives identified any benefits of contact for adoptive parents; some even viewed contact as a disadvantage for them. A small number, however, suggested that an advantage to adoptive parents was that their adopted children's needs were met through contact. Birth relatives recognised the challenge of contact for some adoptive parents. One birth mother said, 'It must be a bugbear to them saying 'Oh my god, here goes, we've got access again.'

Some relatives questioned the motives of a small number of adoptive parents whom they believed viewed contact as the right thing to do but appeared to be just going through the motions. They expressed concerns about the benefits of this for any of the parties.

The importance of the adoptive parents' role in contact meetings

The role taken by adoptive parents in contact meetings varied from situation to situation. In some cases, adoptive parents very much took a back seat and allowed the interactions to be primarily between the birth relative and child for the short time they were together. This was experienced by some people as a demonstration of adoptive parents' respect for the relationship between birth relative and child, and was described by birth relatives as 'not interfering'. Some adoptive parents, while in the background, were also quite active, discreetly facilitating the relationship between the child and birth relative. One adoptive mother suggested ideas for presents for the child to a birth relative to ensure that the gift added to the feeling of connection between the child and birth relative.

For other birth relatives, the presence of adoptive parents in the background took on a more menacing quality and this passive presence was seen as detrimental to the relationship between birth relative and child. In these cases, there was often a lack of trust or respect between the adults involved. The passive role taken by some adoptive parents in contact was also interpreted by some relatives as a lack of active support for the relationship between child and birth family. In some cases, birth relatives felt the adoptive parents did not encourage interactions between themselves and the child. Several birth parents were hoping for a deeper relationship to develop with adoptive parents and were disappointed if this had not happened. One birth mother who had been having contact for more than five years said:

> *They don't have anything to do with me . . . it has been the same from the beginning, exactly the same as when I first met them. They don't say a lot and they don't make any effort, they keep it short, they keep it sweet and they keep it the same as it has been for the last five or six years.*

A birth grandmother also expressed regret about her lack of closeness with the adoptive parents:

> *Maybe if I went to their house and I'd been involved more, it might be different. I'd probably get to know them better. But I only see them once a year . . . we won't be close.*

In other cases adoptive parents interacted more with birth relatives during contact. This was viewed by some birth relatives as positive and by others less so. Where it was welcomed, there were good relationships between birth relatives and adoptive parents. Relatives enjoyed hearing from the adoptive parents about the child's progress at school and the parties considered each other as friends or extended family. Some relatives who had expected adoptive parents to be marginal to the meeting viewed their active presence as problematic and felt adopters dominated interactions. Some relatives were seeking a more shared role during contact. For example, one birth grandfather expressed concern that on a visit to a zoo he did not feel like a full participant in the activity. He said:

> *They were running about and doing different things and you felt as if the family was the family and you were the outsiders . . . I was quite relieved to leave.*

This problem was compounded when the grandfather asked the adoptive family to share the picnic that he and his wife had prepared but the offer was turned down, as the adoptive parents had also brought food. He felt 'rebuffed' by this incident.

Some birth relatives felt that meetings between adoptive parents and birth relatives outside of contact, when the child was not present, could provide a helpful way to build or maintain a relationship with the adoptive parents and, ultimately, the child.

The experiences of birth relatives in cases where contact had stopped

Five of the birth relatives whom we interviewed at Time 2 reported that contact with the adopted child had stopped or been suspended. These relatives included one grandmother and four birth mothers. What they had in common was that in each case the reason for stopping contact was related to the child's reactions to it. In one case the child herself, a teenager, had written to the birth mother to say she wanted to cease direct contact. According to this birth mother, both herself and the adoptive parents had been very happy and comfortable with the contact; in fact, it had gradually increased over the years. The adopted child's decision to terminate contact suggests that she was less happy than the adults with the arrangements. In the other four cases where contact stopped, it seemed this decision had been made on behalf of the child. In one case, a birth mother described how her adopted son was experiencing very difficult feelings about the fact that she had given birth to a new baby and was parenting this child. In a further case (concerning a grandmother and birth mother) the adopted child was showing difficult feelings and behaviours after contact meetings, so contact with both his birth mother and grandmother was stopped. In the final case, the birth mother's child had only recently been adopted and she had just had one contact meeting with him. Her perception was that the meeting had gone well and the child had been comfortable and pleased to see her. However, she was told afterwards that her son (who had special needs related to autism) showed very difficult behaviour, and so it was decided to suspend contact until he was more settled in his adoptive placement.

The reaction of birth relatives to contact stopping was variable. One person (the birth mother whose daughter had stopped the contact) expressed quite mixed feelings. She seemed angry with her daughter for taking this decision. She said that, on the one hand, she would like the contact to continue but, on the other hand, felt it was better it had ceased until, as she put it, 'the storm blows over'. The grandmother whose contact had stopped also expressed mixed feelings and concern that if the contact was bad for the children perhaps it should have been terminated sooner. She explained that she had not been convinced that direct contact was in the children's best interests, hence she was both relieved and 'gutted' that it had stopped. In the other three cases, the birth mothers expressed a lot of concern and empathy for the difficult feelings that children seem to be having after contact. All three were unhappy that contact had stopped or been suspended, but all seemed to have as their primary focus the best interests of their child.

What was common in each case where contact had stopped was that birth relatives expressed high levels of dissatisfaction with the information and support they had been given following that decision. In one case the relative was informed by letter that direct contact was to be suspended. She was told she could write to the child instead. She did so but had not heard whether her letter had been passed on by the agency or received by the adoptive parents. She had no information about if or when direct contact would be resumed, and no information about how her child was getting on. In another case, the birth mother was told her child was having counselling to help her deal with issues relating to the adoption.

The birth mother was anxious to know how her daughter was getting on and whether she was OK, but had received no response to her enquiries.

Summary

This chapter has explored birth relatives' experiences of contact, focusing on the challenges, benefits and success factors. Key findings are as follows:

- Birth relatives identified a number of ways in which they found contact could be challenging. These included:
  - loss of power: the need to manage the relationship with adoptive parents;
  - loss of role: the re-ordering of birth relatives' roles in the lives of adopted children;
  - fear of loss of relationship with the child;
  - the perception of birth relatives as a source of ongoing risk.
- Factors that were identified as contributing to a positive experience of contact for birth relatives included:
  - being able to maintain a continuing connection with the child;
  - their ability to manage the strong emotions raised by contact;
  - developing trust with adoptive parents;
  - the perception of caring as a shared agenda and the role of reciprocity in relationships;
  - feeling valued and included in decision-making;
  - demonstrations of empathy between adoptive parents and birth relatives.
- Birth relatives perceived a number of benefits of contact. These included feeling that contact was in the child's best interests as well as their own. Many relatives felt they could make a positive contribution to their child's life in the adoptive family, and felt it was beneficial for the child to see the two families getting along together.
- Birth relatives described a variety of ways in which adoptive parents participated in contact meetings. Some valued adoptive parents taking a back seat, but others wished they could have more involvement and a closer relationship with adoptive parents.

- Five birth relatives had experienced the cessation of contact because of concerns about the impact of contact on the child. Their feelings about contact stopping varied, but all five were very unhappy with the information and support they had been given following the decision.

11 Support for direct contact arrangements: services received by adoptive parents and how these relate to case factors

This chapter explores adoptive parents' experiences of receiving services to support the direct contact arrangements between their child and the birth family.

The chapter begins by describing five different types of support activity, classified according to their function; following that, the number of people receiving each type is given. We then discuss in more detail adoptive parents' experiences of the roles that support workers play during contact meetings.

In the next section, we describe four different models of contact support, along with profiles of the families receiving them. The number of families where contact was defined as "working very well" is then explored in relation to the four contact support models.

Adoptive parents' experiences of support services – identifying types of contact support

Adoptive parents were asked to describe support they had received in relation to the target contact arrangements. They described a wide range of types of support from both statutory and voluntary agencies. In coding and categorising support activities, we decided to focus on the *functions or purposes* of different activities as opposed to merely the *method* of delivery. So, for example, when an adoptive parent received a phone call from the support worker, the purpose could be to suggest a date for contact, talk through the adoptive parent's feelings about contact or review the child's reactions. Similarly, there could be a variety of purposes for a worker attending a contact meeting.

The analysis focuses specifically on adoptive parents' perceptions of support. We acknowledge that their perspectives may differ from those of service providers. For example, a support worker may believe they offered emotional support during a home visit, but the parent may have experienced the visit as administrative, so the visit would be coded as administrative. Service providers' perspectives on support are explored elsewhere in the study, in both the mapping survey and the economic analysis.

A typology of support services was developed from an initial analysis of the adoptive parents' interview data and five types were identified. Each adopter interview was coded in terms of whether each type of service was reported or not reported.

Types of support services provided to adoptive families

The five types of support activity are described briefly below and in more detail later in this chapter.

1. **Co-ordination and administration**: This type of support was concerned with the practical arrangements associated with contact. It involved agencies acting as go-betweens to agree or advise on the time and place of contact, arranging a venue, providing lifts or escorting a child to contact.

2. **Relationship building**: This category involved interventions specifically aimed at ensuring that relationships between the child and birth relatives, or adoptive parents and birth relatives, developed positively and were supportive of contact. Not included in this category were situations where agency workers were present during contact, were friendly and sociable but did not intervene to build relationships.

3. **Protecting or promoting the interests of the adoptive family**: This involved direct support for the adoptive family because of potential or actual conflicts of interest, a disagreement about how contact should happen or some behaviour that put the child's well-being at risk.

4. **Reviewing arrangements and planning**: This involved assessing individual needs and responding to changes to ensure that contact was of maximum benefit. A review could involve a simple phone call after contact and/or more formal meetings. This category was reserved for agency activities aimed at proactive reviewing and planning rather

than simply responding to problems raised by the birth or adoptive family.

5. **Providing emotional support/therapeutic input**: This was concerned with the psychological aspects of contact. Emotional support could be provided to the child or the adoptive parents as a one-off or ongoing intervention. The provision of specialist interventions such as counselling, life story work or play therapy to resolve distress related to adoption generally was also included in this category.

How many adoptive families were receiving the five types of support services?

An analysis was undertaken to establish the extent to which these types of support were received by adoptive parents. This is summarised in Table 11.1. By far the most common types of support offered to families were co-ordination and administration and protecting or promoting interests. Co-ordination and administration support was provided to 87 per cent of interviewees at Time 1 and 77 per cent of interviewees at Time 2; the key activity that was described was liaison with all parties to set up the contact meeting. Protecting or promoting interests support was provided to 66 per cent of interviewees at Time 2 and 64 per cent of interviewees at Time 2; in most cases this service was delivered via workers attending or supervising meetings. Only a minority of adoptive parents reported receiving services related to the review of contact arrangements; this type of support was reported by 43 per cent of adopters at Time 1 and 33 per cent at Time 2. The two types of support that featured least in adopters' accounts were emotional and therapeutic support and relationship building. Emotional and therapeutic support was provided to about one-quarter of families (parents and/or children) – 28 per cent of interviewees at Time 1 and 24 per cent at Time 2. Relationship building was provided to just 13 per cent of interviewees at Time 1 and 20 per cent at Time 2. It is difficult to determine whether these types of support are provided less often than other types or whether there is less consciousness among adopters of these types of support being provided. Relationship building is, of course, more subtle than direct supervision or phone calls. However, other evidence suggests that these types of support were not

Table 11.1
Types of contact support services received by adoptive parents at Time 1 and Time 2

	Number receiving service at Time 1	% at Time 1 (of 53)*	Number receiving service at Time 2	% at Time 2 (of 53)**
Co-ordination and administration	46	87	41	77
Relationship building	7	13	11	20
Protecting or promoting the interests of the adoptive family	35	66	34	64
Reviewing arrangements and planning	23	43	18	33
Providing emotional support/ therapeutic input	15	28	13	24

* One case was missing because contact had not yet started, one was missing because part of the audio file was incomprehensible
** Two families did not participate at Time 2

only less visible but also less frequently available. Several adopters noted workers' lack of acknowledgment of the deeply emotional aspect of contact and identified the need for more emotional support. For example, some families spoke about the strained relationships between the parties during contact and their frustration at the passivity of the supervising social worker during such a difficult time. Where support was offered it was highly valued by adopters.

The data from adoptive parents support the findings from the case vignette study (Neil, 2007a), which found that adoption professionals did not always recognise the needs of adoptive parents for emotional support in dealing with the impact of contact. Nor did they often recognise the need for intervention to address the nature of the adoptive parents' relationship with birth relatives. Where the findings in this chapter differ from the case vignette study is that, in response to the case vignette, direct work with the child was the service adoption professionals most frequently suggested they would provide. In this chapter, any such work would be categorised under the heading of emotional or therapeutic support. Only a minority of adoptive parents reported receiving support in this category, and in many of these cases the support provided was to the adoptive parents and not the child.

Adopters' descriptions of support received from agencies

In this section, each of the five different types of support service are described in more detail using data from adoptive parent interviews.

Description of co-ordination and administration interventions

As well as liaison with parties and the organisation of meetings, the category of co-ordination and administration included practical support such as providing transport for birth family members to and from the contact meeting, ensuring all information that needed to be shared between parties before contact was shared, tracking down missing birth relatives, formally communicating changes in contact arrangements in writing, arranging specialist support, e.g. an interpreter, and providing financial support. Practical support such as providing lifts to birth family members attending contact was highly valued by adopters and the feeling was often that, without this, contact would not happen.

Costs associated with contact include travel expenses, activity-related costs and entrance fees, meal or refreshment costs, accommodation costs where an overnight stay was necessary, lost earnings when contact required an adult to take time off work and the cost of presents for those attending contact. A minority of adoptive parents received financial help with the cost of contact but it did not necessarily cover everything. There was no evidence of lost income or purchase of gifts being reimbursed, despite these being substantial expenses. While some may question the appropriateness of reimbursing the cost of gifts, these were viewed by adopters as an important aspect of maintaining the relationships within contact. Some adopters who did not receive financial support felt this situation was acceptable, particularly where costs were minimal or where activities and the cost associated with these, such as entrance fees and food, were considered part of everyday family life. Other adopters who did not receive financial support felt strongly that costs should be reimbursed and one adopter suggested that reimbursement should be a *child's right* rather than a means-tested allowance for adopters. Concern was expressed about a lack of clarity regarding what can be claimed and an inconsistent application of the rules. In some cases, the costs of contact were partly met by birth parents; for instance, a birth grandparent paying for a child's meal during contact. This sort of gesture was highly appreciated by adopters. In other cases, adoptive parents paid the costs accrued by birth relatives, who were on a low income.

Description of interventions aimed at protecting or promoting interests

This category included direct supervision of face-to-face contact and, in a smaller number of cases, meetings between the adult parties included in contact to discuss potential or actual conflicts of interest or differences of opinion. Such meetings were felt by the majority of adopters, although not all, to have been a very useful practice. However, they were less successful where the relationship between adults was particularly poor. Problems also resulted when some adult parties were not present at the meeting yet decisions were made and implemented. Some adopters experiencing conflict with birth relatives said they would not welcome a face-to-face meeting between the adults. This is an indication of the anxiety that such a meeting is likely to produce and the need for careful preparation, facilitation and support for all. In one exceptional case, a series of meetings was held between professionals and the adoptive parents before each contact to undertake a risk assessment and agree procedures for the meeting. In this case, the child taking part in contact was deeply committed to contact but also deeply disturbed by her experience of abuse in the birth family.

This category of support also included activities such as establishing a formal written agreement on particular details; for example, the names to be used in contact, whether letters can be exchanged during contact and any boundaries around the exchange of gifts at meetings. These agreements were sometimes drawn up before contact was first established or as a result of issues raised in the course of contact. The agreements were sometimes negotiated by the adults involved in a meeting, sometimes negotiated between the social worker and each individual or sometimes prepared by the adopter and worker only and presented to birth parents as a *fait accompli*. Clarity of expectations was particularly important to adopters whose children were having contact with birth parents who had mental health difficulties, emotional problems or learning disabilities. The protection and promotion of interests were also undertaken by workers in a less formal way when accompanying birth family members to contact. Workers used opportunities immediately before a contact meeting to remind birth family members what is considered acceptable behaviour during contact and to address any negative feelings arising from conflict. One adopter described the social worker as a 'buffer' between her and the birth family.

This category of support was about not only the protection or defence of interests but also the positive promotion of interests and interventions to ensure that contact was beneficial for all. Workers undertook several tasks to achieve this. In some cases workers passed on children's difficult questions about their history to birth family members and helped them prepare to answer such questions helpfully during the contact meeting. Support was also offered by workers with regard to the timing, pacing or intensity of contact where a new and informal arrangement was being established. Workers also helped adopters to develop a positive view of the benefits of contact over time by providing evidence of the value of contact for the child and the importance of the relationship for the birth family member.

Description of review and planning interventions

Where a proactive approach to review was taken it consisted of a number of activities, including phone calls and emails before and after contact to elicit adopters' views about the contact and written questionnaires to them following the meeting. Some workers also informed adopters of birth families' feelings about contact; where this occurred, adopters were very appreciative of this information. Adjustments to contact were sometimes needed to improve the experience and at other times to protect the child.

There were examples in the study of very difficult contact arrangements being effectively turned around through a comprehensive process of planning and review. In one case contact was between a sibling group and their grandmother, who had previously been their main carer. Initially, the two families were largely left to work out contact between themselves. A number of problems quickly arose in relation to different expectations about the frequency and formality of contact, and the adoptive parents were concerned that the children could not understand which family home was to be their permanent base. The adoptive parents' link worker organised a meeting to draw up a contact agreement covering such issues as gifts, involvement of the extended birth family and the frequency, duration and venue of contact. The adoptive parents described this initial meeting as 'very difficult'. Another meeting was held and further work undertaken with the birth family. At the time we followed up this family, the children had been in placement for four years. The early problems with contact had been resolved through the comprehensive planning. The contact remained on track and, through ongoing annual review meetings between the grandparents and adoptive parents, was able to evolve positively. Contact was currently about eight times a year and was very positive for all parties.

It was notable, however, that fewer than half of the adoptive parents (42% at Time 1 and 36% at Time 2) reported a proactive approach to the review of contact arrangements. Instead, many referred to social workers being available if needed, indicating that the onus was on adopters to raise issues and flag up potential problems or the need for change when problems occurred. Given that previous research suggests contact is a dynamic process, changing over time (Neil and Howe, 2004), this reactive approach does not fit well with adoptive families' needs. Some negative consequences of this approach were apparent in the course of the research. In some Time 1 interviews adopters indicated a concern that contact would stop or be suspended; at Time 2, contact had indeed ceased or been suspended in some of these cases. The lack of a mechanism to highlight and address such issues is a concern. In two other cases, data from the Time 2 interview suggested that a contact arrangement was in great danger of breaking down yet there was little evidence of any active review or planning being undertaken by the social worker to avoid this, at least within the adopters' accounts. In one case an adoptive mother described a difficult relationship between her and the birth mother, a tense atmosphere during meetings and the child wanting and needing to see her birth mother but being disturbed in her behaviour after contact meetings. In spite of these warning signals, the agency did not appear to address these concerns. Although the agency supervised the meeting and visited the adoptive family regularly, these interventions did not, from the adoptive parent's perspective, include reviewing the contact arrangements or addressing the problems. In fact, even when the adoptive mother suggested a meeting with the birth mother to 'talk things out' she said the agency told her it was 'not a good idea'. In some cases, the process of the research interview itself gave adopters a chance to reflect on their experience of contact and support, and led them to conclude that a more active approach to review would be more helpful. One adopter expressed her concern about the tendency for potential changes to be discussed informally during contact by one party with the social worker, for instance, while making tea. She feared that this had led to issues being given inadequate consideration and perhaps decisions being made that disadvantaged the birth mother.

Description of interventions providing emotional or therapeutic support

Examples of emotional support offered to children included art therapy, play therapy or life story work to enable children to express feelings about their history and/or contact, and therapeutic work to deal with attachment issues. In one case, direct work was undertaken with a child who feared his birth father would find him and harm him.

Therapeutic input was provided by the local authority, a voluntary adoption support service, a CAMHS service or a private practitioner. At least two families were personally funding direct work with a child in relation to attachment and behavioural issues. While much less common, there was some evidence of therapy or counselling being provided to the adoptive family as a whole in relation to adoption and contact.

Description of interventions aimed at relationship building

Some families described the very careful and often subtle work undertaken during contact by social workers to build relationships between adult birth relatives and adopters, between adopted children and birth relatives, and between siblings reunited in contact. In these cases adoptive parents and workers gave careful thought to the choice of activities during contact. Efforts were made to identify an activity that allowed equal participation of all, including children of various ages and genders and adult birth family members. The activity might be as simple as sharing a meal and chatting or more physically participative, such as bowling or football. Adopters also referred to aids to relationship building such as sharing photographs, exchanging gifts and sharing food. Some social workers intervened directly in activities to help the birth relative participate alongside the child. Some social workers provided food at contact meetings in an effort, it appeared, to make contact as comfortable as possible for everyone and provide an opportunity for relationship building between the parties.

One adoptive mother explained that the worker particularly supported the birth mother's efforts to demonstrate care, such as always ensuring she had chocolate in her cupboards when her birth son visited. In one case where relationships between adults were quite tense, the social worker suggested to the birth mother that she give the adoptive mother a plant as a gift at contact. While the gift did not transform the relationship, it was very much appreciated by the adoptive mother. Some social workers regularly provided adopters with news of the birth family. This was highly valued by adopters as it allowed them to anticipate any tensions in the meetings and to direct conversation sensitively.

The diversity of roles adopted by social workers who are present at contact

Data were collected relating to social workers' presence at contact meetings. Workers were present at about 62 per cent of contact meetings (see Chapter 3). This presence is often referred to as 'supervision' of contact, yet our data indicated that the presence of a worker at contact and a supervisory role are not synonymous; instead, the activities undertaken by workers varied enormously. A more detailed analysis was undertaken, therefore, of the roles undertaken by workers while present at contact meetings. These are described in more detail below.

The approach of some workers was to be little more than a **benign presence**. These workers were described by adopters as very passive and non-interventionist, sometimes to the relief and at other times the frustration of adopters. This was a particular issue where workers were new to a contact arrangement. Some workers took on a role of **inspection and correction**. They were described as alert to conversations and behaviours, stepping in when these became inappropriate. Inspection and correction were consistently described as relating to birth relatives rather than adoptive parents. However, one adoptive mother suggested that a benefit of the worker's presence in contact was to be a **witness** to the adopters' competence as parents in order to avoid false accusations of poor parenting. Some adopters described the worker's role during the meeting as **managing** the contact, i.e. ensuring it started and finished on time. The role taken on by some workers was to make contact a **physically and psychologically comfortable** experience. These workers got conversation started to break the ice and made sure adults had refreshments. Another approach described by adopters was a more active emphasis on **building relationships**. Workers were described as modelling play activities for birth parents or guiding adult conversations so that they were deeper than just social chit-chat. Often workers took on more than one of these roles. Adopters' satisfaction with these various roles and approaches is described further in Chapter 12.

Developing models of contact support

Adoptive parents might receive all, some or none of the five services described above. We felt that just counting the types of service that adoptive parents received would not sufficiently distinguish between different practice models of contact support, and hence we decided to undertake further coding.

Four models of contact support were identified, differing in terms of two key dimensions. The first dimension was whether or not the agency was undertaking **proactive interventions** to facilitate the interactions and dynamics of the contact network, and/or to help people manage their personal reactions to contact. The assumption here is that contact is a dynamic transactional process; each party (child, adoptive parents, birth relatives) will have their own reactions and each will be affected by the behaviour and feelings of other people involved. We were interested in the extent to which contact support interventions worked to address these inter- and intrapersonal dynamics. These processes could be managed through interventions before or after contact; for example, phone support or review meetings, emotional support to children or adults. Sometimes proactive interventions could occur during contact; for example, relationship building between a child and birth family member. The three types of contact support considered to have the specific function of addressing these processes were: relationship building, review and planning and emotional/therapeutic support. Parents who reported receiving any of these services were coded as receiving "proactive interventions".

The second dimension was whether or not an agency worker (or someone appointed on their behalf) **attended the contact meetings**. This is a simple yes/no dimension and does not attempt to take account of the role workers play within meetings. Each case could have neither, one or both of these dimensions of contact support; hence four models were created, as shown in Figure 11.1 and described in detail below.

Figure 11.1
Models of contact support

	Proactive interventions/facilitation	
No	*Yes*	
		No
Model 1: **Administrated contact** – Family-only meetings, but no proactive intervention	Model 2: **Facilitated contact** – Family-only meetings, with proactive intervention	Worker at meetings
		Yes
Model 4: **Supervised contact** – Worker at meetings, no proactive intervention	Model 3: **Supervised and facilitated contact** – Worker at meetings, plus proactive intervention	

Model 1: Administrated contact

In this model, adoptive parents described agencies as having some level of involvement in the contact, usually the type of support coded as co-ordination and administration, such as liaising between parties to arrange meetings. However, meetings were not attended by a worker and none of the three types of proactive contact support services (relationship building, reviewing and planning, and emotional and therapeutic support) were provided outside of meetings.

Case example

Charlene, age 11, has contact with her birth mother for two-and-a-half hours once a year. The meetings are held in a contact centre and she goes with her adoptive parents. The agency phones the adoptive parents and birth mother to agree a date, but otherwise has no contact with the adoptive parents between meetings. The agency books and pays for the venue, but does not attend meetings.

Model 2: Facilitated contact

In this model meetings were not attended by workers, but agencies did provide at least one of the three types of proactive contact support outside of meetings.

Case example

Tyrone, age 8, has contact with four of his siblings once a year. Two of his siblings are also adopted (separately) and two are in foster care. The children and their parents and carers all meet up at a child-friendly public venue; one of the adoptive mothers takes the lead in organising this. No agency worker attends but they are involved in contacting the siblings in foster care and arranging their presence at meetings. They also have organised a meeting for all the adults to get together and discuss the progress of contact.

Model 3: Supervised and facilitated contact

In this model a worker attended contact meetings and the agency also provided at least one of the three proactive contact support services, either within or outside of the contact meetings.

Case example

Norah, age 12, is adopted with her two younger siblings. The three children see their birth mother once a year at a contact centre. Their adoptive parents and a worker attend the meetings. The agency mediates between the two parties to arrange the date. They also ring the adoptive parents soon after a meeting to discuss how it went and then visit the adoptive parents about three months after the meeting to review the contact.

Model 4: Supervised contact

Here, workers attended meetings and agencies often also had a practical or administrative role in supporting contact, or protecting and promoting the interests of adoptive parents. However, none of the proactive contact support services were provided either within or outside of contact meetings.

Case example

Davey, age 7, sees his birth mother for an hour or so once a year at a family centre. His adoptive mother goes with him and a worker is there in the background. The worker brings the birth mother to contact. Apart from a phone call to fix the date, the adoptive parents have no contact from the agency between meetings.

Table 11.2 shows the number and percentage of cases in each of these four models, at Time 1 and Time 2. Because some families had different levels of contact support at both points in time, a third rating was used to describe contact overall, and this was the highest level of support reported. This table shows that the most common model of contact

Table 11.2
Models of contact support at Time 1, Time 2 and overall

	n at T1	% at T1	n at T2	% at T2	n overall	% overall
Model 1: administrated contact (AC)	8	16.3	8	17.4	8	15.4
Model 2: facilitated contact (FC)	8	16.3	8	17.4	8	15.4
Model 3: supervised and facilitated contact (SFC)	21	42.9	17	36.9	27	51.9
Model 4: supervised contact (SC)	12	24.5	13	28.3	9	17.3
Total	**49***	**100.0**	**46****	**100.0**	**52*****	**100.0**

* Four families were not receiving any contact support. One family could not be coded because part of the audiofile was incomprehensible, and one family had just the child placed and contact had not yet begun

** Seven families had no contact support between Time 1 and Time 2. Two families did not take part at Time 2

*** Three families had no contact support at either point in time support received by adoptive families was Model 3 – supervised and facilitated contact. Overall, more than half of the families had received this model of support, with the other half receiving, in approximately equal measures, one of the other three models.

Of the families who took part at both points in time (n = 52), two-thirds (n = 35, 66%) received the same model of contact support at Time 1 and Time 2, but in 18 cases (44%) the model of contact support had changed. Seven families received more support at Time 2 than Time 1. Five of these families were receiving Model 4 at Time 1 (supervised contact) but by Time 2 had some additional facilitation for these meetings (meaning they now had supervised and facilitated contact). One family was managing contact without services at Time 1, but the child had some counselling (related to contact) between the two interviews. The final case where contact support increased was where the contact actually began between Time 1 and Time 2. Eleven families were having less contact support at the time of the second interview. While increases in contact related to increased need by families, decreases in contact support were not always related to a decrease in need; in five of the 11 cases, contact support had decreased because services became less available, for instance, because of staffing issues in the agency. In four cases, the provision of contact support services ceased between Time 1 and Time 2 because families chose to manage contact themselves. In two further cases, no support was received at Time 2 because contact had stopped. In these cases no services were provided to help families manage the impact of contact ceasing.

In order to explore the contact support models in more detail, we looked at which of the five types of contact support people received within the four models, examined at Time 1. The numbers are shown in Table 11.3.

Table 11.3 shows that in most cases across all four models of contact support, the agency was performing some type of co-ordination and administration role.

Model 1 was receiving the fewest services, the agency role here apparently being to set up arrangements and keep contact "ticking over". But there was seemingly no acknowledgement that this was more than a

Table 11.3

Types of contact support received by adoptive parents across the four contact support models (based on Time 1 data)

Contact support type	Co-ordination and administration	Relationship building	Protecting and promoting interests	Review and planning	Emotional/ therapeutic support
Model 1 (AC)	7 of 8	n/a*	3 of 8	n/a	n/a
Model 2 (FC)	7 of 8	0 of 8	2 of 8	8 of 8	2 of 8
Model 3 (SFC)	20 of 21	7 of 21	18 of 21	15 of 21	13 of 21
Model 4 (SC)	12 of 12	n/a	12 of 12	n/a	n/a

* Some cells are marked as "not applicable" because these services are not received by definition

pre-defined group of people meeting at intervals. Hence, there was no emphasis on review, planning, relationships or emotions, and any work in these areas, if required, had to be undertaken by families themselves.

In Model 2, all cases were receiving support with review and planning, with a minority also having emotional/therapeutic support, suggesting that the emotional work of contact is to some extent shared between the agency and the family.

In contrast, Model 3 not only had a worker at meetings but also one-third of cases had relationship building, over 60 per cent had emotional/ therapeutic support and over 70 per cent review and planning. This group clearly was receiving the most intensive level of services, and agencies were heavily involved in helping families manage dynamics and emotions.

Model 4 all had co-ordination and administration and protection and promoting of interest, possibly suggesting a surveillance model of support concerned with co-ordination and supervision, preventing or reacting to problems rather than facilitating positive dynamics.

Which families were having which model of contact support?

This section will explore the relationship between case characteristics and the different models of contact support. For each of the four models of contact we will outline who the contact was with, and the strengths and risks of the adoptive families.

How did the type of birth relatives involved in contact vary by contact support model?

Fitting with what was reported earlier in Chapter 3, there were clear differences in terms of which birth relatives were involved in the contact between the models of contact support that involved supervision (supervised and facilitated, and supervised) and the models that did not involve supervision (Models 1 and 2). As Table 11.4 shows, in the administrated and facilitated contact support models, five of eight cases (63%) in each

Table 11.4

Number of cases by models of contact support (based on the highest level of support) by type of birth relative contact

	Adult contact	*Birth sibling contact*	*Adult and birth sibling contact*	*Total cases*
Model 1: administrated contact	2 (25%)	5 (63%)	1 (13%)	8
Model 2: facilitated contact	2 (25%)	5 (63%)	1 (13%)	8
Model 3: supervised and facilitated contact	17 (63%)	4 (15%)	6 (22%)	27
Model 4: supervised contact	6 (67%)	1 (11%)	2 (22%)	9
No support	1 (33%)	2 (67%)		3
Total	**28**	**17**	**10**	**55**

group involved only birth siblings. In contrast, when contact was super-vised and facilitated, only four of 27 of these cases (15%) were sibling-only contacts, and in the supervised contact model only one of nine cases were sibling only.

The number of contact arrangements involving a main carer who had been involved in the neglect or abuse of the child also varied across the four models, as follows: administrated contact – two out of eight cases; facilitated contact – one out of eight cases; supervised and facilitated contact – 19 out of 27 cases; supervised contact – six out of nine cases. Of the three cases where contact was unsupported, one involved contact with the birth parent who had abused or neglected the child. Clearly, and unsurprisingly, the type of contact support families received was not random; the presence of adult birth relatives, particularly birth parents who had been involved in the abuse or neglect of the child, is a factor that determines whether contact is supervised or not.

The strengths and risks of adoptive families: do these relate to contact support type?

Table 11.5 shows the mean risks/strengths score for adoptive families, the standard deviation, and the lowest and highest scores broken down by the four contact support models. To make the table easier to understand the scores have been adjusted so the lowest score is 1 and the highest 20. Looking at the mean scores, the three families having no support had the highest mean score. This supports data from the interviews, in which these three adoptive parents said they had sufficient resources to manage the contact situation themselves. Looking next at the families who received support, families who had the lowest mean score (11.8) were those having supervised and facilitated contact, and families with the highest mean score (14.6) were those having facilitated contact support. However, the lowest mean score and the highest mean score only differ by less than three points, which on a scale of 1 to 20 is not that substantial. The size of the sample meant it was not possible to examine whether these differences were statistically significant.

Looking now at the highest and lowest scores within each model, it is notable that in the facilitated contact support model, there were no families with a very low score (indicating high risk/low strengths), but in the other three models of support scores ranged from quite low to very high. In this model (facilitated), many families had exchanged identifying details. It may be that this type of exchange only takes place where adoptive parents are communicatively open, and this could explain why there were no very high-risk cases in this model. The type of contact support that most families had – the supervised and facilitated model – included some families with very high scores (indicating low risks/high strengths). However, the adoptive family strengths/risks measure does not indicate the needs of the other parties in contact, or their strengths and risks. Indeed, when the situation of the three families with the highest scores in this model was examined, the reasonably high level of contact support seemed appropriate to the needs of the people involved. In two cases the contact involved the adopted child seeing a number of older siblings who each had different living arrangements and special needs. In another case, the birth mother had mental health problems and learning difficulties and required support in the contact meeting.

Table 11.5

Adoptive family risks and strengths scores across the four contact support models (based on the highest level of contact support the family received)

	Mean risks/strengths	*sd*	*Range*
Model 1: administrated contact	13.4	4.9	4–19
Model 2: facilitated contact	14.6	3.4	10–20
Model 3: supervised and facilitated contact	11.8	5.4	1–20
Model 4: supervised contact	12.7	4.7	3–19
No support	16.7	3	13–20

How did the contact support models relate to whether contact was working well?

At the time of the second interview (or at the first interview for the two families who did not take part at Time 2), contact was working very well in 45.5 per cent of cases (n = 25). Table 11.6 shows the proportion of cases where contact was working very well in each of the contact support models. In Model 1 (administrated contact) and in Model 3 (supervised and facilitated contact) about half of contact arrangements were working very well. However, in Models 2 (facilitated contact) and 4 (supervised contact) only a minority of contact arrangements were working very well. In all three cases where contact was unsupported, contact was working very well, again suggesting that these families did not require any support.

It is difficult to reach any particular conclusions about the data in Table 11.6 because the numbers of cases in three of the four models are quite small. However, the data suggest that each of the four types of contact support may be the right model for some families but not for others. In Chapter 7, the strengths and risks of adoptive families emerged as associated with whether contact works well or not. The impact of contact support on the outcomes of contact for families is something that requires further exploration with a larger sample, and the models of

Table 11.6
The four contact support models, and whether contact was working well or had unresolved issues

	Working very well	*Unresolved issues*
Model 1: administrated contact	4 of 8	4 of 8
Model 2: facilitated contact	2 of 8	2 of 8
Model 3: supervised and facilitated contact	13 of 27	14 of 27
Model 4: supervised contact	3 of 9	6 of 9
No support	3 of 3	

support identified in this exploratory project could be useful in undertaking such research. In the current study, in order to understand if, when and how contact support is valued by adoptive families, and how it might be effective in managing the complexities of contact, it is important to explore the qualitative data. Chapter 12 discusses adoptive parents' views about contact support in much more detail.

Summary

In this chapter, adoptive parents' reports of the contact support services they received have been summarised in terms of the types of support received, and four models of contact support were identified. The profiles of families receiving each of the four different types of contact support were then been looked at. Key points are as follows:

- Five different types of support activity were coded according to the function they appeared to serve:
  - co-ordination and administration;
  - relationship building;
  - protecting or promoting the interests of the adoptive family;
  - reviewing arrangements and planning;
  - providing emotional support/therapeutic input.
- The type of support activity most frequently received by adoptive parents was co-ordination and administration, followed by protecting or promoting of interests. About one-third of adoptive parents received services related to reviewing and planning, about a quarter received emotional support, and only one in five reported relationship-building activities.
- In the majority of cases, adoptive parents reported that a support worker attended their contact meetings. The role that workers took in these meetings seemed variable. In some cases they appeared to play no active part in the meeting – they were just in the background. In other cases they appeared to be trying hard to put people at ease and help the interaction between the parties. Sometimes the worker's role appeared to be to control and correct the birth relative.
- Four models of contact support were generated from the data:

administrated, facilitated, supervised and facilitated, and supervised.

- The first model, administrated contact, was in most cases where the agency retained control of the setting up of contact meetings, but did not attend meetings or facilitate contact further by offering the relevant parties emotional support, relationship building or review and planning.

- The second model, facilitated contact, was again where families met without the support worker – the control of the contact meeting was in the hands of the families themselves. However, in these cases the agency was intervening outside of the contact meeting in terms of emotionally supporting people or planning and reviewing the contact.

- The third model, supervised and facilitated contact, was the model involving the most intensive input of services. Support workers provided high levels of control and support through attending contact meetings and worked proactively at relationship building, reviewing planning, or emotional or therapeutic support.

- The fourth model, supervised contact, was where agencies arranged and supervised the contact, but did not actively facilitate its working; they exercised control, but made little contribution to managing the dynamics of contact.

- About half of the adoptive parents (n = 27) received supervised and facilitated contact support. The remaining parents received, in roughly equal measures, one of the other models of contact support.

- In the two models of support where contact was unsupervised (facilitated contact and administrated contact), most of the contact arrangements were with birth siblings only, and only a small minority involved an adult birth relative who had neglected or abused the child. The opposite situation applied to models of support where contact was supervised (facilitated and supervised, and supervised).

- The group of families having facilitated contact support did not include any particularly high-risk cases. For the other three models of contact support, the strengths/risks scores of adoptive families receiving support varied from low to high. In practice, it is likely that the strengths and risks of birth families also help to determine which model of contact support is used, and this may be why no clear pattern emerges from the adoptive parent data.

- For each of the four models of contact support, there were examples where contact was working very well and others where it had unresolved issues. In practice, different models are likely to suit different families.

12 Support for direct contact arrangements: adoptive parents' perspectives

In this chapter, we discuss adoptive parents' satisfaction with the support services they received. Whether or not they were satisfied is looked at in relation to the four models of contact support identified in Chapter 11. Then, drawing on the interview data we elaborate the key themes that seemed to determine whether or not adoptive parents were satisfied with the support they received. The unmet needs of adoptive parents are also discussed.

Adoptive parents' satisfaction with contact support services

In this section we look at adoptive parents' overall satisfaction with the support services they received, based on what parents said in both of their interviews. Two groups were identified: in the first group were adoptive parents who were "mainly satisfied" with support and in the second were those who expressed "several concerns or anxieties".

Adoptive parents who were mainly satisfied with support

This category included adoptive parents who identified positive aspects of the support they had received. It also included parents who had some reservations about, or suggestions for improvements to, the service but whose positive comments outweighed the negative ones.

Case example: Mainly satisfied

Justin, age 8, had contact with his birth mother three times a year, mediated by the agency and supervised at a contact centre. The agency had also arranged for Justin to have play therapy. On the whole, Justin's adoptive mother was positive about contact support. She felt the worker who attended the meetings got on well with Justin and helped 'keep the flow'. She said the agency had 'always been there for me' and would visit whenever she asked for help. She had some minor concerns about the suitability of the contact venue, feeling the centre was located too close to where members of the birth family lived.

Adoptive parents who expressed several concerns or anxieties about support

This category included adoptive parents who expressed anxieties or discomfort with the ability of either an individual worker and/or the support systems that were available to meet their family's needs and promote their child's best interests.

Case example: Several concerns

Siblings Karl and Kerry (age 12 and 9) had contact with their birth parents twice a year at a contact centre. Their adoptive mother was pleased that the agency worker attended meetings, but felt the worker did not like the birth mother and consequently overreacted to things the birth mother said or did. The adoptive mother felt this could potentially lead to conflict. She also felt the worker misinterpreted the children's feelings. She was unhappy that the agency did not help with the costs of contact, which included a round trip of hundreds of miles.

Over half of the adoptive parents (n = 31, 56%) were coded as being mainly satisfied with the contact support they received, while 44 per cent (n = 24) expressed several concerns or anxieties.

How did satisfaction with contact support vary between the different models of contact support?

Table 12.1 shows the numbers and percentages of adoptive parents who were mainly satisfied with contact support services across the four contact support models. It shows that adoptive parents in the facilitated contact support group were the most satisfied (87%), followed by those who received supervised and facilitated contact support services (70%). In contrast, only a quarter of people receiving administrated or supervised contact support were satisfied with their services.

Table 12.1

Numbers and percentages of adoptive parents mainly satisfied with or expressing several concerns about contact support services across the four contact support models

	Number mainly satisfied	%	Number expressing several concerns	%
Administrated	2	25	6	75
Facilitated	7	87	1	13
Supervised and facilitated	19	70	8	30
Supervised	2	25	7	75

What the facilitated model of support and the supervised and facilitated model have in common is that adoptive parents were receiving some kind of proactive intervention (relationship building, review and planning, or emotional support). The high levels of satisfaction within these two models could be because adoptive parents particularly valued these types of interventions. The following analysis of qualitative data sheds more light on what adoptive parents liked and did not like about their contact support services.

What do adoptive parents value about support services?

Adoptive parents were asked in the interviews to identify what they liked or did not like about the contact support they received. These data were analysed thematically and a number of key themes relating to the quality of contact support are described below.

Importance of the quality of relationship between adoptive parent and worker

One aspect of support that was given great emphasis by a large number of adoptive parents was the quality of the relationship between them and the worker. Adoptive parents valued workers who were approachable, friendly, reliable, supportive and understanding. Some adoptive parents could not speak highly enough of their support worker:

[The service] has been incredibly supportive and useful ... [the worker] is amazing. I feel completely comfortable to say anything I need to say to her about any of it ... she's incredibly supportive of me and [the adopted child] ... I feel very empowered by her ... she's very approachable, very professional, fantastic communication. She is warm and friendly but without being friends, you don't feel ... you know she is there to do a job and she does it incredibly well. There is mutual respect and trust.

Where the relationship was good, adoptive parents expressed greater levels of satisfaction with support and greater confidence in the worker's abilities. Adoptive parents also felt it was important that the adopter and worker were on the same wavelength and that a lack of compatibility or agreement could lead to conflict or tension in the contact meeting that could negatively affect the contact. One adoptive parent whose first language was Hindi had not had access to a Hindi-speaking support worker. She felt this had affected the extent to which she could form a relationship with a worker, particularly in terms of her ability to communicate effectively her needs and feelings. As she explained:

I have to struggle for words in my mind. Even now I have to think what I'm going to say next. To emotionally think you need your own language to make other people understand what you have inside you.

Those adoptive parents who felt their relationship with the worker was poor described a very impersonal service. Parents complained that the worker had knowledge of the file or case but not the individuals involved in contact or that too much communication was by letter rather than face to face. One described the service as 'a bit third party somehow'.

Many adoptive parents felt that without continuity it was difficult to build a close and trusted relationship with the worker. An absence of a named worker also caused problems for some adoptive parents. One person explained:

You have to steel yourself and you have to be quite strong because you know that you are going to be put through to so many different departments and wait for them to call back.

225

Many adoptive parents had experienced high turnovers of support staff and found this negatively affected the quality of the support service offered. This was often the case for siblings in foster care where there could be frequent changes of these older siblings' social workers. Some people's experience had been that they had to repeatedly contact newly allocated workers to ensure that support was provided and in one case the changeover resulted in a contact meeting not being organised. Uncertainty was a feature of some people's experiences of support, uncertainty about who would provide support, who would supervise contact, when a worker would be in touch and the quality of the service that would be provided.

This was not everyone's experience, however. Some adoptive parents were incredibly positive about how reliable and available their support worker had been. As one mother put it:

If she says she's going to phone, she does. If you email she replies. If she says she is going to do something you know it will happen and that's reassuring . . . If I phoned up and said I needed something to be different then it would be looked at.

Some adoptive parents praised services that ensured there was a well-organised handover from one worker to another. This was seen as particularly important for the child. Adoptive parents felt that workers needed to get to know children and adults before undertaking any direct work with them such as supervising contact. This did not always occur. Some people expressed an appreciation when workers ended relationships with children appropriately, marking the ending with a small gesture such as a card.

As well as a lack of continuity, there were other aspects of the service that had a negative impact on the adoptive parent's relationship with the worker. Some people's experience was that workers were so busy that phone calls were often interrupted or workers had to end a call quickly to deal with a more urgent matter. In the opinion of some interviewees, this "fire-fighting" approach to support did not allow a close and trusting relationship to build. Adoptive parents valued support that allowed them to talk without feeling they were taking up too much of the worker's time. They valued workers who listened and treated them as an individual.

Importance of the knowledge, skills and approach of the worker

Another aspect of support to which adoptive parents frequently referred was the knowledge, skills and competence of the worker as well as their approach. Adoptive parents valued workers whose actions demonstrated that they were experienced and professional. One adoptive mother said:

> We did happen to have a very good social worker . . . one of the senior ones who had been there donkey's years . . . the one with the most experience and it helped us immensely. She was very good and I would recommend [the support service] to anyone.

It was important for parents to have confidence that the worker had a degree of expertise in relation to adoption and contact in order to provide insight into, for example, the child's perspective. Parents highlighted as important the ability to deal with conflict, interpersonal skills and the ability to understand the particular needs of birth relatives, such as mental health issues.

Some people referred to the importance of a personalised service. They wanted services to be well informed about their individual situation and to have an intimate knowledge of the people involved in contact. One adoptive parent described her worries about the new social worker allocated to her child's older sibling saying:

> [The new social worker] doesn't know about their background at all . . . she'll probably do her best but it's very difficult without having the background knowledge to be so effective as the other [social workers] who were involved from the start.

A deep and genuine interest in the family and a caring attitude were also seen as important aspects of a good service. Adoptive parents did not assume, however, that this necessarily meant regular face-to-face contact with a worker. For example, one family's contact meeting was arranged through the letterbox service. The adoptive mother typically spoke to the workers annually when they liaised with a birth relative to set up a meeting. However, this adoptive mother believed she got a very personal service. Her view was shaped by the interest shown by the workers in her adopted daughter when she rang the service. She said that often the worker would comment on the photographs of the child sent through the letterbox service saying, 'Doesn't she look so grown up?' It appears that relatively small gestures such as this, when genuinely expressed, can have a positive impact on the adoptive parents' satisfaction.

Authority and control: getting the balance right

The most common theme in adoptive parents' accounts of their satisfaction or dissatisfaction with support services related to issues of authority and control, that is, the extent to which workers or adopters were or were not in charge of contact arrangements. The "right" point on this continuum differed from person to person; some people emphasised how much they valued workers taking control, while others preferred to take charge themselves.

Several adoptive parents valued the role that workers could play in taking control of boundaries or agreements set around contact, stepping in when these are breached and being an authoritative voice. For example, one parent involved in a large sibling group contact described the social worker supporting the meetings as 'absolutely excellent', saying:

> She is very good with [the siblings] . . . Because sometimes it can be a bit iffy if there's not a social worker around and some of the older ones try to do things that they're not supposed to be doing. So you're in a difficult position sometimes if you're not their carer . . . It's nice when someone else is there to sort of step in . . . it makes it more relaxing, comfortable having them there.

Another adoptive mother said she wanted contact to be supervised by a worker because 'We wanted it very much to be taken out of our hands . . . it's security. It's taking the pressure off us.'

This was seen as particularly important where there was some level of conflict in the relationship between adoptive parents and birth relatives, but was also judged to be important by some adoptive parents who felt contact was working well and their relationship with birth relatives was good. Some felt that having clear and structured boundaries in place early in the process enabled a trusting relationship to develop, so that later on boundaries could be relaxed. In some cases adoptive parents felt it was helpful that decisions were seen to come from the worker rather than from themselves. In two cases where contact had stopped, adoptive parents wanted the worker to convey this decision to the child as they were worried the child would otherwise blame them for the cessation of contact.

Some people felt that workers had not got this aspect of the service right and described the worker as either too controlling or too passive. One adoptive parent felt that the supporting agency was quite disengaged from the contact and did not want to take any control. He described how the support worker used to drive the adopted child's siblings to the meeting but then would go off and read a book while the contact happened: 'I think she was of the attitude that "I'll drive them there but don't expect anything else".' This left the adoptive parents having to manage a difficult situation where the older birth siblings showed their seven-year-old adopted child photographs of the birth family on their mobile phones. Overall, this parent doubted the commitment of the agency to this contact, saying:

> I felt in some of those visits that if the social worker at that time could have got it down to half an hour then she would have been really quite happy to. I think she didn't want to be there at all . . . We don't want that much – it's just that . . . if we are expected to commit to this, the least the council can do is commit the same.

In some cases, the reasons why adoptive parents wanted to be in control of contact were largely practical. For example, in a case involving contact with older siblings in foster care, the adoptive parents had decided to organise the contact directly with the older sibling's foster carer. As she explained:

> We just found it was so much to-ing and fro-ing; the social worker would phone up and ask us when we could make it, then she had to phone someone else, then phone us back to say that they can't do that exact time – so in the end we decided it would be easier to work it out ourselves.

Although this adoptive parent was happy to take a lot of control of the contact she was pleased that the agency remained involved and appreciated the occasional phone call from them, saying 'there's always that fallback if you need it'.

Where the control and authority of the worker were important, adoptive parents valued the formality that agency involvement brought to the contact arrangement. Family centres, written rules and agreements and social work presence at contact meetings were generally seen as helpful when formality was desirable. Some adoptive parents saw these as positive ways to formalise not only the contact but also the relationship. One adoptive parent explained that it was easier to decline a birth relative's request for increased contact when it was made through a third party, i.e. the worker, rather than directly from the birth relative.

Some adoptive parents were anxious that changes in worker might lead to inappropriate changes in control. Where adoptive parents were concerned about the risks of contact, they were anxious that any new worker brought in to supervise contact fully understood the potential risks. Some families had had poor experiences of new workers being unaware of risks within contact and not taking action to avoid these. For example, personal information might be exchanged between a child and birth relative without the knowledge of the worker due to a lack of awareness of the danger of this happening and a lack of action to avoid the opportunity for such an exchange to take place.

For some adoptive parents it was important for them to feel they were in the driving seat; not everyone wanted the support worker to be "in charge". One adoptive mother expressed her satisfaction with the worker who was 'not too supervisory' but instead took the lead from her about the style of contact and level of supervision. Some adoptive parents challenged the view that workers are the experts and, instead, suggested that families have expertise based on their intimate knowledge of the child. One person said:

> *I have come to the conclusion that social workers know their job and I will take their professional advice, but actually on a day-to-day basis I know my child and I know what works for her and at the end of the day I know what impacts on me, so I am not shy in saying that what*

they have suggested isn't going to work. It might work in other circumstances, but it is not going to work here.

Some adoptive parents sought an approach to support that provided them with the information needed to see the perspectives and understand the motivations of all parties, but ultimately allowed them to make their own decisions about contact.

This dimension of authority and control was quite different for the four foster carers interviewed. Foster carers, even those designated as permanent carers for the child, do not have parental responsibility for the child, which remains in the hands of the local authority and birth parents. The ability of the foster carers, therefore, to exercise control of contact was quite limited compared to adoptive parents. One foster carer, whose foster child was having contact with adopted siblings, wanted to accept an invitation from the adoptive parents to have contact at their house. However, she was told by the local authority that she must not do this; the adoptive parents were free to invite her, but she was not free to accept. Another foster carer of an older sibling felt that the adoptive parents involved in the sibling contact were allowed much more say in the contact arrangements than she was; for example, the adoptive parents would set the time and date and she would be expected to fit in.

Addressing multiple needs and competing interests

Some people described effective contact support as support that balanced the needs and interests of children, birth relatives and adoptive parents. In some cases, adoptive parents emphasised that what was helpful to both them and their child was that the birth relative's needs were recognised and met by the support agency. This was seen as particularly important by adoptive parents when birth relatives had high support needs, perhaps because of a mental health problem or a learning disability. One adoptive mother said that she saw the contact worker as being mainly 'there for the birth mum', adding that this was 'really important' and without this support the birth mother 'probably wouldn't end up getting [to contact]'. In this case, the adoptive mother was very positive about the support the worker had provided to the birth relative. In other cases, adoptive parents were concerned that birth relatives were not sufficiently supported or their interests were overlooked, and that this affected the workings of the contact arrangements. One adoptive mother recognised the birth mother's vulnerability and her unpredictability, and therefore the need for her to be both supported and controlled during contact. Her expectation of support was that:

> *The support person would be looking after [birth mother] and meeting her needs . . . to look after her and make sure the contact was within the guidelines . . . that is, things like [birth mother] doesn't step out of line, doesn't start asking the children questions that aren't appropriate, that sort of thing. The role of the social worker is to look after [birth mother] and make sure she's behaving as she should do.*

She felt, however, that the supervisor's approach to the birth mother was too heavy handed, and she worried this was not only detrimental to the birth mother but also unhelpful for the children:

> *She doesn't handle [birth mother] as well she should . . . it needs to be more gentle . . . I think the person doing it needs to be very well trained, because it's such a key thing for the children . . . I think the personality of the person doing it may not be helping . . . I think she's too hard and organising . . . [birth mum] is being ordered about a little too much, as if she was a child.*

Conversely, in a small number of cases adoptive parents felt the support agency focused too much on the birth parent's needs and not enough on the child's. One adoptive mother said: 'I do feel that [birth mum] has too much say in the contact . . . I feel that sometimes social workers in the past have namby-pambied her.' She felt that the birth mother was able to have this influence because 'if she doesn't get her way somebody suffers'.

Adoptive parents valued information being passed on to them about birth relatives' well-being, circumstances or views on contact – and some specifically said they would like this to happen more. Adoptive parents also appreciated efforts made by workers to ease the discomfort of adults during contact and to get conversations started.

In most cases, it was the same worker who supported the adopter and the birth relatives with contact. Therefore, a worker's ability to offer support in an equitable fashion was important. Some adoptive parents questioned the ability of one worker to achieve such equity but several praised the skills of the worker in achieving a balance between often competing interests. Where there was more than one worker or agency involved, adoptive parents appreciated their efforts to communicate closely and co-ordinate efforts. Where this was not achieved it led to great frustration on the part of adoptive parents. The effective co-ordination of arrangements involving a number of different parties was often an issue, particularly in relation to sibling group contacts.

Support workers' attitudes to contact were mentioned by some adoptive parents. People often found it encouraging when workers promoted contact as a good thing. One adoptive parent put it like this:

I think we are where we are at because of [our social worker]. I think [she] took us on a journey about contact, you know from a place where we weren't really comfortable with contact to a place where we are more than comfortable with it.

In a small number of cases the confidence of adoptive parents about the value of contact appeared to be undermined by professionals. One adoptive mother, who was generally positive about contact, had some concerns about an early meeting. When she tried to discuss these with the social worker, his response was '. . . well, I didn't think he should have contact anyway'. In the adoptive mother's view, the social worker was 'always anti-contact. I think he is anti-contact in all circumstances, anti-direct contact.'

The need for a planned approach to contact

A further aspect of quality to which adoptive parents referred was the presence (or absence) of a review and planning system. As we reported in Chapter 11, only a minority of adoptive parents had their contact formally or informally reviewed and planned. Not everyone felt the need for a formal review system but several people did express concern about the reactive approach taken by agencies and a lack of proactive review and planning. They were frustrated with a lack of effort to anticipate changing needs and circumstances. One adoptive mother whose child had been placed 12 years previously felt that her daughter's needs and wishes had changed over the years but the contact plan had not altered:

> *Those arrangements appear to be set in stone or are quite hard to modify or adjust and certainly for us there was never any forum to sit down and review those arrangements ... to me the most important thing is building in some form of review and not leaving it to chance but building in a way of reviewing it, representing all the parties.*

Several adoptive parents wanted more feedback about the birth relative's experience of contact and some did not know whether birth relatives received support. One parent said:

> *My biggest thing is the fact that after the contact [birth relatives] go off and we never hear anything more ... sometimes I think it would be really nice if whoever it was that did the contact just followed through with a phone call to say 'I think it went really well' or '[birth mum] was really positive ...'. But you know there's none of that. It's just like that is it for the year – see you – bye.*

Where reviews did take place they were often instigated by the adoptive parent or, when instigated by the worker, were viewed by adoptive parents as brief and cursory. Two adoptive parents reported that ad hoc review meetings had been arranged at short notice and they were unable to attend. One adoptive mother reported that, without first consulting her, a worker had suggested to her adopted child that the frequency of contact be increased.

Unmet needs

It was clear that both the type and amount of contact support that adoptive parents desired varied from case to case. Some people received a lot of services and yet still felt they had unmet needs. Other people received very little or even no services and were satisfied with this arrangement, often because they felt it was less complicated than having an agency involved and gave them a greater sense of control. Some families with minimal support expressed a wish to be 'left alone to be a family' and others feared that more involvement would feel intrusive or interfering. There were a number of adoptive families across the range of service provision who felt there were contact support services they required that were not being provided. Many of these have already been discussed in the preceding section. The following is a list of other services that some adoptive parents wished had been available to them:

- recognition of the role change from foster carer to adoptive parent and training or advice to deal with this;
- feedback from an independent observer about how contact is progressing;
- more advice about likely changes to contact when the child reaches age 18;
- funding for therapy related to behavioural or attachment issues;
- awareness and consideration of the needs of disabled adopted children;
- advice and guidance about suitable venues for contact;
- training beyond adoption preparation to allow for the shift from the theory to the practice of contact;
- opportunities to talk one to one with another adoptive parent who has experience of direct contact;
- opportunities to discuss direct contact in a peer group situation.

Summary

This chapter has looked at adoptive parents' overall levels of satisfaction with contact support services, and has explored themes related to the determinants of satisfaction. Key findings are as follows:

- Over half of the adoptive parents (56%) were mainly satisfied with the contact support they received, while 44 per cent expressed several concerns or anxieties.
- Satisfaction with contact support varied according to the model of support adoptive parents received. Adoptive parents who received the facilitated model of support or the supervised and facilitated model

were the most satisfied (87% and 70% respectively). In contrast, only a quarter of parents who received administrated contact support or supervised contact support were satisfied.

- Aspects of contact support that were valued by adoptive parents were as follows:
  - a good relationship between the adoptive parent and the support worker;
  - workers demonstrating knowledge, skills and a personalised approach to support;
  - a balancing of authority and control shared between adoptive parents and the support agency;
  - addressing the needs of children, birth relatives and adoptive parents;
  - a forward-thinking and planned approach to contact and to contact support.
- The amount and type of contact support that adoptive parents desired varied from case to case. Some specific unmet needs were identified in the chapter.

13 Support for direct contact arrangements: services received by birth relatives

This chapter outlines the experiences of the 39 birth relatives of services received to support direct contact with their adopted child. The number of relatives receiving each of the six types of contact support is documented and further detail of the types of activity under each broad category is given. The five types of contact support provided to adoptive parents were also identified in the birth relative sample along with one further type of intervention. Birth relatives' experiences of having contact supervised by a worker was a significant theme in the interviews, and this is discussed. Using their self-reports, relatives were coded according to the model of contact support they received (the same categories used for adoptive parents). In this chapter, the four models of contact support are then compared in terms of which type of birth relative received which model of contact support. Models are also compared in terms of birth relatives' satisfaction with contact.

Type of support services provided to birth relatives

Birth relatives, like adoptive families, were receiving various types of contact support from statutory services or voluntary agencies working on behalf of statutory agencies. Our starting point for identifying different types of support service was to consider whether the categories developed on the adoptive parent sample could also be applied to birth relatives. We found that each of the five categories could be used with slight amendments to fit the birth relative data; in addition, we identified a sixth type of intervention experienced by birth relatives, that is, risk management or minimisation.

1. **Co-ordination and administration**: This type of support was concerned with the practical arrangements associated with contact.
2. **Relationship building**: This category involved interventions aimed at

ensuring that relationships between the child and birth relatives, or adoptive parents and birth relatives, developed positively and were supportive of contact.

3. **Protecting or promoting the interests of birth relatives**: This category of service was concerned with direct support provided to birth relatives to protect or promote their specific interests, opinions or needs in relation to contact with the child where these come into conflict with the needs of the adoptive family.

4. **Reviewing arrangements and planning**: This involved assessing individual needs and responding to changes to ensure that contact was of maximum benefit. This category was reserved for agency activities aimed at proactive reviewing and planning rather than simply responding to problems raised by the birth relative.

5. **Providing emotional support/therapeutic input**: This was concerned with the psychological aspects of contact. Emotional support could be provided to birth relatives as a one-off or ongoing intervention. The provision of specialist interventions such as counselling or psychotherapy to resolve distress related to adoption generally was also included in the category.

6. **Risk management or minimisation**: This was concerned with interventions to control or minimise risks that the birth relative might pose to the child or adoptive parents. It included a worker describing the rules or boundaries of contact, and activities aimed at monitoring or enforcing these boundaries.

How many birth relatives were receiving the six types of contact support service?

Table 13.1 shows how many birth relatives were receiving each of the six types of contact support at Time 1 and Time 2. The service most commonly received was co-ordination and administration, with 90 per cent of birth relatives receiving this at Time 1 and 80 per cent at Time 2. Only a minority of relatives received each of the other five types of support service. It is notable that whereas the majority of adoptive parents (between 62 to 66%) received support services that had the function of protecting and promoting their interests, for birth relatives this type of service was the least likely of the six types to be received, with only 11–17 per cent of birth relatives reporting this type of service. Relatives were much more likely to report receiving interventions that appeared to protect and promote the interests of the adoptive parents or the child – the category of risk management or minimisation. About one-third of birth relatives received this "service", although perhaps that is not the right word to use, as generally birth relatives did not experience this activity as serving their needs. Roughly one-quarter of relatives reported relationship building or review and planning services. Looking at emotional/therapeutic support, 40 per cent felt they had this type of service at Time 1, but only 23 per cent at Time 2.

Three of the 38 birth relatives at Time 1 received no formal support service. In these three cases, contact was arranged directly between the birth relatives and adoptive parents. In two of the three cases, the contact had been initially arranged and supervised by the agency, but over time

Table 13.1
Frequency of provision of various types of support to birth relatives

	n at Time 1	*% at* Time 1 *(of 38)**	*n at* Time 2	*% at* Time 2 *(of 35)***
Co-ordination and administration	34	90	28	80
Relationship building	8	21	8	23
Protecting or promoting interests	4	11	6	17
Reviewing arrangements and planning	11	29	9	26
Providing emotional support/therapeutic input	15	40	8	23
Risk management or minimisation	12	32	12	34

* In one case the child was recently placed and contact had not yet started.
** Four birth relatives did not take part at Time 2.

the families began managing the arrangement themselves. In both of these two cases the birth relative was happy to have no services. In the third case, the relative (the grandparent) was unhappy with a number of aspects of contact and would have valued some review or renegotiation of the arrangement. At the time of the second interview, this person was still not receiving any contact support services. In the other two cases, one person was not able to take part in the second interview. The other person was receiving a minimal level of service at Time 2 because the agency had become involved in arranging the dates for contact.

At Time 2, six birth relatives were not receiving any contact support services – this included the person mentioned above who continued to have unmet needs. In two of the other five cases, contact support appeared to have stopped because it was no longer needed, and birth relatives were content with receiving no support. In one case the child had reached the age of 17 and was having direct unmediated contact with the birth relative. In two of the six cases, contact had stopped; in each of these cases the birth relative had received no further communication or support from the agency. Finally, there was one case where contact had moved from being organised by the agency to being organised by the adoptive parents and birth mother. Although the birth mother was very happy for the agency to relinquish their organisational and supervisory role, she did feel she had unmet needs in relation to emotional support.

Some birth relatives had general ongoing support needs that were not specific to adoption or contact, which were met by care workers or the community mental health team. These workers tended to provide some support in relation to adoption contact in addition to that provided by adoption support services. This applied to a birth mother with a learning disability, a birth mother with a severe mental health problem, a sibling who was looked after by the local authority and a sibling who had learning difficulties. Where such support was available, the relative appeared to get a more comprehensive range of support types, including emotional support, and less common support types, such as the promotion of their interests. This range of supports was very welcomed by these relatives who saw the workers as 'there for them'. If birth relatives received support for contact from these other sources, it was included in the coding reported above only if it was clearly provided on behalf of the adoption agency or adoption support agency, for instance, where support was provided by a worker from the "leaving care" team in the same local authority.

Birth relatives' descriptions of the support services received from agencies

Birth relatives' descriptions of co-ordination and administration services

As stated above, the most frequent support service reported by birth relatives was the co-ordination and administration of contact arrangements. However, the range of support offered was fairly narrow. The most frequent service activity mentioned by birth relatives was the setting up of contact meetings. All 33 birth relatives receiving co-ordination and administration services at Time 1 reported that the agency was involved in arranging the meeting. Occasionally this was arranged by the worker during a visit to the relative's home but more typically it was done by phone or letter. Where arrangements were made by letter there was very little scope for the birth relative to have an input into decision-making around contact. In almost a third of the 33 cases, relatives were informed of the date and venue rather than consulted about it. The amount of notice given varied, but in some cases was as short as two weeks. In two cases, birth relatives were informed of the time and venue of contact indirectly through other relatives.

The other main practical support offered to about one-quarter of birth relatives was the provision of a lift to and/or from a contact meeting. This was usually provided by a social worker, though in one case a volunteer driver was used.

Very few birth relatives appeared to be receiving any financial help with contact. For some there were no costs, or minimal costs, involved in a contact meeting. In two cases this was because the meeting took place at the relative's home. In a small number of cases the meeting was held at a local public venue and travel and entrance fees were minimal. For some birth relatives contact involved no costs, as it took place at a family centre and the relative was taken to and from contact and not allowed to bring presents. For most relatives, however, contact did involve some financial outlay and this could include travel costs, entrance fees or activity costs, the cost of eating out and the cost of gifts for children and, in some cases, adoptive parents. These expenses ranged from about £10 to £60–£70. For some birth relatives, therefore, the costs could be quite significant. One birth mother was spending approximately £150 on gifts for her birth children, though this was exceptional. Several contacts made use of free venues to try to keep down costs.

Only three birth relatives mentioned getting help with travel expenses to and from contact. Another two mentioned that the costs of an activity or refreshments had been reimbursed. For some who were on low incomes, the lack of financial support was problematic and provided a barrier to contact. One birth family said they found it difficult to participate fully in contact due to financial constraints. At a previous contact, the families had gone to a McDonalds restaurant but because it was before pay day the birth family could not afford to eat. They pretended they weren't hungry and sat and watched the children and adoptive parents eat. A birth sibling also reported that she had to put off contact for a month because she could not afford it. Another had to pay for herself and her care worker to take part in activities when attending contact and was struggling to meet this double cost. Where it was allowed, birth relatives were very keen to give a gift to their birth children, but for people on a low income this was sometimes very difficult. One birth mother talked about 'scraping money together' to give the children a gift.

In three cases adoptive parents and in three cases the mothers of birth parents were subsidising contact costs for the birth relative in modest ways, such as bringing refreshments to a meeting or paying for a meal or an entrance fee. In one case, the adoptive parent offered to meet the costs of a birth sibling who was unable to attend contact because of financial difficulties but social services would not allow it, and the agency did not provide financial help in this case. One birth sibling reported that she had to arrange contact at times when her neighbour could take a day off work and babysit for her child, as she received no financial support with child care.

In the small number of situations where financial help was available, it was not always taken up by birth relatives. One birth mother explained that her relationship with social services was so poor that she would never consider taking financial help from them. She said, 'I wouldn't ask them for nothing. I would walk to that venue if I had to. No, I don't want anything from them.'

Birth relatives' experiences of relationship-building services

While birth relatives acknowledged the great importance of the relationship between them and the child, and between them and the adoptive parents, very few reported receiving any support with relationship building.

In the few cases where some sort of relationship-building intervention was initiated by the worker, it was almost always directed at building or strengthening the relationship between the birth relative and the child. It included the worker offering guidance before the meeting about how to play and interact with the child, advising the birth relative how to sensitively answer a child's questions about their previous experiences and adoption or advising a birth relative about appropriate toys or gifts for the child. This support was often, therefore, about building the skills and confidence of relatives when interacting with the children. One birth mother felt that formal meetings at a contact centre helped her to develop a repertoire of shared activities with the child and this then prepared her for doing shared activities outside of the centre. There were two examples of workers offering to take photographs during contact specifically to avoid the birth relative's attention being taken up with this at the expense of interaction with the child.

There were just two examples offered of agency interventions that were intended to build a relationship between the adults involved in contact. One birth mother spoke about the active efforts of the supervising social worker to encourage interaction and dialogue between her and the adoptive parents. In another case an annual meeting between the adoptive parents and birth relatives was facilitated by the agency in order to agree dates for contact, provide feedback to the birth relatives about the children's progress in their new family, discuss issues that had arisen during contact meetings and negotiate ways to address these. The relatives believed these meetings had been instrumental in the development of a trusting and positive relationship between them and the adoptive family.

Birth relatives' experiences of services aimed at protecting or promoting interests

This category of support was reported by only four birth relatives at Time 1 and six at Time 2. One of the roles played by the agency could broadly be described as negotiating with adoptive parents on behalf of the birth relative. One birth grandmother reported that the contact between her, her birth grandchild and the adoptive parents had been very fraught. The adopters had on several occasions changed the date of contact at short notice and had cancelled some meetings. The grandmother saw the adoption support service's role as ensuring that the contact order granted by the court was adhered to. She felt that the social worker had been firm with the adoptive parents to ensure this was achieved. In another case, the support worker had talked to the adoptive parents about the birth relative's wishes to exchange telephone numbers and have more frequent contact. In a case where adoptive parents had not been happy with a birth sibling taking photos during contact, the support worker had reached an agreement with the adoptive parents that she could take photographs on behalf of the sibling. In other cases in this category, the intervention was only with the birth relatives. For example, a birth father whose birth son was approaching age 18 said he had got in touch with the adoption support service to seek advice about his rights in relation to contact when his son became an adult. In another case, a support worker kept the birth relative regularly updated about the child's progress between the widely spaced out contact meetings. An adult sibling who had decided to suspend his contact with his adoptive brothers and sisters had been helped by the support worker to think through the implications of this for all involved. Finally, a birth grandmother reported that her adoption support worker was very good at helping her reflect on the dynamics of contact and emphasising the importance of her role in her grandchildren's lives. She felt this gave her the confidence to take a less passive role in contact.

Birth relatives' experiences of services for reviewing arrangements and planning

Less than one in three birth relatives reported that the supporting agency had undertaken any proactive reviewing or planning activities. Of the relatives coded as receiving this type of support, in almost all cases the review or planning of contact was undertaken rather informally. Relatives most frequently referred to informal chats with social workers about how contact was going, which took place either on the telephone between contact meetings, immediately before or after contact, and sometimes on the journey to and from contact. A small number of relatives reported that they received a home visit to discuss contact.

Even where some sort of review activity was taking place, the effectiveness of this was variable. Reviewing contact did not necessarily lead to planning or implementing changes and some birth relatives who described review activities also told of a number of unacknowledged and unmet needs. Some relatives, however, gave examples of adjustments that had been made to contact arrangements, such as a change of venue or some evidence of anticipation of children's needs and advice being given to birth relatives to enable them to meet these needs. One birth mother reported that the social worker had visited her at home to help her plan how she would answer her children's questions that might arise during contact. One particularly successful model of review was described by a birth grandmother who has an annual meeting with the adoptive parents, facilitated by an agency worker, to review how things are progressing, raise issues and negotiate solutions. This is then followed up by regular phone calls to the grandmother throughout the year to make any necessary adjustments. However, this was the only example of a systematic, regular cross-party review process.

It was also some birth relatives' experience that one social worker would specifically ask for their views and opinions about how contact was progressing while others within the same agency would not. This suggests there is not a systematic approach to the review of contact support and the service relies instead on individual workers using their initiative. There were also examples of changes to contact happening as much by accident as through planning. For example, an older sibling was having supervised contact with her younger sister. When the social worker was on leave the adoptive parents agreed to go ahead with contact without supervision and this then became the established pattern.

Birth relatives' experiences of emotional support and therapeutic interventions

As stated earlier, 16 (42%) birth relatives who were having contact at Time 1 reported receiving some level of emotional support from the support agency. The way this was delivered and the degree to which these relatives felt emotionally supported varied greatly. The support was often provided solely on the day of contact, either immediately before or after a meeting. For example, social workers would use the time spent transporting birth relatives to and from a contact meeting to chat and provide emotional support. Some workers arranged to meet the birth relative privately before or after contact to check out how they were feeling about the meeting. One birth mother said that the social worker always walked her to the bus stop after contact to chat about how she felt things had gone. A small number of birth relatives reported receiving emotional support from a worker between contact meetings, with either a visit or a phone call. In one case the support was very well structured. This contact was not supervised but the birth relative had an annual face-to-face meeting with the agency and was phoned three times a year for review and support purposes. The relative found this very valuable. Only one birth relative said she was currently receiving formal counselling services; two reported receiving counselling or psychotherapy in the past.

Regardless of the way that support was delivered, some birth relatives said they felt very well supported emotionally by the worker, while others did not. Where birth relatives did feel supported, they had a very good relationship with their worker, they felt the worker cared about them as an individual, was concerned to meet their needs and was a 'shoulder to cry on' or 'took the time to listen'. They also felt that the support provided had helped them to cope with their situation. Some relatives, however, did not feel adequately supported. In some cases the historical relationship between social services and relatives within an adversarial legal system had an impact on the relative's willingness to take up an offer of emotional support or counselling.

Interventions aimed at minimising the perceived risks of direct contact

Some birth relatives referred to interventions that were directed towards them but were provided to meet a perceived need of another party. These interventions were intended to anticipate, assess and tackle perceived risks presented by contact to the child's well-being or the relationship between the child and the adoptive family. We categorised these as risk management or minimisation, and about one-third of birth relatives reported this type of intervention. The risk could be perceived by the worker, the adoptive parents or both. This category included interventions such as birth relatives being given instructions about what they were or were not allowed to say or do during contact. Topics of conversation that were considered unsuitable included the children's schooling or hobbies, birth parents or members of the extended birth family. In some cases these topics were not allowed in order to avoid identifying information being revealed to birth relatives. In other cases they were seen as potentially distressing for children. However, in some cases the rationale for avoiding certain topics was not very clear to the relative. It was also unclear to what extent children had been involved in decisions about what were and were not appropriate topics of discussion and what support and guidance they had been given in order to avoid such topics. This lack of clarity appeared to be a source of some stress for birth relatives.

This category also included active monitoring of conversations between children and birth relatives, and clarifying or reinforcing rules and boundaries during contact meetings or outside of the meetings. In order to be included in this category, intervention had to be more than passive supervision or the mere presence of a worker at contact. While adoptive parents had described such interventions in terms of conflict resolution, birth relatives' descriptions were of an intrusive and controlling style of "support".

Birth relatives' experiences of contact meetings "supervised" by a worker

Over 60 per cent of contact meetings were attended by a worker (see Chapter 5). This section reports on birth relatives' experiences of having a worker at contact.

As we reported from the perspective of adoptive parents in Chapter 11, support workers attending contact meetings could take on a number of different roles. While all the different roles of workers generated from adoptive parent reports were also visible in the accounts of birth relatives, it is fair to say that the "inspection and correction" role dominated birth relatives' narratives.

Where supervision was provided, relatives who had a positive experience of contact often commented on the low-key nature of the supervision and described supervisors as 'fading into the background'. These workers were conspicuous in their absence in the accounts of birth relatives' "benign presence". One birth mother contrasted the supervision she received before and after the adoption, greatly preferring the style of supervision provided after the adoption, where the workers were, 'not watching for things to go wrong'. Some relatives definitely found the presence of a worker at contact a positive thing. As one birth mother said, 'I would never not have her in contact with me.'

In many cases where contact was problematic, however, the supervisor loomed large. Supervision as described by birth relatives usually involved a worker being present during contact, often in the background, observing and listening in on conversations between the child and birth relative and stepping in to interject when necessary. Often contact was governed by a series of rules that emerged as time went on. These rules were sometimes very restrictive and were felt by birth relatives to negatively affect the quality of the contact or the relationship with their child. The rules included: no taking of photographs, no hugging children, no talking about the children's school, no refreshments to be taken into the room where contact takes place, no personal objects to be taken into contact and shared with children, no discussion about the child's birth mother or other relatives.

Some birth relatives struggled to understand the justification for such restrictions, some of which were felt to be unreasonable. Relatives were particularly confused by the prescription that they must not discuss other members of the birth family during contact. This was perceived as nonsensical, when children had had established relationships with these relatives in the past; it was even perceived by some as "underhand" or dishonest in some way.

Rules relating to gifts and cards were also confusing to birth relatives. They were often told they must limit the number of gifts or the amount of money given to children; in some cases gifts and cards were not allowed. Some supervisors appeared to view gifts as detrimental to the relationship between the child and birth relative. One social worker advised a birth mother to reduce the number of gifts so that she was not viewed by the children as merely 'the present lady'. Birth relatives, however, viewed gifts as a tangible expression of love and care and as integral to the maintenance of their relationship with the child. They, therefore, viewed the restrictions placed on gift-giving as a restriction on their ability to maintain a loving relationship.

Unsurprisingly, birth relatives often described a feeling of discomfort with supervision. They took issue not only with the rules they were expected to follow but also with the manner in which these rules were communicated to them. Many had experienced workers breaking into conversations between birth relatives and children and declaring certain topics or questions out of bounds. Others had experienced rules being laid down to them by social workers at the beginning of a contact meeting in front of their birth children. Some relatives, therefore, experienced supervision as a form of control and somewhat undermining. In some cases this was experienced so negatively by relatives that contact was compared to prison visits. One birth grandmother reported:

> . . . it's like prison visiting virtually, and that is so painful . . . I find it very upsetting really because, although you're longing to see them and it all goes as well as it can, it's still like a prison visit . . . you're not allowed to do that, you can't do this, you can't do that, and it is, it's very, very upsetting.

One birth mother expressed her distress when she left the room to go to the toilet and a supervisor told her in a stern way, in front of her birth children, that she must not have a cigarette. The mother had not disclosed to her children that she smoked, as she did not want to be a negative role model for them.

For some birth relatives contact felt like a very public affair and this sat uneasily with their wish to achieve a level of intimacy with the child. Relatives felt observed by adoptive parents, supervisors and even other adult birth relatives who were present. One birth mother had three supervisors present at contact with her children who were 'all stood around'. She described her feelings in the following way: 'I found it one hundred per cent intimidating'. One birth mother described supervision as inducing in her a feeling of being 'monkeys in a cage, on display for you to sit and analyse'.

Contact supervision appeared to produce self-consciousness in birth relatives, which added to a feeling of inhibition and led to the stifling of interactions and relationships with children and sometimes the silencing of those present. One relative explained that she had decided not to hug or kiss the adopted child at the end of contact because she felt such awkwardness during contact and feared she would become upset, and that would upset the child. Where rules about what was permitted and what was not permitted were vague, this appeared to result, in some cases, in a virtual shutting down of communication and interaction between the child and the birth relative, as relatives feared 'stepping out of line' and this leading to some loss of privilege. One birth mother explained:

You don't know what to say to the children . . . you're not allowed to ask them what schools they go to because then they are giving you too much information, information that I'm not supposed to have . . . There are questions there that you want to ask like 'What's your new school like? Have you got lots of friends?' You know general chit-chat like you do with a normal child. But you just feel restricted in what you can say.

It was not always clear in birth relatives' reports whether rules were set by the supervising agency or whether agencies were carrying out the wishes of adoptive parents in imposing rules and restrictions. Some birth relatives felt disempowered by the contact process. In some cases the contact arrangements were not adequately communicated to birth relatives, leaving them uncertain about when they would next see the child.

Developing models of contact support

The support received by birth relatives was further coded using the same four models developed on the adoptive parent sample. In other words, cases were categorised according to whether a support worker attended the contact or not, and whether or not any of the pro-active interventions (relationship building, reviewing and planning, or emotional support) were provided, generating four categories of support: administrated contact, facilitated contact, supervised and facilitated contact, and supervised contact. However, because the receipt of services here was from the birth relative's perspective, it is not necessarily the case that a birth relative was receiving the same model of contact support as the adoptive parent within the same arrangement. For example, in some cases where we interviewed the birth relative and the adoptive parent, the adoptive parent recived a follow-up phone call or visit but the birth relative did not. Because these models of contact support look slightly different from the birth relative perspective, further case examples of each type of support are given below.

Model 1: Administrated contact

Case example

Birth mother Jackie sees her daughter twice a year with the adoptive parents at a neutral venue such as a garden centre or swimming pool. In the past, the agency had supervised the contact meetings but this had now stopped and the only contact Jackie had with the agency was a letter she received twice a year to tell her the time, date and venue of the contact.

Model 2: Facilitated contact

Case example
Tyson is the 18-year-old sibling of Noah, aged four. His contact with Noah is twice a year, in a public place. Tyson has his own support worker for the contact who arranges everything. The support worker speaks to the adoptive parents and finds out the times, date and location. He sometimes takes Tyson but no longer stays with him during the meeting. He is available to help prepare Tyson for the meetings, e.g. by talking through questions that Tyson wants to ask the adoptive parents. The support worker has also helped Tyson choose presents appropriate for Noah's age.

Model 3: Supervised and facilitated contact

Case example
Birth father Gavin sees his children twice a year. He meets with them and their adoptive parents in a public place, e.g. a museum. A support worker from the adoption team arranges the dates with the adoptive parents and accompanies Gavin to the contact meeting. During the meeting the support worker's role is low key: 'She mainly walks along with the adopters, while I'm playing with the kids . . . and just takes photos and that.' The worker then phones Gavin a few days after the visit to get his feedback on how it had gone and to discuss any issues that may have arisen. He felt he could phone the support worker and said she would 'explain anything that I want to know'.

Model 4: Supervised contact

Case example
Grandmother Sylvia had contact with her two teenage grandchildren once a year for an hour-and-a-half. The meetings were held at a neutral venue and attended by the adoptive parents and the contact worker. Sylvia said she got a letter telling her where to turn up and on which day. During the meeting, she felt the worker's role was to observe the visit and make sure Sylvia didn't do anything wrong. Sylvia felt she

got no preparation or support in relation to the contact. She explained that the only time the worker ever got in touch with her outside of the meeting was not to support her, but to correct her, saying the agency only got in touch 'if they have felt that things have been wrong'.

Table 13.2 shows the number and percentage of cases in each of these four models, at Time 1 and Time 2. Because some families had different levels of contact support at both points in time, a third rating was used to describe contact overall, and this was the highest level of support reported. The table shows that when we look at the highest level of contact

Table 13.2

Models of contact support for birth relatives at Time 1, Time 2 and overall

	n at T1	% at T1	n at T2	% at T2	n highest level	% highest level
Model 1: administrated contact (AC)	4	11	3	10	3	8
Model 2: facilitated contact (FC)	8	23	7	24	9	25
Model 3: supervised and facilitated contact (SFC)	13	37	10	35	16	44
Model 4: supervised contact (SC)	10	29	9	31	8	22
Total	**35***	**100**	**29****	**100**	**36****	**99*****

* In one case the child was recently placed and contact/contact support had not yet started. Three people received no contact support.

** Four birth relatives did not take part at Time 2. Six people had no contact support.

*** Three people did not have contact support at either point in time.

**** Percentage does not equal 100 because of rounding.

support received by birth relatives the most common model was Model 3 – supervised and facilitated contact. Forty-four per cent of families had received this model of support. The next two most common models were facilitated contact (25%) and supervised contact (22%). Only a small minority of birth relatives (8%) were in the administrated contact model.

Table 13.3 shows in more detail the services that birth relatives received within these four models of contact support, based on service use at Time 1. This shows that those who received the fewest types of services

Table 13.3

Types of contact support received by birth relatives across the four models of service delivery (based on Time 1 data)

Contact support type	Co-ordination and enablement	Relationship building	Protecting and promoting interests	Review and planning	Emotional/ therapeutic support	Risk management
Model 1 (AC)	4 of 4	n/a*	0	n/a	n/a	0
Model 2 (FC)	7 of 8	3 of 8	2 of 8	5 of 8	4 of 8	1 of 8
Model 3 (SFC)	13 of 13	5 of 13	2 of 13	6 of 15	11 of 13	4 of 13
Model 4 (SC)	10 of 10	n/a	0	n/a	n/a	7 of 10

were those receiving Model 1 (administrated contact) – in all cases in this model, agency involvement was restricted to the co-ordination role. Relatives receiving facilitated contact support and supervised and facilitated contact support often received quite a number of different services. However, of those having facilitated contact, only one person out of eight reported intervention focused on risk management. This could suggest these cases were a lower risk, or at least that risks were not perceived by the agency. For those relatives in the supervised contact model, as with the adoptive parent sample, it does appear that support for these contact arrangements was delivered with a risk orientation; seven out of ten birth relatives reported interventions aimed at controlling risks that they were perceived to bring to contact, whereas no relatives in this group reported interventions aimed at protecting or promoting their own interests.

How did the birth relative involved in contact vary by contact support model?

Table 13.4 shows which birth relatives (birth parents, adult siblings or grandparents/others) were receiving which models of contact support. Numbers in each group are very small so it is hard to reach any conclusions, but there were examples in the study for each model of contact support being used for different birth relatives.

Table 13.4
Number of cases by models of contact support (based on the highest level of support) by type of birth relative

	Birth parent	*Adult sibling*	*Grandparent or other*	*Total cases*
Model 1 (AC)	1	1	1	3
Model 2 (FC)	4	2	3	9
Model 3 (SFC)	11	2	3	16
Model 4 (SC)	4	1	3	8
No support	1	1	1	3
Totals	**21**	**7**	**11**	**39**

It would be interesting to know whether the strengths and risks of birth relatives bore any relationship to the contact support models they received. However, the number of birth relatives within each model of contact support was quite small (under ten for three of the four models). Furthermore, the combined strengths/risks scores could not be calculated for every birth relative (see Chapter 6), reducing the numbers in each group even further. Hence, it was decided not to attempt to compare these four contact support models in relation to birth relatives' strengths and risks.

Did birth relatives' satisfaction with contact vary by contact support type?

In Chapter 9 we reported how birth relatives' satisfaction with contact was coded in terms of three groups: mainly satisfied, mixed satisfaction and mainly dissatisfied. Just over half of birth relatives were satisfied with contact, and just under half mixed or dissatisfied. In this analysis, we compared birth relatives who were mainly satisfied with those in the other two groups. The data in Table 13.5 show that all relatives who received administrated or facilitated models of contact support were satisfied with their contact. In comparison, only a minority receiving either of the other two types of contact support were satisfied with contact (five out of 16 of those receiving supervised and facilitated, and one out of eight of those receiving supervised). A chi-squared test looking at satisfaction with contact (satisfied versus mixed or unsatisfied) and whether contact support included supervision by a worker. (Models 1 and 2 versus Models 3 and 4) showed there was a statistically significant association between these two variables, with relatives whose contact was supervised being significantly less likely to be satisfied with contact than would be expected by chance ($\chi^2 = 18$, $df = 1$, $p<.001$). This could suggest that the experience of having supervised contact impacts negatively on birth relatives' feelings of satisfaction with contact, and interview data suggest this is certainly the case for several relatives. But, as the table shows, there were six relatives in the study whose contact meetings were supervised and who were satisfied with contact, thereby suggesting that it is not supervision *per se* but the manner in which it is conducted that is important. It is also worth considering whether relatives' levels of satisfaction with contact have a bearing on whether contact is supervised or not. In Chapter 9 we reported that birth relatives' levels of coping with adoption predicted whether they were satisfied with contact. In other words, birth relatives who were not satisfied with contact may well be low in terms of coping with adoption and this may be a reason why agencies wish to supervise contact.

Table 13.5
Numbers and percentages of birth relatives who were mainly satisfied with contact across the four contact support models

	Number satisfied with contact	%	Number mixed or dissatisfied with contact	%
Administrated	3	100	0	0
Facilitated	9	100	0	0
Supervised and facilitated	5	31	11	69
Supervised	1	12.5	7	87.5

Summary

This chapter has outlined the type and range of services to support contact that were described by the 39 birth relatives in the study. Key findings are as follows:

- Thirty-six of the 39 birth relatives had received contact support services. Six different types of support activity were coded according to the function they appeared to serve, as follows:
  - co-ordination and administration;
  - relationship building;
  - protecting or promoting the interests of the birth relative;
  - reviewing arrangements and planning;
  - providing emotional or therapeutic support;
  - risk management or minimisation.

- The first five of these types of support were similar to those identified in the adoptive parent sample. The sixth category – risk management or minimisation – was concerned with interventions that appeared to have the function of controlling or minimising risks which the birth relative might pose to the child or adoptive parents.
- The service most commonly received was co-ordination and administration, with 80–90 per cent of birth relatives receiving this service. Only a minority of birth relatives received each of the other five types of support service. Compared to adoptive parents, birth relatives were much less likely to receive a service that protected and promoted their interests (64–66% for adoptive parents; 11–17% for birth relatives).
- In the majority of cases where contact was supervised by a worker, birth relatives perceived that the focus of the worker was to control and correct the relatives' behaviour. The majority were uncomfortable with supervision, but a minority found it helpful.
- The same four models of contact support that were identified in the adoptive parent sample were applied to the birth relative sample. Sixteen birth relatives received supervised and facilitated contact support; nine relatives had facilitated contact support; eight had supervised contact support; and three had administrated contact support.
- For each of the four models of contact support, there were examples of this model being used with adult siblings, birth parents and grandparents or other relatives.
- Birth relatives whose contact was supervised (i.e. those having supervised contact or supervised and facilitated contact) were significantly less likely to be satisfied with their contact than relatives whose contact was not supervised (i.e. those having administrated contact or facilitated contact). All of the birth relatives who received these latter two models of support were satisfied with their contact.

14 Support for direct contact arrangements: birth relatives' perspectives

This chapter outlines birth relatives' satisfaction with support services. Ratings of satisfaction with support are looked at in relation to the four contact support models described in the previous chapter. The key themes that emerged from the qualitative analysis of interview data in relation to the factors that underpinned satisfaction (or dissatisfaction) are elaborated.

Birth relatives' satisfaction with contact support services

The birth relatives' satisfaction with the contact support services they received was coded using the same framework that was used with the adoptive parent sample. In other words, people were categorised into those who were mainly satisfied with support (including those who may have had some small suggestions for improvement) versus those who expressed several anxieties or concerns. These ratings were based on both interviews or if the person only took part at Time 1, just that one. The satisfaction of birth relatives with contact support was very similar to that of adoptive parents; just over half of birth relatives (n = 21, 54%) were mainly satisfied with support and just under half (n = 18, 46%) expressed several dissatisfactions.

Case example: Mainly satisfied with support
A birth mother who received supervised and facilitated contact support did not identify any negative aspects of the support service. On the positive side, she felt she had plenty of time to talk to the contact worker before and after meetings on their one-hour car journey. She felt the worker was friendly, noticed how she was feeling and took "the time to listen" to her experience of contact. The mother

was positive about the worker's role during contact, saying that she was 'not watching for things to go wrong' but instead had advised her on how to interact with her son. She expressed confidence that the agency would always warn her if any changes in contact were required – that she would not be 'pounced on' with this news.

Case example: Expressing several anxieties or concerns

A grandmother who received supervised and facilitated contact support expressed both positives and negatives about it, but the latter outweighed the former. On the positive side, she felt the contact was arranged at a time to suit her. She described her social worker as 'very sweet and kind' and she related well to the children. The grandmother was looking forward to attending an event for birth relatives which the local authority was organising. On the negative side, the worker's presence at contact meetings made her feel as if she was under surveillance. She felt that because the social worker was also representing both the adoptive parents and the child, this meant the worker could not really be on her side. She said: 'They got what they want . . . they're not concerned about my feelings too much.' When she enquired about the possibility of having more frequent contact she was told she should feel lucky with what she had already, which made her feel like she was 'asking for the world'.

How did birth relatives' satisfaction with contact support vary by support model?

The proportion of birth relatives who were mainly satisfied with contact support varied across the four models of support, although because of low numbers in some groups caution in interpretation is required.

The numbers and percentages in Table 14.1 show that where the contact support model involved proactive interventions (facilitated contact support and supervised and facilitated contact support), the majority of birth relatives were satisfied with the support (eight of nine for facilitated support, and nine of 16 for supervised and facilitated support). One of the three birth relatives who had administrated support was happy with it, and only one of eight of those having supervised support was happy with this

Table 14.1

Numbers and percentages of birth relatives who were mainly satisfied with contact support across the four contact support models

	Number mainly satisfied	Percentage	Number expressing concerns	Percentage
Administrated	1	33	2	67
Facilitated	8	87.5	1	12.5
Supervised and facilitated	9	56	7	44
Supervised	1	14	7	86

support. This pattern, that contact support models which involved proactive intervention were more popular than models which did not, is the same as that observed in the adoptive parent sample (see Chapter 12).

These findings suggest, therefore, that facilitation (comprising one or more of the following activities: emotional support, relationship building and review and planning) is an important determinant of satisfaction with service provision for both adoptive parents and birth relatives. This may be because these types of services more directly address the adults' feelings, concerns, needs and strengths. In contrast, when contact is administrated or supervised, although overt risks may be controlled (e.g. the full identity of adoptive parents can be protected, and the risk of the birth relative saying or doing the "wrong" thing may be guarded against), these interventions may do little to change deeper issues, e.g. how adults feel about the contact and each other. Although these models of contact support work well for a minority, most people may experience this type of intervention as controlling but not supportive.

The differences in birth relatives' satisfaction between the supervised and facilitated model (where 56% of birth relatives were satisfied with support) and supervised model (where 12.5% of relatives were satisfied) could suggest that relatives may be more able to accept the supervision of contact where it is accompanied by emotional support, relationship building or review and planning. When supervision is undertaken in the absence of any of these, birth relatives may experience support as intrusive and controlling. In some cases, it may be that it is difficult for some relatives to accept having contact supervised no matter how well this role is undertaken; this could be related to their history and previous experiences with the local authority.

What aspects of support do birth relatives value?

In this section we look at the key themes relating to the aspects of support services which appeared to underpin birth relatives' satisfaction or dissatisfaction with support.

A good relationship with the worker

Birth relatives particularly valued being able to establish a good relationship with the support worker and/or contact supervisor. A good relationship was seen as one where there was a rapport between the relative and the worker, where the worker displayed sensitivity and was non-judgemental. Characteristics of the worker such as trustworthiness, friendliness, calmness, kindness, helpfulness, reliability, experience, approachability and a caring attitude were seen as important. One birth mother described the contact support worker in the following terms:

> She was really nice . . . I think she had been a counsellor . . . she was just so calm in her ways. She was an older lady but she had obviously been through a lot, seen a lot and she was just excellent – a natural.

Relationships that were maintained over long periods were particularly valued. As one birth mother said:

> . . . it is nice in the fact that it is not someone different every year. It is nice that we know there is that regularity and it has always been [the same person], because otherwise it could be confusing for [the child] and me.

Emotional support to deal with the stress and emotional turmoil of contact was highly valued and birth relatives were very appreciative when workers demonstrated a trust in them, for example, by reducing or withdrawing supervision. The availability of support workers was important. Relatives appreciated having access to a named worker whom they could reach easily by phone and who would return their calls if they were out. Birth relatives were frustrated when they experienced workers as unavailable or unresponsive, and it was very difficult to build a relationship in such circumstances.

Obviously many birth relatives had been through an adversarial process with social services, and building trusting relationships with a social worker did not necessarily come easily to them. One birth mother said the social worker who had taken her child away came to see her before her first contact meeting; she described this as 'the final insult'. In another case the birth relative used the term 'dealing with the enemy'. However, in some cases, including that of the previous birth mother, it seemed that the introduction of a new worker from the adoption team or adoption support team opened up a new opportunity for relatives to relate to children's services on a more positive platform. One said that the people supporting the contact had been 'pretty good', though she quickly qualified this by saying 'but I don't mean normal social workers, I mean just social workers that deal with placements and things to do with adoption.'

What particularly helped birth relatives trust social workers was the feeling they would be listened to and respected. As one sibling commented about the social worker supporting contact, 'She would listen before she judges someone.'

Acting as an intermediary and balancing everyone's needs

Birth relatives also stressed the importance of the worker's role as intermediary in the relationship between the birth relatives, child, adoptive parents and agency. They particularly valued the efforts of workers to maintain clear channels of communication between the parties, both during and outside of contact meetings. Relatives described a number of tasks associated with this role, such as listening, explaining and reassuring, acting on concerns and communicating decisions. They valued having their views communicated to adoptive parents and getting feedback about the child's experience of contact and the adopter's point of view. If this did not happen, they often felt disempowered, marginalised and unable to raise concerns. Where there was such communication, relatives felt involved in contact and, in turn, involved in promoting the best interests of the child. They also trusted workers to act on their concerns. This sometimes meant birth relatives were included in decision-making about contact. This was not always possible, but where this was the case, relatives found it helpful when support workers at the very least explained why certain decisions had been made. Where it was clear that these were in the best interests of the child and it was explained fully to the relative, they were usually very accepting of such decisions.

Birth relatives felt it was important for workers to remain impartial and consider all points of view. They believed that workers should be sympathetic to their position while at the same time focused on the child's welfare. A key skill for workers, therefore, was negotiation and managing conflict. There were a small number of examples where changes had been made to contact to meet the birth relatives' needs; for instance, changing the time of year or day of the week for meetings. Where rules and restrictions related to contact were necessary, it was important for support workers to explain to relatives the reasons behind them. If relatives understood why certain boundaries were necessary, it was easier for them to accept them. For example, one mother was reminded to turn up at the right time, that is, not to come too early. When it was explained to her that it was important that she was introduced properly to her child rather than bump into him in the car park, her response was:

> . . . it just helped you understand where you stand – everything is clear. You know it is all set for a reason and all the procedures you can understand.

This birth mother was happy to have received a very detailed written plan for the contact, saying it made everything clear to her, 'it's all been written out like child's play'.

Examples such as these suggest that it is not the imposition of boundaries *per se* that is difficult for birth relatives, but the appropriateness of the boundaries and the manner in which they are explained that is important. One mother was reminded not to tell members of the extended birth family where she would be meeting the adoptive parents. She was happy to agree to this, saying 'They said that – but not in a horrible way . . . so I was happy to agree with that.'

When these issues were handled sensitively by support workers, birth relatives could experience this type of intervention as supportive. As the birth mother quoted above said:

> *Obviously, when you first start doing these contacts you are frightened to death of breaking the rules for fear that the contact will be stopped for doing something out of place. So I think it is just really good to understand what the boundaries are so you don't overstep them.*

Birth relatives particularly appreciated interventions designed to build their resourcefulness, skills, competence or confidence and, ultimately, improve the experience of contact for them and the child. This capacity-building support was closely related to the relationship building undertaken by workers. Relatives also focused on the supportive ways in which workers provided advice and guidance rather than rules and diktats about their conversations and play with children during contact.

Planning, review and predictability

In some cases, the support that people described appeared organised and predictable and it involved birth relatives as active participants, negotiating the arrangements for contact. One birth mother described how, right from the early stages of her children's adoption placement, she was prepared and supported in relation to contact, at that stage by the children's social worker (this was an example where the birth relative was able to work co-operatively with her children's social worker). She was helped to prepare for an initial meeting with the adoptive parents and was consulted about the venue for the first contact meeting, to which the children's social worker accompanied her. Once the adoption order had gone through, support for contact was taken up by the post-adoption team. This birth mother explained how the contact support worker 'sorts everything out'. She contacts the mother before every meeting, by phone or arranges a home visit, and they discuss the plans for the next meeting. The worker uses these meetings to explain any changes to the contact arrangements and the boundaries of contact are clarified. After each contact, the support worker phones or writes to the birth mother to give her feedback about how contact went from the children's point of view, and to seek feedback from the birth mother that she could take to the adoptive parents and the children. The mother felt this was useful 'because you could let each other know if there was anything that you didn't like, which you could change for the next time'. This approach to support helped this birth mother feel that her opinions and feelings were valued and that she was an active participant in the arrangements. Although this contact was quite controlled (meetings were supervised and boundaries were clear), the mother felt comfortable with the agency intervention, clearly experiencing it as supportive. About the worker, she commented, 'it's good to know she will always be there' and she said the agency had been really good with 'all the help they have given me – they have helped me cope'.

In other cases, contact support seemed far less empowering and organised. The dissatisfaction with support raised by more than half of the birth relatives interviewed related to the degree to which they were involved in decision-making. The accounts of many relatives suggested they had come to expect that their views would often not be sought and they would be peripheral to any decision-making. The expectation of support services appeared to be that birth relatives would fit in with plans made by the worker and adoptive parents. Some relatives had ideas for changes to contact that would improve the experience for them and their birth children. However, there did not appear to be a forum or process in which these could be raised. Therefore, relatives often kept ideas to themselves, often fearing that such suggestions would be seen as "rocking the boat" or confrontational. The lack of forum for review, therefore, appeared to have the effect of silencing many birth relatives. There was at least one case where contact appeared to be at risk of ending because of unspoken, and therefore unresolved, issues. In some cases, this poor planning on the part of support services had very detrimental effects on the relative's, and ultimately the child's, experience of contact. One grandmother explained that she once missed half of a contact meeting as the arranged time clashed with her medical needs.

Birth relatives commonly expressed a sense of discomfort with the level of uncertainty they faced in relation to contact. The areas of uncertainty included what was expected of them inside and outside of contact, when contact would next be arranged and what would happen when the child reached the age of 18. The lack of review and planning also seemed to indicate a view that needs would not change over time. One birth sibling said she had been offered the opportunity, in the early days of contact, to meet the adoption support team. At the time, she turned this down. She later felt confident enough to take it up but had not been offered the chance again and did not feel able to suggest it herself. One birth mother proposed that an independent advocacy service should be available to birth relatives to ensure their views were taken into account.

Birth relatives were asked if they had taken up any opportunity to meet adoptive parents (separately from a contact meeting with the child) at the beginning of the child's placement. Twenty-four birth relatives (63% of 38; data were missing in one case) said they did have such a meeting. It was clear, however, that these initial encounters between birth relatives and adoptive parents were rarely used to discuss contact plans in any detail. Birth relatives frequently described these occasions as highly charged emotionally. This type of meeting, in most cases, is probably not the right forum to conduct a detailed planning of post-adoption contact. However, the opportunity for adoptive parents and birth relatives to meet without the child being present was very rarely offered at a later stage. Several relatives felt it would be very helpful. In some cases, they were seeking a separate meeting or discussion with adoptive parents to keep up to date with the child's progress, interests and friendship groups so they could talk about them with the child. In other cases, people were looking for an opportunity to build bridges with the adoptive parents. One grandmother said that she felt there was 'a huge gulf' between the birth family and adoptive family and that:

> *Nobody seems to make any effort to actually help either side to deal with this . . . nobody seems to want to go there . . . We don't get any sense that anybody is trying to hear what differences there are, not making any positive move to say 'Look, we've got a difficult situation here – what can we do to make it better?'*

Being bounded by formality and rules

Approximately a third of birth relatives were concerned about the degree of formality and the rules of conduct that were imposed by support agencies. Relatives saw these as creating an unnatural or uncomfortable context for contact and some felt these rules were highly controlling. They also expressed uncertainty about the purpose or rationale for certain rules.

As already noted, some birth relatives perceived supervision as confrontational, negative, watchful, monitoring risk and expecting the worst: one birth relative said it was like being in a goldfish bowl. In some cases, the degree of control maintained by the support agency appeared to be disproportionate and unhelpful. For example, a birth mother who was having contact with her son had exchanged mobile phone numbers with him and his adoptive father. The support agency intervened and said this was not allowed. There was no evidence that the birth mother would present any risk to the child or adoptive family by having this number. The contact had been taking place over a number of years, it was considered to be going well, it was unsupervised and very informal, and the child was almost 18. However, it was clearly practical to exchange phone numbers, as the meeting took place on a weekend when the support agency was unavailable to relay a message if there was a problem or one party was delayed.

Detrimental effects of disproportionate rules and boundaries were evident in a few cases. In one case, a grandmother had initially agreed with the children's adoption. Despite the fact that she had been a stable and caring influence in the children's lives, and was the carer of the older sibling, contact with her grandchildren after adoption was very brief, supervised, infrequent and rule bound. Although the grandmother emphasised that she would never want to disturb the children's placement, the experience of contact was beginning to affect her feelings about it. She had moved from feeling positive about the adoption to feeling deeply unhappy, resentful and full of regret that she did not have the children living with her. We did not interview the adoptive parents in this case, but it is easy to imagine that this contact is no more comfortable for the children and the adoptive parents than it is for the grandmother.

The importance of emotional support

For a number of birth relatives contact could give rise to numerous and mixed feelings, as we reported in Chapter 10. It is unsurprising, therefore, that for many of our interviewees, the presence or absence of emotional support was the key determinant of their satisfaction, or dissatisfaction, with contact support. A third of birth relatives reported feeling dissatisfied with the emotional support available to them. Some felt totally unsupported, while others felt the support they received was inadequate. Birth relatives referred to the strong emotions raised by contact and the lack of a proactive service to help them deal with these. Some felt that, while their worker would respond to their expressed needs, what was actually required was for the worker to make the first move. One birth relative explained that she felt totally overwhelmed at her first contact with the child, and that following this meeting 'I was crying for two days.' During this period, she had to phone the worker for another reason, and in the course of the phone call explained how she felt. Although she found the worker's response reassuring, she remarked that, 'If I hadn't had phoned her up about something . . . I don't think she would have phoned me up.' For this birth relative, a proactive approach to emotional support would have been helpful because she was, in her words, 'old school', that is, she felt she should deal with problems herself. She reflected that:

> If someone had told me, 'You are entitled to feel that emotional and
> upset, and maybe if you can't cope with it, maybe you should go find
> someone to talk to' – if someone had given me that advice maybe I
> would have taken it.

Some people reported that they had had to ask for, or even demand, support or counselling. In some cases, the impersonal way in which support was provided was problematic for birth relatives and did not allow them to express distress. One birth mother said she would prefer support to be given face to face rather than over the phone.

Unmet needs identified by birth relatives

Birth relatives identified a number of unmet needs that are not included under the main headings above. These are:

- advocacy, information and legal advice about what happens when the adopted child reaches the age of 18;
- an independent mediation/advocacy service that can negotiate contact before the adoption order;
- greater mental health awareness by service providers;
- more support for letterbox contact;
- more support for members of the extended family, such as grand-parents and siblings of the adopted child who have remained within the birth family.

Summary

This chapter has explored the satisfaction of birth relatives with contact support services. Ratings of satisfaction with support were looked at in relation to the four contact support models described in Chapter 13. Central themes in relation to the factors that underpinned satisfaction (or dissatisfaction) have been described. Key points are as follows:

- Birth relatives were categorised into those who were mainly satisfied with support and those who expressed several anxieties or concerns. Twenty-one birth relatives (54%) were mainly satisfied with contact support and 18 (46%) expressed several dissatisfactions.
- Satisfaction with support was looked at in relation to the four contact support models. One of the three people receiving administrated support was satisfied. Eight of nine people receiving facilitated support were satisfied. Nine of 16 people having supervised and facilitated support were satisfied. Only one of the eight people having supervised support was satisfied. Thus, as was found in the adoptive parent sample, service users were happier with support services that included proactive interventions.
- A number of themes related to aspects of support that appeared to underpin birth relatives' satisfaction with services were identified, as follows:

- – a good relationship with the worker;
- – the worker acting as an intermediary, balancing everyone's needs;
- – attention to planning, review and predictability;
- – the availability of emotional support.
- A concern about contact support raised by approximately one-third of birth relatives was the feeling that they were bounded by formality and rules which they did not always understand, and which did not always appear to them to be necessary or appropriate.

15 The costs of supporting contact

This chapter reports the findings of our costing of contact support services. The provision of support services by support workers is described, and estimates of the time spent providing such services and the subsequent cost of this provision are outlined. Estimates of the use of services by individuals in the intensive study and, ultimately, the total cost of service provision for the "average" adoptive parent and the "average" birth relative, are presented. The chapter then looks at the relative costs and services of the four contact support models, presenting descriptive statistics for these. Finally, correlation analyses are used to explore whether the strengths and risks of adoptive families and birth families were related to the costs and resources of their service provision.

Caseworker diaries

Twenty caseworkers from seven agencies (five local authorities, one adoption support agency and one voluntary adoption agency) agreed to complete the caseworker time diaries. All respondents were female. A number of them described their role as a project (or support) worker (n = 11), six described themselves as social workers, two were social work assistants and one was a manager.

Eleven respondents were employed full time, averaging 37 hours a week (range: 36–37.5). Nine respondents were part time, working an average of 20 hours a week (range: 13–27).

Table 15.1 reports the results of the aggregation of all respondents' time diaries, displaying (in minutes) the mean, median and interquartile range. In terms of time commitment, the analysis shows that a session to plan contact takes nearly two hours (117 minutes) to organise and deliver. Supporting contact meetings takes the most time, an average of 152 minutes, and support before and after contact takes 83 minutes, while other support for contact takes just over an hour (70 minutes). The median time commitment is lower than the mean for planning contact, support before and after contact and other support. This suggests that the data are positively skewed, i.e. some caseworkers spend considerably more time providing some support services than other workers. This skewed distribution could be due to differences in the complexity of cases assigned to caseworkers, the quality or degree of support they provide, caseworker training or experience, models of support used or promoted by the agency, or a combination of these factors.

Table 15.1
Time commitment for each contact support activity (minutes)

	Number	Mean	Median	Interquartile range
Planning contact	17	117	98	42–195
Supporting contact meetings	16	152	174	67–210
Supporting people before/after contact	16	83	80	36–123
Other support for contact	12	70	62	28–120

The data collection tool allowed for a comparison of direct and indirect time commitments. Direct time was the time the worker actually spent meeting with the service user or talking with them on the phone. Indirect time included activities related to facilitating the support (e.g. case recording, administration, liaising with colleagues, travelling, email or letter contact with service users). Table 15.2 presents the split of time commitments between direct and indirect work. The indirect time commitments were, in all but one instance, greater than the direct time commitments. When planning contact, a case worker spends on average 32 minutes of their total time directly with a client and 92 minutes on indirect work; 91 minutes are spent directly with a client when supporting meetings, compared with 79 minutes of indirect work. These differences are perhaps not unexpected; contact planning, by its very nature, should involve more administration and less direct client work, while supporting contact should be more client based.

Table 15.2
Average direct and indirect time commitment for each support activity (minutes)

	Number	Mean
Planning contact		
Total direct	16	32
Total indirect	16	92
Supporting contact meetings		
Total direct	13	91
Total indirect	16	79
Supporting people before/after contact		
Total direct	15	47
Total indirect	11	57
Other support for contact		
Total direct	9	43
Total indirect	9	50

Valuing resource use

The average time commitments for the different support activities presented in Table 15.1 above were valued using the unit cost of one hour of service-user related work. The resulting unit costs of providing each specific service are presented in Table 15.3.

Service use diaries

Ninety-four individuals were recruited to the evaluation study. This included one adoptive parent who was interviewed twice in relation to two

Table 15.3
Unit costs of contact support services (£ sterling, 2007 prices)

	Cost
Planning contact	76.04
Supporting contact meetings	99.04
Support people before/after contact	54.15
Other support for contact	75.28

children from different birth families. Eighty-seven completed service use diaries were returned, giving a response rate of 93 per cent. In these diaries, agency workers kept a record of all the activities they had undertaken in supporting individual birth relatives and adoptive parents in the study over a 12-month period. Only one diary was returned for the adoptive parent with two children; a review of the interviews with this parent suggested that roughly equal amounts of contact support were received in relation to both children; as such, the recorded resource use was halved for each child and the analysis considers the resource use in relation to each child separately. The total sample includes data on 36 birth relatives, 50 adoptive parents and two foster carers. Due to the small number of foster carers in the sample, they are excluded from subsequent analyses.

Resource use by adoptive parents

Resource use by adoptive parents over a 12-month period, as recorded in the service use diaries, is described and summarised in Table 15.4. Most of the support provided by case workers came in the form of assistance with direct (face-to-face) contact; over a 12-month period, 6.10 support sessions were received by the "average" adoptive parent. They also received 1.10 information and advice sessions, 1.58 sessions providing assistance with indirect contact and 1.14 sessions of casework. Minimal amounts of needs assessment, support groups, counselling and advocacy were provided, while no adoptive parent received therapy. An average of 1.64 "other" services were provided, including transport, newsletters and finance. To aid the costing of services each specific "other" was (where possible) re-categorised to fit with the categorisation of support services provided by caseworkers (for example, emotional support was recoded as counselling).

In aggregate, the "average" adoptive parent in the contact study received 12 sessions over a 12-month period (range = 0–49). Three adoptive parents received no support sessions during that period, and there is a very long tail to the distribution. This skewness means it may be more informative to consider the median value (9). If the three adoptive parents who used no services are excluded, the mean number of services increases

Table 15.4
Summary of resource use by adoptive parents over a 12-month period (n = 50)

	Mean number of sessions	*Standard deviation*	*Minimum*	*Maximum*	*Total number adoptive parents receiving service*
Needs assessment	0.12	0.52	0	3	3
Information and advice	1.10	2.27	0	12	17
Support groups	0.06	0.42	0	3	1
Therapy	0.00	0.00	0	0	0
Counselling	0.10	0.42	0	2	3
Assistance with face-to-face contact	6.10	8.25	0	35	43
Assistance with letterbox contact	1.58	2.33	0	10	23
Casework	1.14	2.13	0	10	17
Advocacy	0.16	0.55	0	3	5
Other	1.64	2.65	0	9	18
Total service provision	**12.00**	**11.39**	**0**	**49**	**47**

slightly to 12.77. However, given that the "average", or typical, adoptive parent (or birth relative) includes individuals who are offered services but do not use them, it is important to include these non-users in the mean estimations.

Caseworkers also recorded the number of planned but missed appointments, so-called "did not attends", or DNAs. There was one instance where an adoptive parent failed to attend a session during the 12-month period. Including this DNA appointment in the estimation of the mean would result in a relatively unchanged average of 12.02 sessions per adoptive parent. The fact that only one adoptive parent missed one support session in the 12-month study period is an interesting finding. It suggests that adoptive parents in the study were highly motivated to receive services relating to their child's contact with birth relatives, and thus possibly reflects commitment to contact in general.

Resource use by birth relatives

Resource use by birth relatives over a 12-month period as recorded in the service use diaries is summarised in Table 15.5. The most support for birth relatives came in the form of assistance with direct (face-to-face) contact. Over a 12-month period nearly five sessions were received by the "average" birth relative. In addition, the "average" birth relative receiving support for contact also received assistance with indirect contact 1.17 times, 0.72 sessions of casework and 0.53 sessions of information and advice. Needs assessment, support groups, counselling and advocacy were rarely provided. No birth relative received therapy during the 12-month period. Notably, not all birth relatives in the study received support for direct contact – only 31 of 36 (86%). Few "other" services were provided. When they were, they were described as transport, letter writing and/or phone calls. As described above, to aid the cost analysis, these were subsequently recoded.

In total, the "average" birth relative received 8.92 services/sessions over a 12-month period. This ranged from 0 to 23. Only two birth relatives received no services or support during this time, while six service users received 15 or more services. The median value of service support is 9.5.

In terms of missed appointments, in the sample of 36 birth relatives there were only two DNAs over the 12-month period. Including these missed appointments in the estimation of the mean would result in a slightly higher average of 8.97 sessions per birth relative. The very low levels of birth relatives missing appointments demonstrate the motivation of birth relatives to maintain direct contact with the child and their willingness to receive services in support of this. It is interesting that the birth relatives in the study were able to work with local authorities, even though in most cases these will have been the same authorities that had removed the child.

Table 15.5
Summary of resource use by birth relatives over a 12-month period (n = 36)

	Mean number of sessions	Standard deviation	Minimum	Maximum	Total number of birth relatives who received service
Needs assessment	0.08	0.28	0	1	3
Information and advice	0.53	1.03	0	5	11
Support groups	0.06	0.23	0	1	2
Therapy	0.00	0.00	0	0	0
Counselling	0.14	0.59	0	3	2
Assistance with face-to-face contact	4.75	4.66	0	17	31
Assistance with letterbox contact	1.17	1.61	0	6	15
Casework	0.72	1.49	0	5	10
Advocacy	0.22	0.76	0	4	4
Other	1.25	2.57	0	12	11
Total service provision	**8.92**	**6.04**	**0**	**23**	**34**

Total cost of providing contact support services

Total cost of providing services to adoptive parents

For the 12 services received by the "average" adoptive parent in a 12-month period the estimated cost was £999. The interquartile range was £198 to £1,226. Table 15.6 presents the number of sessions used and cost for the average adoptive parent for the sample as a whole, and also specifically for the four local authorities which made up most of the sample. This shows that the average costs and number of sessions per person varied quite considerably between agencies, being almost twice as high in local authority LA3 as in LA1. This may reflect different

Table 15.6
Total resource use and total cost for adoptive parents for four largest contributing local authorities

		Number of sessions		Cost	
	n	*Mean*	*Range*	*Mean*	*Range*
LA 1	12	9.92	3–16	£842	£251–1,294
LA 2	7	17.00	2–49	£1,268	£198–3,456
LA 3	11	18.45	0–45	£1,594	£0–4,052
LA 4	10	12.40	5–38	£1,137	£450–3,671
Total sample	**40**	**12.00**	**0–49**	**£999**	**£0–4,052**

approaches to supporting contact in different authorities. However, as the numbers of cases in each group are quite small and group differences were not tested, caution should be taken in interpreting the results.

Total cost of providing services to birth relatives

For the 8.92 services received by the "average" birth relative in a 12-month period the estimated cost was £757. The interquartile range was £328 to £956. Table 15.7 presents the resource use and cost for the average birth relative, for the sample as a whole, and also specifically for the four local authorities which made up most of the sample. Once again, it appears that LA3 may provide relatively more services at a higher average cost than the other three authorities and the sample as a whole. The agency providing the least services/costs to birth relatives was LA2.

It is not possible to tell from our data why these differences in service provision between local authorities may have occurred. It might be simply that some authorities are prepared to devote more resources to supporting direct contact than others. Or it might be that authorities differ in terms of the extent to which they promote post-adoption contact, and there is certainly evidence of this from our mapping survey and from other research (Neil, 2002a). Local authorities may differ in the level of risk they are prepared to consider when promoting direct contact. An agency may only wish to promote direct contact in cases where they consider it to be very safe and to need few resources. They may, for example,

Table 15.7
Total resource use and total cost for birth relatives for four largest contributing local authorities

		Number of sessions		Cost	
	n	*Mean*	*Range*	*Mean*	*Range*
LA 1	9	10.11	5–18	£840	£403–1,579
LA 2	5	6.6	2–11	£540	£198–861
LA 3	7	13.14	7–23	£1,148	£514–1,984
LA 4	11	8.82	1–20	£745	£54–1,890
Total sample	**32**	**8.92**	**0–23**	**£757**	**£0–1,984**

consider direct contact between siblings in two different adoptive placements but be wary of contact with birth parents. Other agencies may consider direct contact in a broader range of cases, including those where risk is present and the need for supervision or other expensive resources is required.

Costs and services in relation to the four models of contact support

In this section, the costs and services for people in the study are detailed in relation to the contact support models which were outlined in Chapters 11 and 13. The following data are preliminary. We did not test group differences (compare cost or service outcome by model of support) because the number of people served (or cases) in three of the four contact support groups was very small (less than ten).

Costs and services for adoptive parents

Table 15.8 shows the total number of sessions and total cost of services for adoptive parents in the four different models of contact support. Adoptive parents receiving supervised and facilitated contact support were reported to have received on average 16.23 services in a year. This was almost twice as many as parents who received supervised contact support services (mean = 8.88). Adoptive families receiving the facilitated model received a number of services (9.83) similar to those having supervised support, indicating that although workers were not attending meetings, work was being undertaken behind the scenes. Adoptive parents who received the least number of services were those in the administrated support model; they received, on average, five services in one year.

The cost of services provided to families in the study also varied across the four models. The most expensive model was supervised and facilitated, costing on average £1,371 in one year; the cheapest model was administrated, incurring an annual average cost of £395. The costs of providing facilitated and supervised contact support were similar – £734 and £776 respectively.

Table 15.8
Mean number of sessions and mean cost for adoptive parents for each of the four contact support models

	Sample size (max)	Total number of sessions	Range	Total cost	Range
Administrated	7	5	0–11	£395	£0–863
Facilitated	6	9.83	6–16	£734	£392–1,226
Supervised and facilitated	26	16.23	0–49	£1,371	£0–4,052
Supervised	8	8.88	3–18	£776	£251–1,580

The number of sessions which caseworkers provided for birth relatives also varied across the four groups (see Table 15.9). The most sessions were received by those in the "supervised and facilitated" model (an average of 11.43 sessions were provided) and the least by those in the administrated group (mean = 3), and this is the same pattern as seen in the adoptive parent sample. Birth relatives having facilitated contact support received on average 6.56 sessions in the year. Whereas in the adoptive parent sample those having supervised and facilitated support received almost twice as many sessions as those having supervised support, in this birth relative sample the two figures were very similar (11.43 versus 11.38). This could possibly indicate that the supervised model of contact

(Model 4) involves more input with birth relatives (presumably focused on managing risk) than with adoptive parents. Indeed, the most expensive model of contact support for birth relatives was the supervised model, costing on average £1,004 per year. The costs of providing "supervised and facilitated" support were only slightly lower, at £960 per year. The cheapest model was administrated (£246) while facilitated contact support cost £536.

Table 15.9
Mean numbers of sessions and mean cost for birth relatives across the four contact support models

	Sample size (max)	Total number of sessions	Range	Total cost	Range
Administrated	3	3	0–7	£246	£0–540
Facilitated	9	6.56	1–15	£536	£54–1,188
Supervised and facilitated	14	11.43	2–23	£960	£198–1,984
Supervised	8	11.38	5–21	£1,004	£403–1,996

Do costs and services provided relate to the strengths and risks of families receiving services?

In order to understand whether adoptive families and birth relatives who had fewer strengths and greater risks received more services (as measured by the number of sessions and total cost of services), we undertook correlation analyses (using Spearman's Rho) using the composite strengths/risks scores for adoptive parents and birth families. For adoptive parents, both services and costs were negatively correlated with the strengths/risks scores (services: $r_s = -.29$, n = 52, p<.05; costs: $r_s = -.29$, n = 52, p<.05). This indicates that the greater the strengths of the adoptive family, the fewer costs and services the agency provided. Looking at birth relative data, there were no statistically significant correlations between costs and services. However, as was the case with the adoptive parent sample, correlations were negative (services: $r_s = -.24$, $n = 28$, $p<.2$; costs: $r_s = -.21$, $n = 28$, $p<.3$).

Summary

This is the first research project which has attempted to systematically cost services to support post-adoption contact. A process of bottom-up costing was used to estimate the costs of a range of activities that support workers employ to provide support services to adoptive parents and birth relatives. These unit costs were then used to value the support services provided to adoptive parents and birth relatives over a 12-month period. This was done using data supplied by caseworkers about the services provided to adoptive parents and birth relatives in the study; an excellent response rate of 93 per cent was achieved. Key findings are as follows:

- The "average" adoptive parent was estimated to have used 12 support services over a 12-month period at an average cost of £999. This included three adoptive parents who incurred no costs (as they did not use any services) and some users who greatly utilised the services that were on offer; the maximum cost was £4,052.

- The "average" birth relative received 8.9 services (range 0 to 23) and the average cost over the 12-month period was £757, with the maximum being £1,984.

- There was considerable variation between service users as to the number of sessions they received and the total cost of that provision over the study period. This variation in level of support required by different people is something agencies will need to take into account when planning their work commitments and allocating cases to workers.

- The number of missed appointments for adoptive parents and birth relatives was very low. This could suggest the commitment of both parties to the continuation of contact and may indicate that people both want and need contact support services.

- There was a suggestion that the level of services provided to support contact may vary according to the agency providing the service. When the four local authorities from whom most cases were drawn were

283

compared, one of the large authorities seemed to be providing more services at greater cost than the other three.

- Descriptive data were presented comparing the four contact support models in terms of their relative costs and services. For adoptive families, the model with the highest costs was supervised and facilitated contact (an average cost of £1,371) and the cheapest was administrated contact (an average cost of £395 per year). For birth relatives, the most expensive model was supervised contact (this costing on average £1,004) and the least expensive model was administrated contact (£246 on average per year). Although the data presented are exploratory, they do suggest that some models of supporting contact are more expensive than others and, therefore, it is important that services are targeted appropriately to needs.

- The composite strengths/risks scores of adoptive families were correlated with both costs and number of sessions provided. This indicated that families with more needs tended to receive more services. The composite strengths/risks scores of birth relatives were not significantly correlated with the number of services they received, or the costs of these.

16 Discussion

This chapter draws together findings from across the study. It begins with a reminder of the aims of the research, then discusses the complexity of direct post-adoption contact. The balance of challenges and benefits of contact is discussed and the case factors that may affect contact are outlined. The chapter then looks at people's experiences of support services and what works in supporting direct contact. It ends with a summary of the strengths and limitations of the research.

Summary of the aims of the research

The aims of the study were to explore the provision of support services to help birth and adoptive families manage direct post-adoption contact arrangements. The specific research questions we strove to answer were as follows:

1. What are the characteristics of adoptive parents, adopted children and birth relatives who are involved in complex direct contact arrangements?
2. What are the experiences of adoptive parents and birth relatives of direct contact arrangements?
3. What types of services to support contact do birth relatives and adoptive parents report using?
4. What are adoptive parents' and birth relatives' experiences of using contact support services?
5. How much do support services for direct contact cost?

The research was carried out in collaboration with eight agencies involved in providing contact support services. Fifty-one adoptive parents, four foster carers and 39 birth relatives took part; both qualitative and quantitative data were collected.

What is complex about direct contact?

In order to think about the provision of services to support contact, it is essential to understand the complexities of direct contact. In this section, we draw on the accounts of adoptive parents and birth relatives about their experiences of contact, which were described in Chapters 7–10. The child's perspective is represented by the accounts of adoptive parents. What emerges from our data is a picture of contact as something which inevitably involves some level of challenge, but which for most people is worthwhile and beneficial in spite of its complexity.

For children, contact is about birth family connections but such connections are rarely straightforward for those adopted from care. Herein lies the emotional complexity of contact. Some children may have good relationships with their birth relatives, unmarked by any history of abuse and neglect. This may be especially true of sibling or grandparent relationships. However, even when relationships are excellent, contact raises complex feelings such as loss, sadness, excitement and questions about why separation was necessary. The gap between meetings – often six or 12 months – makes it hard to maintain feelings of comfort and familiarity with each other. When relationship histories are more complex, feelings are inevitably a more complicated mix of both positive and negative emotions, and happy, sad or scary memories may rise to the surface. In some cases, birth relatives may behave in ways that disappoint or frighten children, or make them feel torn between their two families. For some children, these feelings manifest themselves through anxious, disturbed, withdrawn or defiant behaviours before, during or after contact. Some children will not necessarily know or remember birth relatives; the challenge for them may be to develop some kind of relationship but without the regular, day-to-day interactions upon which family relationships are usually built.

Children have to deal not just with how they feel within relationships; they have to make sense of who they are to birth family members, who their birth family members are to them, and how these relationships fit in with relationships in the adoptive family. What does it mean to have two mums? Who is your real sister – your adoptive sister with whom you live, or your birth sister whom you see once a year? These types of questions constitute the emotional backdrop of contact for the child. The contact event itself has its own complexities. Aside from the feelings the child brings to contact, the event itself can be strange – infrequent, attended by people you don't know and whose role is unclear to you, little to do, no refreshments, long car journeys. Meetings may remind the child of past contact sessions with birth family members during care proceedings, especially when the same venue is used. To add to all this, the child is likely to be aware that the event is not emotionally neutral to anyone else in the room.

For adoptive parents, contact is about the child's birth family connections, but the contact meeting requires the adoptive parent also to connect with the birth family. This can raise complex feelings, especially for parents who find it hard to think about the child having another family. Psychologically speaking, adoptive parents have to find a space in their minds for another mother, father, grandparent or sibling. Meeting with these people can remind them that the child has not always been "theirs". The adoptive parent is required to relate to the birth relative. In some cases they already know each other and past experiences impinge on the present. This can be positive – for example, foster carers may adopt the child and there may already be a co-operative relationship with birth relatives. However, some of the most complex cases in our study were kinship or foster care adoptions: people knew each other but the relationships were troubled. A history of directly contested adoption proceedings seemed particularly difficult to overcome. For the majority of adoptive parents, however, the child's birth family members are strangers and a relationship must be established. There are a number of challenges here. Birth relatives often have very different needs and lifestyles from adoptive parents. They come to adoption from different points – birth families are losing a child, adoptive families are gaining one. Adoptive parents' feelings about birth relatives may be influenced by information given to them by the agency, information that may focus on the negative. Parental feelings about the harm experienced by the child can affect feelings towards birth relatives, especially if they have been involved in bringing about the harm. The opportunities for adults to talk through issues of concern without children being present are often very limited. The time and space within contact meetings in which to build a relationship is limited. As well as having strong feelings of their own, adoptive parents are also likely to feel protective of their child and to be investing much emotional energy in considering their child's emotional reactions. They are often faced with the difficult emotions of birth family members. They have no script to help them deal with this complexity. They may share the child's feelings about the strangeness or unnatural nature of the event. Adoptive parents often have busy lives, working and caring for children, and fitting in birth family meetings can present logistical challenges.

For birth relatives, contact is an opportunity to maintain a connection with the child, an opportunity that most people really treasure. Relatives value this opportunity, for their own sake and also because they hope to continue contributing to the positive development of their child. So, in some respects, birth relatives approach contact with much to gain. But the contact is complex because it makes real the way in which their connection to the child has changed, reduced and to some extent been replaced by her or his connections to the adoptive family. This is probably the central challenge of contact for birth relatives: that the child now has a new family. This may be no less difficult to come to terms with for siblings and grandparents than it is for birth parents. This reality leaves the birth relative with an undefined role in relation to the child – are they still a sister, mother, grandfather, father? What sort of sibling, parent or grandparent can they be when their contact with the child is limited to a few hours once or twice a year? Birth relatives are challenged in terms of maintaining their relationship with the child: how to keep alive some sort of connection in such limited circumstances and with such an undefined role. They also experience challenges in relating to adoptive parents, e.g. feelings of resentment, sadness or envy about the adoptive parents taking over the primary role as the child's psychological parent. Relating to adoptive parents may be made more difficult because of lack of information, such as their names, where they live, their jobs, their family history, why they wanted to adopt, etc. Birth relatives' experiences of contact may be clouded by their previous experiences with professional agencies. Many will have a history of conflict with children's services, and will have been judged to have failed as parents. They then have to cope with rules and restrictions in contact, rules put in place because they are perceived to be a risk to their child.

To summarise, for everyone involved in the contact there are a number of needs or challenges:

- building and sustaining relationships;
- understanding one's role and the role of others;
- making sense of family boundaries;
- coping with the strangeness of the event;
- dealing with complex feelings.

People's experiences of contact: the balance of challenges and benefits

All contact arrangements appeared to involve a level of challenge, and in all cases some level of benefit was apparent. But the balance between these two sets of factors was very different in different cases. In some situations, many benefits were experienced with few challenges. In other cases, the challenges were many and the benefits few. The majority of people were somewhere in between these two positions with, in most cases, the balance tipped in favour of benefits.

As reported in Chapter 7, in our adoptive parent sample we categorised contact arrangements into two groups – "working very well" and "unresolved issues and concerns". The former group included only cases where, at least from the adoptive parent's perspective, there were no significant issues. Over four out of ten cases (42%) were categorised as "working very well". All remaining cases were classed as having "unresolved issues and concerns". In some of these cases, the issues and concerns were relatively minor and, overall, adoptive parents were much more positive than negative about the contact arrangements. Often concerns were practical or logistical, or to do with the adoptive parents themselves, as opposed to a negative impact on the child. This is why we did not choose to describe this second category as "contact not working" because, on balance, many cases in this group were working at a level at which adoptive parents felt quite happy to continue with the arrangement. They felt the benefits outweighed the challenges.

The group where contact had "unresolved issues" did, however, contain some cases that were quite worrying. This group included five cases where contact had stopped owing to concerns about the impact on the child, but also a small number where contact was continuing but it was unclear to the adoptive parent, and sometimes to the research team, whether the benefits were indeed outweighing the challenges, particularly in terms of the impact on the child. An important role for contact support services is to work with adoptive parents to keep under review this balance of challenges and benefits, helping adoptive parents to ensure that the child's welfare is protected.

The benefits of contact felt by adoptive parents were different from case to case but three particular themes were evident; each were mentioned by at least half of all adoptive parents. First, adoptive parents highlighted the contribution contact could make to their child's identity development. Second, they saw the value to the child of being allowed to continue birth family relationships, and they felt it an advantage that the child's loss did not have to be total. Third, parents felt that contact benefited their relationship with the child, confirming them in their status as the psychological parent and creating an atmosphere of openness and trust within the family.

Over half of the birth relatives (53%) were mainly satisfied with contact. They emphasised the reassurance that contact afforded them about the child's well-being, and they hoped and believed that through contact the child would know their birth family still cared. Eighteen per cent of birth relatives expressed an equal number of satisfactions and dissatisfactions about contact, and 29 per cent expressed more dissatisfactions than satisfactions. Despite the fact that a significant minority of birth relatives (47%) were either mixed or dissatisfied with contact, all birth relatives were happy to be able to see and spend some time with the adopted child or children; hence, they felt the benefits of contact outweighed the negatives. Some of the reasons why birth relatives were unhappy with contact were about dealing with issues of loss or role change. Others were to do with the nature of the contact event and birth relatives' feelings that they had little say over arrangements, that they were seen as a risk not a resource and that their behaviour needed to be monitored and controlled. Thus, birth relatives' satisfaction with contact overlapped greatly with their satisfaction with contact support. If birth relatives are unhappy with contact arrangements, this may have an impact not only on them, but also on adoptive parents and children.

Understanding how case factors impact on contact

In this research we explored the case factors that might determine how well contact works out from the perspective of adoptive parents and birth relatives. The strengths and risks that we looked at in the adoptive parent sample were: whether or not the child had emotional or behavioural problems; whether or not the adoptive parent and the child had a positive and unproblematic relationship; whether or not, based on parent report, the child had complex feelings about adoption; whether or not the child was under two when placed with the adoptive family; and whether or not the child was having contact with the birth relative who had been their main carer and been involved in neglecting or abusing them. We also looked at whether the adoption communication openness of adoptive parents predicted whether contact was working very well. In the birth relative sample we examined: whether or not the birth relative had clinically significant mental health problems; whether or not the birth relative had been the main carer for the child and been involved in their abuse or neglect; and the extent to which the birth relative was coping well with adoption. Drawing on these quantitative findings (see Chapters 7 and 9), and the qualitative data about people's experiences of contact (reported in Chapters 8 and 10), a relatively clear picture emerges about the cases in which contact has a good chance of being viewed positively by adoptive parents and birth relatives, and the cases where there are likely to be challenges and a greater need for support services. These are summarised below.

Factors contributing to contact that was viewed positively by adults

- There is a commitment to contact on all sides, a positive attitude and an awareness of the benefits.
- There is a clear connection between the child and birth relative in the

presence of an equally strong attachment to the adoptive family.

- There is acceptance on the part of birth relatives of the child's adoption and their changed role in the life of the child.
- There are good enough relationships between the adoptive parents and birth relatives.
- There is a consensus among birth relatives and adoptive parents about what is in the child's best interests.
- Efforts are made by birth relatives and adoptive parents to demonstrate that they value the other's role in the child's life.
- The child is developing well.

Factors contributing to contact that was viewed by adults as problematic

- There is poor adjustment to the adoption and poor acceptance of dual connection by birth relatives.
- There is poor commitment to contact or a negative attitude to it by either birth relatives or adoptive parents.
- There is a lack of connection evident between the child and birth relative or a fear of loss of connection resulting from the structure or process of contact (infrequent, highly formal).
- There is a poor relationship between the child and adopters.
- The child is struggling to cope with emotional or behavioural issues.
- The contact includes a birth relative who neglected or abused the child.
- There are poor relationships between the adoptive parents and birth relatives.
- There are unresolved and competing needs.
- There is poor communication or a lack of clarity about expectations, rules and the rationale for these.
- There are high levels of emotional distress in one or more of the parties.

These findings could potentially inform the development of services to support contact. They suggest that both adults and children may need individual help with aspects of their adjustment, e.g. to understand and deal with their own feelings and to understand their relationship to other people in the adoption kinship network. A picture of contact not as an event but as an evolving network of relationships emerges, suggesting that work between people to help understand and negotiate these relationships could be indicated. The structure of post-adoption contact arrangements needs to be appropriately matched to the levels of risk inherent in each case. A clear understanding of boundaries is likely to be necessary in every case, and in some situations it will be important to adhere firmly to certain restrictions. This may be especially true when the birth relative involved in contact has, in the past, neglected or abused the child, and careful thought is needed about who in the birth family can offer most to the adopted child through contact (see also Wilson and Sinclair, 2004; Wade *et al*, 2010). Contact should be regularly reviewed. If it does not appear to be working well, work should be undertaken with all parties to assess whether and how the difficulties could be overcome. Finally, an important role of contact support services should be to monitor the balance of challenges and benefits to ensure that, where problems are insurmountable, contact that is not in children's best interests is not allowed to continue. In cases such as these, services should be provided to support all parties in the process and aftermath of stopping contact.

What are people's experiences of contact support services?

Almost all adoptive parents and birth relatives who took part in the study had used some contact support services. From people's self-reports, we coded support services in terms of their function. The functions served by contact support services appear largely to match the needs for support that we have summarised above, although by no means everyone felt that all of these needs were met.

Managing emotions

The emotional challenges of contact are experienced differently by different people. Contact support services must recognise that contact can have an emotional impact on children, adoptive parents and birth relatives: a contact support service must be more than just an administrative venture. Professionals' accounts of how they would respond to a fictional case suggest that workers give high priority to the child's emotional needs (Neil, 2007c). It is less clear that the emotional impact of contact on adults is always recognised. This was suggested in the case vignette study (Neil, 2007c) and it also appeared to be the case for some of our interviewees. About one-quarter of adoptive parents were receiving emotional support. For birth relatives, 40 per cent felt they received emotional support at Time 1, but only 23 per cent at Time 2. Although not all service users will require emotional support from the contact support service (many people will have their needs met elsewhere), some adoptive parents and birth relatives clearly had unmet needs. It seems essential, therefore, that support providers consider the emotional impact of contact on children and adults, and that they provide opportunities to allow these feelings to be expressed and managed. For both adoptive parents and birth relatives the opportunity to form a relationship with the person supporting contact was valued. A named worker who was easy to contact and responsive, who understood adoption-related issues and who had the personal qualities of warmth and empathy helped people to make sense of their own emotions. Detailed advice about offering emotional support to children and adults before and after contact is provided by Bond (2007).

Building and maintaining relationships

Post-adoption contact is a relationship-based experience, as has been noted by a number of authors (e.g. Logan and Smith, 2004; Beek and Schofield, 2004; Neil and Howe, 2004; Grotevant, 2009), and this research reinforces that message. Our case vignette analysis (Neil, 2007c) highlighted that few contact support professionals thought about support in terms of working jointly with adoptive parents and birth relatives. Actively attempting to build a shared understanding of the goals of contact, establishing collaborative relationships – a sense of working together to make contact better – was not a feature of many contact support arrangements that we studied. Where such work was undertaken, however, it was highly valued. There were few opportunities for adults to meet together without children being present. Reviews of contact were only held in a minority of cases (at Time 1, 43% of the adopters and 29% of birth relatives reported receiving "reviewing and planning" support) and reviews were often informal, unilateral or carried out with each party separately. For both birth relatives and adoptive parents, relationship-building support was reported by less than one-quarter. Our research suggests that a focus on relationship building would be a useful constit-uent of many contact support plans. In some cases, it might be that the child and the birth relatives need help in relating to each other, and in other cases it is the adults who will need such support.

Grotevant (2009, p 295) argues that adoptive parents and birth relatives need to find a 'mutually agreeable degree of closeness in their relationships', a process he refers to as 'emotional distance regulation'. He argues that a family systems perspective can be useful. He concludes that adoptive parents and birth relatives may need help to consider themselves part of a broader adoption kinship network and recommends that they are taught skills and strategies to help them negotiate emotional distance regulation. These strategies might include birth relatives and adoptive parents working together to present the same messages to the child and recognising each other's different but unique contributions to him or her. Grotevant also argues that people may need help with negotiating the boundaries of their relationship.

Negotiating and managing risk

Themes related to how risks were managed, and to the rules and bound-aries of contact, were apparent in the reports of both adoptive parents and birth relatives, although the experiences of these two groups were quite different. At Time 1, two-thirds of adoptive parents reported receiving services that protected or promoted their interests or the interests of their child. Such services included the supervision of contact meetings and the management of risks and boundaries. In contrast, at Time 1 only 11 per cent of birth relatives felt their interests were protected or promoted by the support agency. Almost three times that many (32%) reported being on the receiving end of interventions that had the function of managing or minimising risks which, it was perceived, they presented to the child or adopters. Adoptive parents were concerned that contact should not impact negatively on the child, and they frequently highlighted risk and boundaries issues. Birth relatives were often uncomfortably aware that they were perceived to be a risk to the child.

While many adoptive parents felt rules and boundaries were necessary to protect their confidentiality, or to protect the feelings or physical safety of the child, risk was not perceived in the same way by all adoptive parents. Some were very worried about the risk of siblings exchanging information with each other in contact. Other adoptive parents accepted that it was inevitable that brothers and sisters would talk to each other about their schools and their home town, and that they would wish to exchange mobile phone numbers. They might even have seen these exchanges of information as benefiting the sibling relationship. Some adoptive parents appreciated the help of agencies in managing risks. Others felt able to exercise this control themselves. In some cases, the accounts of adoptive parents reinforced the views of some birth relatives that the approach of agencies towards relatives might be unnecessarily restrictive or heavy handed. Help for birth and adoptive families to reach agreement about what risks there are in contact, and how they might best be managed, would seem to be an essential component of contact support services. Certain people may need structured and controlled arrangements in the beginning but over time, as trust develops, these can be relaxed. The role that support workers play during meetings needs careful consideration. Managing risk and boundaries may be a necessary part of this role, but should not be the only function. As Bond (2007, p 59) argues:

> *Good supervision during contact is open and supportive and aims to facilitate rather than to control or direct, but is ready to intervene when issues occur and help participants to breed solutions.*

Offering practical help

People may need help with the provision of appropriate venues, help with transport, help with the financial cost of contact, or practical assistance in co-ordinating times and dates of meetings. These considerations, if not attended to, add to the stress of contact. A number of sibling group contacts were included in the study. The practical issues involved in simply getting together children from several different families at a time and place that suited everyone were often immense, and it could be unclear who was in charge of these practicalities. Some practical problems were especially concerning to birth relatives who had physical and mental health problems, who lacked confidence using public transport or were on a low income. Practical and administrative services are therefore a necessary, although not in many cases sufficient, aspect of contact support.

What works in supporting contact?

Matching services to the needs of families – an individualised approach

Service users were most happy with their contact support if it met their needs and was attuned to their circumstances. Some families required very little from support agencies – they preferred to undertake most of the work of contact themselves, and had the capacity to do so. Other families both wanted and needed more intensive services, and they highly praised agencies' responses to their needs. But about half of both adoptive parents and birth relatives had a number of dissatisfactions with the support they received. Some families had unmet needs; others felt they had services they did not require or had the wrong services.

Our research identified four different models of contact support. There did not appear to be one that was right for everyone, and each model seemed to work for some people. The four models were generated by looking at two different dimensions. The first dimension was whether a worker attended the contact meeting (i.e. the contact was supervised). The second was whether one of three proactive interventions were provided: emotional support, relationship building and review and planning. We would argue that in all post-adoption direct contact cases, the contact scenario is likely to engender an emotional response in participants, that relationship building will be a necessary task, and that the arrangement ought to be appropriately planned, monitored and reviewed. However, there may be cases where adoptive families and birth relatives are capable of managing some or all of these tasks themselves. Therefore, when deciding which model of contact support is appropriate, it will be necessary to consider the ability and willingness of families to manage these aspects of contact themselves. Below, we discuss the different models of support and when they may or may not be useful.

In the first model, *administrated contact*, the agency retained control of setting up contact meetings, but did not attend these or facilitate contact by offering parties emotional support, relationship building or review and planning. For both birth relatives and adoptive parents, this model of contact support delivered the fewest number of services over the year (an average of five for adoptive parents and three for birth relatives). In both the adoptive parent and the birth relative sample this was also the cheapest model of support, costing on average £395 for adoptive families and £246 for birth families. In the adoptive parent sample, in almost two-thirds of cases this model was used in relation to sibling contact. When adoptive parents received this model of support, contact was working very well in half of the cases, the highest proportion of any of the four models. In the birth relative sample, 100 per cent of people receiving this model were satisfied with contact. Levels of satisfaction with *support for* contact, however, were low in both the adoptive parent and the birth relative samples. In each case under a third of service users were happy with their contact support: the majority of people felt they had unmet needs.

This model of support is only appropriate in cases where it has been assessed that either the birth relatives present no risks to the child during contact, or that any risks that may be presented can appropriately be recognised and managed by the adoptive parents. The model is also only appropriate where both the adoptive parents and birth relatives involved can manage their own, and the child's, emotional responses to contact without the need for support from the contact support service. In some cases, adoptive parents and birth relatives (or the two or more sets of adoptive parents/foster carers in sibling contact arrangements) can manage emotional issues by themselves. In other cases, they will have resources in their personal network to help them manage these issues. Some birth relatives may have other professionals involved in their lives who are well placed to support them in dealing with the emotional impact of contact; for instance, mental health workers, learning disability support workers, or specialist birth relative support providers.

If the families involved can manage the risks of contact, the emotional demands, and the relationships involved, the question is raised as to whether there is any role for the agency at all. What agencies can offer in the administrated contact model is a means for adoptive parents to keep their identifying details confidential. No matter how well the adults engaged in contact get along, there are still likely to be situations where adoptive parents do not wish to exchange identifying details with birth relatives (or with the carers of siblings), and therefore a third party is needed to help make the arrangements. There may be some situations where administrated contact may be used as a stepping stone to help families move towards self-managing arrangements. Some families may require the cushion of quite minimal agency involvement for a year or two, until trust is firmly established. Other families may want this type of support service in the longer term because it gives them the reassurance of having a third party involved. Families may value the service because of the practical expediency of having somebody else to remember that contact is due, and to remind people to make the arrangement. This may be particularly important for people with busy lives. Overall, therefore, the type of cases for which this support model is appropriate is likely to be very similar to that where families can manage the contact themselves. They may be working towards reaching this position, or may need this fairly low level of support over a number of years.

The second model, *facilitated contact*, was where families met without the support worker but the agency was intervening outside of the contact meeting to provide emotional support, relationship building or contact planning and review. In both adoptive parent and birth relative samples, the costs of this model of support were the second lowest (£734 for adoptive parents and £536 for birth relatives). This model was mainly used to support sibling contact (63% of cases in the adoptive parent sample). In the adoptive parent sample, contact was considered to be working very well in only one in four cases. This is in contrast to the birth relative sample where 100 per cent of birth relatives were satisfied with contact. Satisfaction with contact support, however, was very high in both samples; all birth relatives were happy with this model of support, as were 83 per cent of adoptive parents.

Like the previous model, facilitated contact does not involve any worker supervision of meetings so the provisos about risk management outlined above also apply. Families utilising this model of support need to have sufficient strengths and resources to deal with issues that might arise on the day of the meeting. Facilitated contact support, however, enables the agency to help families with some of the complexities of contact outside the actual contact event. There may be arrangements that do not involve any great risks (e.g. contact between two siblings in different adoptive families, or with a grandparent who has not been involved in the ill-treatment of the child), but where contact is practically or emotionally challenging, or where the different families involved have different expectations of the contact. For some families, contact may generally run smoothly but because children grow and change there is a need to keep it under review.

The third model, *supervised and facilitated contact*, involved the most intensive input of services. Support workers attended contact meetings and provided input aimed at relationship building, reviewing and planning or emotional or therapeutic support. In both samples, this model of contact support provided the highest number of services per year (16 for adoptive parents and 11 for birth relatives). In the adoptive parent sample, this model was clearly the most expensive (costing £1,371 on average). However, in the birth relative sample the average costs (£960 per year) were very similar to the expense of supervised contact. From the adoptive parent sample, it can be seen that this model was used mainly to support contact involving one or more adult birth relatives; it was only used to support sibling contact in a small minority of cases (15%). Contact was working very well for almost half (48%) of adoptive families receiving this model of support, but looking at the birth relative sample only about a quarter (27%) were satisfied with contact itself. Over half (56%) of birth relatives were satisfied with this model of contact support (the second highest proportion of satisfied people of the four groups) and two-thirds of adoptive parents (69%).

This model is likely to be the most appropriate in cases where either a number of risk factors are present (or even one risk factor which is very concerning) and/or where the strengths of adoptive parents or birth relatives are low. It may also be appropriate in cases where there are no particular concerns about the risks to the child during contact, but where one or more of the parties require emotional support during the meeting. For example, it might be that the child feels more comfortable having a trusted social worker at the meeting, or that a birth mother with learning difficulties or who is depressed needs the supportive presence of a professional. In other cases, adoptive parents may get on well with birth relatives and not be worried about any risks for the child, but contact can still raise a lot of emotions that are easier to cope with if a third party is present. Some adoptive parents may feel able to manage the contact meeting themselves, for instance, managing boundaries and risks, but nevertheless prefer to be freed from the responsibility of having to do so. They may feel more able to focus on the child's needs when they are sure someone is there for the birth relative, or they may feel their relationship with the birth relative will be improved if someone else reinforces the boundaries. In cases where there are a number of risk factors, but where contact is considered nevertheless to be in the child's best interests, the supervised and facilitated model of support can allow agencies to try and build strengths, monitor and reduce risks, and keep the arrangement under review to ensure that the challenges and benefits of contact do not tip too far in favour of the former. This model of support was the most commonly used in both adoptive parent and birth relative samples. This reflects the complexity of cases in the sample and suggests that many support workers and agencies already recognise and provide the help people need. Some families may need this model of contact for several years. Others may require it just for an initial period as they move towards unsupervised meetings.

The fourth model, *supervised contact*, was where the agency arranged and supervised the contact but did not actively facilitate its working; they exercised control, but made little contribution to managing the dynamics of contact. Adoptive parents receiving this model had, on average, nine services per year, and birth relatives had 11. In the birth relative sample this model of support was the most expensive (£1,004 per year on average) and in the adoptive parent sample it was the second most expensive (£776 per year on average). This model was used mainly for contact involving adult birth relatives (only 11% of cases involved sibling-only contact in the adoptive parent sample). Satisfaction with it was very low in both adoptive parent and birth relative samples (25% were satisfied in the former and 12% in the latter). Where adoptive families had this model of support, contact was working well in one in three cases. In the birth relative sample, less than one in five birth relatives (17%) were satisfied with contact.

The outcomes of this model of contact support seem to compare less favourably to the other models, although we did not systematically compare them and a larger sample would be required to do this. It makes sense, however, that people are unlikely to be happy with contact support where the agency's role is to monitor but not to support, and clearly the majority of adoptive parents and birth relatives in the study felt this was the case. In what circumstances, therefore, might this model be appropriate? Some people in the study did value having a worker at contact meetings purely to be in the background, to be called upon if needed or to mark the beginning and ending of sessions. They did not particularly want this person to intervene much during the meeting. Just being there was enough. There may be cases, therefore, where birth relatives and adoptive parents do not require emotional support from the agency either during or outside meetings, where they can handle the dynamics of their relationship without professional support, where they can undertake the review and planning arrangements themselves, where adoptive parents can manage the risks and boundaries of the arrangement, but where a third party in the background is considered helpful. In most cases, however, we would suggest that if agencies consider that contact is sufficiently complex to require supervision, it will almost certainly require reviewing and planning, and people may require emotional support or help with relationship building.

Involving families in assessment
As outlined in the literature review, adoptive parents and birth relatives are often not involved in the initial plans for post-adoption contact and the arrangements may be imposed upon them rather than being decided by them. We suggest that it may be useful for contact support providers (often these will be located in the post-adoption team) to be included at

the pre-adoption stage, where their role would be to involve children (where their age and understanding allows), adoptive parents (once they have been identified) and birth relatives in the process of both contact planning and the planning of contact support. Ideally, support for contact and the resources required for this should be specified in the adoption support plan. Where it is not possible to involve families in these early discussions, the contact plan will be largely driven by the local authority which is placing the child. However, although the contact plan may be outlined, exactly how it should take place and the agency role in supporting it need to be discussed when the court proceedings are over. The resources required to support contact also ought to be discussed at an early stage. Early attention to the detail of contact plans and plans for contact support may be important in getting contact arrangements off to a good start. It may prevent problems arising, such as misunderstandings about the frequency of contact, the exchange of presents, the suitability of particular venues or names to be used during meetings.

Meeting the needs of all parties

Many adoptive parents whom we interviewed recognised the support needs of birth relatives and felt it was important that these were met. Similarly, birth relatives recognised that contact might be difficult for children and adoptive parents, and that if these needs were not met contact might not work well. It is important that contact support addresses the needs of all involved. Those of the child must remain the central focus, but if contact does not work for the adults it will not work for the child. A number of accounts demonstrated how professionals were able to manage the diverse, and sometimes competing, needs of all involved in contact without appearing to be on any one person's side. Workers' skills, experience, attitudes and values enabled this sophisticated work to take place. In other cases, support for one or more of the parties was lacking. Sometimes agencies appeared to have a negative opinion about the value of contact, or a pessimistic view of what birth families might have to offer. Both adoptive parents and, more commonly, birth relatives may have had difficult experiences with local authorities in the past (Charlton et al, 1998; Neil et al, 2010). Often, the introduction of a new worker from the post-adoption team offered a fresh start and constructive relationships were built.

There were a few cases in our study where people received contact support from the independent sector, and where this was the case people appeared to value a new and independent view on the situation. In our parallel study, "Helping birth families", where we investigated the role of independent support services for birth relatives (Neil *et al*, 2010), we highlighted the potential of these services to help birth relatives engage constructively in contact arrangements. Birth relatives needed help with contact after adoption, but too often they had been excluded, or had excluded themselves, from arrangements to plan contact in the pre-adoption stage. Very few birth relatives in the current study had even heard about, let alone used, independent support services. This reflects the fact that in most cases we followed up people several years after the adoption, and independent services for birth relatives are a relatively recent innovation. There may be a much more significant role that these independent support agencies could play in representing or directly meeting the support needs of birth relatives in relation to direct contact.

Recognising the dynamic nature of contact

Both adoptive parents and birth relatives identified the different ways that contact could change over time. Children grow and change. Some children wanted to see less of their birth family members as they grew closer to their adoptive parents. Others became more concerned with their friendships and activities as they moved into their teenage years, while some became more interested in their birth family members. Adoptive parents' and birth relatives' own feelings and views about contact were dynamic and transactional. Some birth relatives started off feeling hostile towards adoptive parents but over time grew to accept and like them. Some adoptive parents felt that contact was very difficult in the early days of placement when their relationship with the child was not yet established firmly. A couple of years later, they felt much more open and relaxed. People entered and left the adoption kinship network. Birth siblings were born, adoptive siblings arrived. Birth relatives could go missing. "Life", with all its unpredictability, moved on. All these changes could have an impact on contact and a chance to review plans was helpful and welcomed. Both birth relatives and adoptive parents seemed to appreciate regular reviews, even if they were quite low key, as opposed to having to initiate the process.

People's needs for contact support are also likely to change over time. Some contact arrangements may need less support as adoptive parents feel more confident, children feel more secure in their new family, and trust builds between parties. Some adoptive families could be encouraged to consider whether they might prefer to move to a facilitated model of support, as opposed to supervised and facilitated. Contact arrangements which are supervised are likely, in most cases, to cost more than those which are not. Saving money should never be the main reason to stop supervising contact but neither, where resources are scarce, should services that are no longer needed continue to be provided simply because of a lack of review. Sometimes more resources may need to be put in as the situation changes. For example, several adoptive parents in our study said their children found it difficult when their birth mother had another baby. There may be times such as this in adopted children's lives when they might benefit from extra support, or where their adoptive parents or birth relatives might need extra advice.

Supporting the termination of contact

We have mentioned several times in this report that a legitimate role of contact support providers is to assist adoptive parents, where necessary, to keep the balance of challenges and benefits in contact under review, especially in high-risk cases. There will be situations where direct contact with birth relatives is attempted but is later assessed as not in the best interests of the child, and some of these cases were included in our study. Where terminating direct contact is necessary, we would suggest that the role of the support agency ought not to end there, though sadly it did for several people in the study. Where children, adoptive parents and birth relatives have had unsatisfactory experiences of contact, they are likely to need help to make sense of what has happened. The ending of contact will probably give rise to a range of feelings, maybe relief but also possibly guilt, anger or a sense of loss. Birth relatives who have been told that contact must stop because the child has been so troubled by it are likely to feel quite anxious about how their child is getting on. The need for support after ending direct contact is therefore indicated. The support agency may also have an important role to play in facilitating alternative arrangements to meet the child's needs, for instance, letterbox contact or life story work with the child. The decision to cease contact may also need to be kept under review, as in the future it may be in the child's best interests to re-start meetings.

Evaluation of the project and suggestions for future research

The strengths of this research are that we have collected data from a number of key informants. Service providers were included in the mapping stage of the project and the economic analysis. Adoptive parents and a broad range of birth relatives, including young adult siblings, have contributed their views. The recruitment and retention of service users into the study was very successful. We have collected a broad range of qualitative and quantitative data and have been able to compare and contrast these. We succeeded in our aim to develop distinct service typologies from service users' reports, and four different models of contact support were outlined. These models could be applied in future research to conduct a more systematic comparative examination of the outcomes of contact and contact support. This study is the first to have systematically attempted to cost the provision of face-to-face post-adoption contact support services, and this was achieved through the excellent return of data from agencies offering support services to the adoptive parents and birth relatives who took part.

The study succeeded in gathering and analysing birth relatives' and adoptive parents' experiences of contact arrangements and their views about the services they received to support contact. This provided an account of "what works" in contact support that focused on the perspectives of adoptive parents and birth relatives, which can be used by service providers in shaping future services.

We successfully involved adoptive parents and birth relatives in the research process at three stages: the planning of data collection and recruitment; data analysis; and understanding implications for practice. We used innovative methods for involving service users and this project is an example of collaborative research (Hanley, 2003).

There are a number of limitations of this research, which future projects may seek to address. Our cost analysis employed published unit costs representative of the social work system in 2007 (Curtis, 2007). These unit costs were estimated from much earlier work that attempted to cost childcare provision (Knapp *et al*, 1984). The methodology of estimating unit costs is complex (see Beecham, 2000), and new research has recently come to light suggesting that the previous estimate of overheads (e.g. running costs, personnel and management costs, and building costs – i.e. costs that cannot be attributed to any one case) was an underestimate (Selwyn *et al*, 2009). Therefore, the costs presented in this report are likely to also underestimate the true cost of providing contact support services; the absolute differences (between adoptive parents and birth relatives and between service typologies and risk groups) will, however, remain.

This research project does not represent directly the views of adopted children and young people about their experiences of contact with birth relatives, or of contact support services. The views of children and young people may differ from those of their adoptive parents or birth relatives, and further qualitative research with adopted children and young people is needed. In addition, the adoptive parent interview sample consisted mainly of adoptive mothers. There is some evidence that adoptive fathers may feel less positive about post-adoption contact than adoptive mothers (Selwyn, 2004), and it would be helpful to include fathers' perspectives more thoroughly in future research.

This research is exploratory and the sample size did not allow for a systematic evaluation of the comparative benefits of different models of contact support. Any such investigation would need to take account of whether the families using different types of support services had different strengths and risks, as these have been shown to be related to how contact works out. In investigating the outcomes of contact in relation to the contact support services provided, an important outcome to be included in any such research is the child or young person's perception of contact. This study focused, in the overwhelming majority of cases, on contact support services provided by local authorities, and the mapping stage of our project indicated that this is the norm. A small number of families in our project used specialist contact support services provided from the independent sector, but we have not compared such specialist services with mainstream provision. Future research may wish to address this gap.

Summary

This chapter draws together and discusses findings from across the report. It also evaluates the study's strengths and limitations. Key points are as follows:

- The aims of this study were to explore services provided to support direct post-adoption contact. Fifty-one adoptive parents, four foster carers and 39 birth relative took part. Economic data were collected from caseworkers over a one-year period.

- Direct post-adoption contact is complex in different ways in different cases, but a number of key needs or challenges for people involved in having such contact emerged. These include building and sustaining relationships, understanding one's role and the role of others, making sense of family boundaries, coping with the strangeness of the event and dealing with complex feelings.

- All contact arrangements appear to involve some level of challenge, but in every case some level of benefit was apparent. The balance between these two sets of factors was very different in different cases.

- How well contact arrangements progressed seem to be influenced by a number of factors to do with the child, adoptive parents, the birth relatives and the relationships between them. Taking account of these strengths and risk factors when planning contact and contact support is likely to lead to more case-sensitive decision-making.

- Important roles that contact support services can play include helping people manage emotions, building and maintaining relationships between people, negotiating and managing risk, and offering practical help.

- Suggestions for the provision of contact support services include:
  - ensuring that the model of contact support is matched appropriately to the needs and wishes of families and the strengths and risks in the case;
  - including families in the assessment of contact plans and contact support plans;
  - ensuring that attention is paid to the needs of all parties;
  - recognising the dynamic nature of contact;
  - where it is necessary for direct contact to be stopped, seeing that people are supported through and after this process.
- Strengths of the research include:
  - data were collected from a number of key informants: adoptive parents, birth relatives and service providers. The retention of service users over the follow-up period was exceptionally high, as was the return of data from caseworkers;
  - distinct models of contact support were identified and costed;
  - adoptive parents and birth relatives were successfully involved as consultants to the research process.
- Limitations of the research include:
  - the unit costs employed on the project may underestimate the true cost of contact support;
  - the views of adopted children and young people were not included;
  - the research did not include contact support provided by specialist services in the independent sector.
- Future research could build on the current study by systematically evaluating the comparative benefits of the different models of contact support identified in this study. A much larger sample size would be needed to take account of all the relevant factors. It will be important in any such research where the outcomes of contact are to be studied, that the views of adopted children and young people are sought.

17 Service users' suggestions for practice

In this final chapter, we wish to present the suggestions for practitioners that were generated by our groups of birth relative and adoptive parent consultants. During these group meetings, we presented the key themes from our data about the challenges of contact for all parties, and we invited adoptive parents and birth relatives to contribute their suggestions for addressing these issues. We would like to give the last word in this report to our service-user consultants, by ending with their suggestions for practice.

Values and principles
- The overall aim of services should be to enable, facilitate and empower all involved to make contact work for them.
- Support providers should respect the personal knowledge that adoptive parents and birth relatives have – not override this with their own expertise.
- It may be better if the support worker involved in contact is not a social worker – or at least not the social worker involved in the adoption of the child, but someone independent. Perhaps a charitable and completely independent organisation should lead a service for managing and supporting contact arrangements.
- All parties should be helped to focus on the positives that contact can bring – what good can the sharing of information and meeting each other bring about? What do the adoptive parents and children want to know about birth relatives that will help them? In turn, what does the birth relative want to know about the child that will help them?

The role of support workers
- Education for social workers is needed to ensure they hear and understand the views of birth families.
- All parties should make clear what they would like from the worker.

- The role of the worker should be clearly defined but flexible, to fit in with the requirements of each case.
- The worker should be adequately skilled and trained. They need to be attuned to what is occurring in contact for all parties and what is needed.
- Social workers should use language that is understood by everyone.
- If at all possible, there should be consistency of worker.
- Individuals need to have the opportunity to change worker if necessary.
- People should be able to opt out of support if they feel they don't need it.
- Birth parents could have a mentor or advocate to ensure they have a say.

Planning contact

- Preparation of adopters prior to adoption should make it clear that adoptive parents need to accept or take on the child's birth family to some extent. Adopters must be prepared from the beginning to see contact as important. Workshops and meetings with birth relatives/ adult adoptees should be used to help them experience contact from different perspectives.
- Adoptive parents' attitudes about contact need to be taken into account before deciding whether they are right for the child. The ability of parties to work together at the matching stage also ought to be considered. There has to be a positive working relationship between adults.
- Adoptive parents need to feel they have choice over contact.
- Prior to the adoption, the child, if old enough, could write down how they feel about contact in a book for the adoptive parents.
- Older children should be enabled to have contact without their adoptive parents if they wish.
- Birth parents have to be supported to accept the adoptive parents as part of their extended family. They need help to have empathy for adoptive parents. Birth relatives who cannot accept the child's adoption need special help so they can understand how the children will be feeling.

- Birth relatives should have plenty of support and preparation focusing on contact and what it means for the adopters and child. They need help to understand the benefits of good contact for all, and their own continuing importance in the children's life.
- Extra support needs should be provided when birth parents have other children. Birth parents will need advice on how to explain the adoption of a sibling to the child they are parenting.
- As contact comes at the end of a lengthy legal process – starting with care proceedings and leading to adoption – preparation is vital from the outset to ensure a successful outcome in contact arrangements. If emotions and difficulties are not dealt with properly from the start, problems over contact may well ensue.
- Ensure birth relatives and adopters meet together at least once prior to the adoption to make sure they can work together. Arrange a meeting for all adults with the contact support worker to talk through everyone's wishes and needs for contact. Think, 'What is the aim of contact? How can we all make it positive in this particular case?'
- Each party involved in contact could have their own person to listen to them and support them.
- A clear and long-term plan for support and resources for contact should be made at the time of adoption. Contact needs should be adequately resourced.
- Adoptive parents should not have to suffer financially because of contact.
- Mid-week contact can be a burden for adoptive families who often need to use up valuable holiday time. Contact needs to be resourced to enable support workers and supervisors to work at weekends.

Making contact meetings positive
- Prior to each contact there should be a call or visit from a support worker to find out what is going on for the individuals who are to meet. They can provide advice for the contact session and feedback from the other party, so all are prepared for each other and any issues/questions that may come up.
- On the morning of a contact meeting, birth relatives could receive a phone call from a fellow birth parent supporter.

- There should be support for birth parents to prepare for contact, with opportunities to think through things that may be done or said and questions that may be asked of them.
- Help adopters to get to know the birth relative, such as by telling them about their hobbies or interests. They can then use contact time productively to engage with the birth relative and help the child to get to know them.
- Adoptive parents need to be told what the birth relative is keen to know about the child, so that they know what to bring and share with them.
- Ensure contact is at a neutral venue – not the same place where the assessments were carried out.
- Adoptive parents need to be told the full facts of the case and given explanations for suggested boundaries and rules around contact.
- Don't make blanket rules but think about what is helpful in each particular case. Explain any rules clearly to all parties.
- Emergency contact numbers should be exchanged so that all can contact the other party (via an intermediary if necessary) in case of last-minute problems on the day of contact. A mobile phone could be allocated with this as its sole purpose.
- Be creative – venues and activities could be chosen to fit in with both child and birth relatives' hobbies and interests – an art gallery? A football match? Plan to do something constructive – where siblings can engage with each other and play together.
- Sometimes contact should focus on the real issues that are going on for the children and their families. Games and activities or drama can be used to help children explore what is happening for them.
- Sometimes it may be useful to do life story work in contact meetings – the child can suggest gaps they would like filled in or periods of the birth relative or family's life they want to know more about. The birth relative could come with photos, old school reports or items related to current or past hobbies/talents. There could be "getting to know each other" sessions. There can be a huge advantage in children seeing the positive side of their birth family/genetic history.
- Look for a solution that suits all parties in areas such as present giving.

Dealing with emotions

- Group/peer support for birth relatives, adoptive parents and children should be available so people do not feel isolated and can learn from others who have been through similar experiences.
- Internet groups can provide additional support – particularly for sharing ideas about venues and other practical issues.
- Therapeutic support for children and adults should be available.
- Understand that saying goodbye for the birth relative is like losing their child all over again.
- Counselling or support should be available to children, adoptive parents and birth parents to help them deal with their feelings about the contact. Counselling or support ought to be available to the wider birth family members, even if they are not involved in the contact.
- The mental health of clients needs to be taken into account and where necessary cases taken up by counsellors with a working knowledge of mental illness. Mental health services should get funding to assist in providing this service.
- Adoptive parents need help to deal with the child's feelings and behaviour after contact. They should be encouraged to use the life story book and create opportunities for the child to talk through feelings.
- Youth and children's workers ought to be available after adoption to help children with contact. Ideally, older adoptees could help younger children.
- If the child has a bad reaction to contact, help everyone to understand this. Work through possible reasons and ways of helping the child and don't just assume contact should be stopped.
- Services need to be provided to children who cannot talk to their adopters. An anonymous helpline should be available.

Keeping contact going

- Review contact arrangements regularly to ensure they are still relevant, and so that new concerns can be discussed. Once contact is working well, the gaps between reviews can be lengthened.
- If something inappropriate has been said or done at contact, this needs

to be explained clearly and discussed, showing the reasons why it is inappropriate. Help birth relatives rather than stick rules on them.

- Provide good, full feedback after contact showing how all are feeling about the way things are going.
- After each contact, a questionnaire could pick up feelings about how it went – positives and negatives – from all parties.
- There should be a system so that anyone can report a problem or issue with contact, and mediators will help the parties deal with it together.
- There should be the assumption that regular adult-to-adult meetings will occur to deal with issues, build relationships and avoid suspicions/assumptions.

References

Achenbach T. M. and Rescorla L. A. (2001) *Manual for ASEBA School-Age Forms & Profiles*, Burlington, VT: University of Vermont, Research Center for Children, Youth & Families

Adoption Policy Review Group (2005) *Adoption: Better choices for our children. Adoption Policy Review Group Report of Phase II*, Edinburgh: Scottish Executive

After Adoption (2007) *Moving from the Sidelines: A study of the provision of independent support in Wales for the birth parents and relatives of children in the adoption process*, Cardiff: After Adoption

Atkinson A. and Gonet P. (2007) 'Strengthening adoption practice, listening to adoptive families', *Child Welfare*, 86:2, pp 87–104

Barth R. P. and Berry M. (1988) *Adoption and Disruption: Rates, risks and responses*, New York: Aldine de Gruyter

Beecham J. (2000) *Unit Costs — Not exactly child's play: A guide to estimating unit costs for children's social care*, Joint publication from Department of Health, Dartington Social Research Unit and Personal Social Services Research Unit, Canterbury: University of Kent,

Beek M. and Schofield G. (2004) 'Promoting security and managing risk: Contact in long-term foster care', in Neil E. and Howe D. (eds) *Contact in Adoption and Permanent Foster Care: Research, theory and practice*, London: BAAF

Berry M., Cavazos Dylla D. J., Barth R. P. and Needell B. (1998) 'The role of open adoption in the adjustment of adopted children and their families', *Children and Youth Services Review*, (1–2), pp 151–71

Bond H. (2007) *Top Ten Tips for Managing Contact*, London: BAAF

Bouchier P., Lambert L. and Triseliotis J. (1991) *Parting with a Child for Adoption: The mother's perspective*, London: BAAF

Bowlby J. (1988) *A Secure Base: Parent-child attachment and healthy human development*, New York: Basic Books

Boyatzis R. E. (1998) *Transferring Qualitative Information: Thematic analysis and code development*, Thousand Oaks, CA: Sage

Brodzinsky A. B. (1990) 'Surrendering an infant for adoption: the birth mother experience', in Brodzinsky D. M. and Schechter M. D. (eds) *The Psychology of Adoption*, New York: Oxford University Press

Brodzinsky D. (1987) 'Adjustment to adoption: a psychosocial perspective', *Clinical Psychology Review*, 7, pp 25–47

Brodzinsky D. (1990) 'A stress and coping model of adoption adjustment', in Brodzinsky D. M. and Schechter M. D. (eds) *The Psychology of Adoption*, New York: Oxford University Press

Brodzinsky D. (2005) 'Reconceptualizing openness in adoption: implications for theory, research and practice', in Brodzinsky D. and Palacios J. (eds) *Psychological Issues in Adoption: Research and practice*, New York: Greenwood

Brodzinsky D. (2006) 'Family structural openness and communication openness as predictors in the adjustment of adopted children', *Adoption Quarterly*, 9, pp 1–18

Brodzinsky D., Singer L. M. and Braff A. M. (1984) 'Children's understanding of adoption', *Child Development*, 55, pp 869–78

Brooks A., Allen J. and Barth R. P. (2002) 'Adoption service use, helpfulness, and need: a comparison of public and private agency and independent adoptive families', *Children and Youth Services Review*, 24:4, pp 213–38

Charlton L., Crank M., Kansara K. and Oliver C. (1998) *Still Screaming: Birth parents compulsorily separated from their children*, Manchester: After Adoption

Christian C. L., McRoy R. G., Grotevant H. D. and Bryant C. M. (1997) 'The grief resolution of birth mothers in confidential, time-limited mediated, ongoing mediated and fully disclosed adoptions', *Adoption Quarterly*, 1, pp 35–58

Coast J. (2004) 'Is economic evaluation in touch with society's health values?', *British Medical Journal*, 329 (7476), pp 1233–6

Crank M. (2002) 'Managing and valuing contact with contesting birth families', in Argent H. (ed.) *Staying Connected: Managing contact arrangements in adoption*, London: BAAF, pp 98–114

Curtis L. (2007) *The Unit Costs of Health and Social Care 2007*, Canterbury: Personal Social Services Research Unit

Cushman L. F., Kalmuss D. and Brickner Namerow P. (1997) 'Openness in adoption: experiences and psychological outcomes among birth mothers', *Marriage and Family Review*, 25, pp 7–18

Department for Children, Schools and Families (2009) *Statistical First Release: Children looked after in England, including adoption and care leavers, year ending 31 March 2009*, London: DCSF

Derogatis L. R. (1993) *BSI: Brief Symptom Inventory: Administration, scoring and procedures manual*, Minneapolis: National Computer Systems, Inc

Dozier M. and Rutter M. (2008) 'Challenges to the development of attachment relationships faced by young children in foster and adoptive care', in Cassidy J. and Shaver P. (eds) *Handbook of Attachment*, New York: Guilford Press

Drummond M., O'Brien B., Stoddart G. and Torrance G. (1997) *Methods for the Economic Evaluation of Health Care Programmes*, (2nd edition), New York: Oxford University Press

Egeland B., Sroufe L. A. and Erickson. M. (1983) 'The developmental consequence of different patterns of maltreatment', *Child Development*, 52, pp 44–52

Etter J. (1993) 'Levels of co-operation and satisfaction in 56 open adoptions', *Child Welfare*, 72, pp 257–67

Festinger T. (1986) *Necessary Risk – A study of adoptions and disrupted adoptive placements*, Washington: The Child Welfare League of America

Frasch K. M., Brooks D. and Barth R. (2000) 'Openness and contact in foster care adoptions: an eight-year follow up', *Family Relations*, 49, pp 435–46

Fratter J. (1996) *Adoption with Contact: Implications for policy and practice*, London: BAAF

Fratter J., Rowe J., Sapsford D. and Thoburn J. (1991) *Permanent Family Placement: A decade of experience*, London: BAAF

Freeman P. and Hunt J. (1998) *Parental Perspectives on Care Proceedings*, London: The Stationery Office

Ge X., Natsuaki M. N., Martin D. M., Leve L. D., Neiderhiser J. M., Shaw D. S., Villareal G., Scaramella L., Reid J. B. and Reiss D. (2008) 'Bridging the divide: openness in adoption and post-adoption psychosocial adjustment among birth and adoptive parents', *Journal of family Psychology*, 22:4, pp 529–40

George C. and Main M. (1979) 'Social interactions of young abused children: approach, avoidance and aggression', *Child Development*, 50, pp 306–18

Gross H. E. (1993) 'Open adoption: A research-based literature review and new data', *Child Welfare*, 72, pp 269–84

Grotevant H. D. (1997) 'Coming to terms with adoption: the construction of identity from adolescence into adulthood', *Adoption Quarterly*, 1, pp 3–27

Grotevant H. D. (2009) 'Emotional distance regulation over the life course in adoptive kinship networks', in Wrobel G. and Neil E. (eds) *International Advances in Adoption Research for Practice*, Chichester: Wiley

Grotevant H. D. and McRoy R. G. (1998) *Openness in Adoption: Exploring family connections*, Thousand Oaks, CA: Sage

Grotevant H. D., McRoy R. G. and Ayres-Lopez S. (2004) 'Contact in adoption: outcomes for infant placements in the USA', in Neil E. and Howe D. (eds) *Contact in Adoption and Permanent Foster Care: Research, theory and practice*, London: BAAF

Grotevant H. D., Perry Y. and McRoy R. G. (2005) 'Openness in adoption: outcomes for adolescents within their adoptive kinship networks', in Brodzinsky D. and Palacios J. (eds) *Psychological issues in adoption: research and practice*, New York: Greenwood

Grotevant H. D., Ross N. M., Marcel M. A. and McRoy R. G. (1999) 'Adaptive behaviour in adopted children: predictors from early risk, collaboration in relationships within the adoptive kinship network, and openness arrangements', *Journal of Adolescent Research*, 14, pp 231–47

Grotevant H. D., Wrobel G. M., Von Korff L., Skinner B., Newell J., Friese S. *et al* (2008) 'Many faces of openness in adoption: perspectives of adopted adolescents and their parents', *Adoption Quarterly*, 10:3/4, pp 79–102

Haight W. L., Black J. E., Mangelsdorf S., Giorgio G., Tata L., Schoppe S. J. and Szewezyk M. (2002) 'Making visits better: the perspectives of parents, foster parents and child welfare workers', *Child Welfare*, 81, pp 173–202

Haight W. L., Mangelsdorf S., Black J., Szewczyk M., Schoppe S., Giorgio G., Madrigal K. and Tata L. (2005) 'Enhancing parent-child interaction during foster care visits: experimental assessment of an intervention', *Child Welfare*, 84, pp 459–81

Hanley B. *et al* (2003) *Involving the Public in NHS Public Health and Social Care Research: Briefing Notes for Researchers* (2nd edition), London: INVOLVE

Harris R. and Lindsey C. (2002) 'How professionals think about contact between children and their birth parents', *Clinical Child Psychology and Psychiatry*, 7, pp 147–61

Harrison C. (1999) 'Children being looked after and their sibling relationships: the experiences of children in the working in partnership with "lost" parents research', in Mullender A. (ed.) *We are family: Sibling relationships in placement and beyond*, London: BAAF

Hart A. and Luckock B. (2004) *Developing Adoption Support and Therapy: New approaches for practice*, London: Jessica Kingsley Publishers

Head A. and Elgar M. (1999) 'The placement of sexually abused and abusing siblings', in Mullender A. (ed.) *We are Family: Sibling relationships in placement and beyond*, London: BAAF

Henney S. M., McRoy R. G., Ayers-Lopez S. and Grotevant H. D. (2003) 'The impact of openness on adoption agency practices: a longitudinal perspective', *Adoption Quarterly*, 6, 31–51

Hoopes J. (1990) 'Adoption and identity formation', in Brodzinsky D. M. and Schechter M. D. (eds) *The Psychology of Adoption*, New York: Oxford University Press

Howe D. (1998) *Patterns of Adoption*, Oxford: Blackwell Science

Howe D. and Feast J. (2003) *Adoption, Search and Reunion: The long-term experience of adopted adults*, London: BAAF

Howe D., Sawbridge P. and Hinings D. (1992) *Half a Million Women: Mothers who lose their children by adoption*, London: Penguin

Howe D. and Steele M. (2004) 'Contact in cases in which children have been traumatically abused or neglected by their birth parents', in Neil E. and Howe D. (eds) *Contact in Adoption and Permanent Foster Care: Research, theory and practice*, London: BAAF

Kedward C., Luckock B. and Lawson H. (1999) 'Mediation and post-adoption contact: the early experience of the Post-Adoption Centre Contact Mediation Service', *Adoption & Fostering*, 23, pp 16–26

Jones C. and Hackett S. (2007) 'Communicative openness within adoptive families: adoptive parents narrative accounts of the challenges of adoption talk and the approaches used to manage these challenges', *Adoption Quarterly*, 10:2/3, pp 157–78

Kirk H. D. (1964) *Shared Fate*, New York: Free Press

Knapp M., Bryson D. and Lewis J. (1984) *The Comprehensive Costing of Child Care: The Suffolk cohort study*, PSSRU Discussion Paper 355, Personal Social Services Research Unit, Canterbury: University of Kent

Lee J. S. and Thwaite J. A. (1997) 'Open adoption and adoptive mothers: attitudes towards birthmothers, adopted children, and parenting', *American Journal of Orthopsychiatry*, 67, pp 576–84

Logan J. and Smith C. (1999) 'Adoption and direct post-adoption contact', *Adoption & Fostering*, 23, pp 58–9

Logan J. and Smith C. (2004) 'Direct post-adoption contact: experiences of birth and adoptive families', in Neil E. and Howe D. (eds) *Contact in Adoption and Permanent Foster Care: Research, theory and practice*, London: BAAF

Logan J. and Smith C. (2005) 'Face-to-face contact post adoption: views from the triangles', *British Journal of Social Work*, 35, pp 3–35

Lowe N., Murch M., Borkowski M., Weaver A., Beckford V. and Thomas C. (1999) *Supporting Adoption: Reframing the approach*, London: BAAF

Lyons-Ruth D., Alpern L. and Repacholi B. (1993) 'Disorganised infant attachment classification and maternal psychosocial problems as predictors of hostile-aggressive behaviour in the preschool classroom', *Child Development*, 64, pp 572–85

Macaskill C. (2002) *Safe Contact? Children in permanent placement and contact with their birth relatives*, Lyme Regis: Russell House Publications

Main M. and Hesse E. (1990) 'Parents' unresolved traumatic experiences are related to infants' disorganized attachment status: Is frightened and/or frightening parental behaviour the linking mechanism?', in Kearns D. and Richardson R. (eds) *Attachment in Middle Childhood*, New York: Guilford Press

Mauskopf J. A., Paul J. E., Grant D. M. and Stergachis A. (1998) 'The role of cost-consequence analysis in healthcare decision-making', *Pharmacoeconomics*, 13:3, pp 277–88

Milan S. E. and Pinderhughes E. E. (2000) 'Factors influencing maltreated children's early adjustment in foster care', *Development and Psychopathology*, 12, pp 63–81

Millham S., Bullock R., Hosie K. and Haak M. (1986) *Lost in Care*, Aldershot: Gower

Morgan R. (2006) *About Adoption. A children's views report*, Newcastle: Office of the Children's Rights Director, Commission for Social Care Inspection

Neil E. (1999) 'The sibling relationships of adopted children and patterns of contact after adoption', in Mullender M. (ed.) *We are Family: Sibling relationships in placement and beyond*, London: BAAF

Neil E. (2000) 'The reasons why young children are placed for adoption: findings from a recently placed sample and implications for future identity issues', *Child & Family Social Work*, 4, pp 303–16

Neil E. (2002a) 'Contact after adoption: the role of agencies in making and supporting plans', *Adoption & Fostering*, 26, pp 25–38

Neil E. (2002b) 'Managing face-to-face contact for young adopted children', in Argent H. (ed.) *Staying Connected: Managing contact in adoption*, London: BAAF

Neil E. (2003a) 'Understanding other people's perspectives: tasks for adopters in open adoptions', *Adoption Quarterly*, 6, pp 3–30

Neil E. (2003b) 'Adoption and contact: a research review', in Bainham A., Lindley B., Richards M. and Trinder L. (eds) *Children and Their Families: Contact, rights and welfare*, Oxford: Hart Publishing

Neil E. (2004a) 'The "Contact after Adoption" study: face-to-face contact', in Neil E. and Howe D. (eds) *Contact in Adoption and Permanent Foster Care: Research, theory and practice*, London: BAAF

Neil E. (2004b) 'The "Contact after Adoption" study: indirect contact and adoptive parents' communication about adoption', in Neil E. and Howe D. (eds) *Contact in Adoption and Permanent Foster Care: Research, theory and practice*, London: BAAF

Neil E. (2007a) 'Supporting post adoption contact for children adopted from care: a study of social workers' attitudes', *Adoption Quarterly*, 10:2/3, pp 3–28

Neil E. (2007b) 'Post-adoption contact and openness in adoptive parents' minds: consequences for children's development', *British Journal of Social Work – Advance Access*: DOI: 101093/bjsw/bcm087

Neil E. (2007c) 'Coming to terms with the loss of a child: the feelings of birth parents and grandparents about adoption and post-adoption contact', *Adoption Quarterly*, 10:1, pp 1–23

Neil E. (2009) 'The corresponding experiences of adoptive parents and birth relatives in open adoptions', in Wrobel G. and Neil E. (eds) *International Advances in Adoption Research for Practice*, Chichester: Wiley

Neil E., Cossar J., Lorgelly P. and Young J. (2010) *Helping Birth Families: Services, cost and outcomes*, London: BAAF

Neil E., Grotevant H. G. and Young J. (2006) *Adoptive Communication Openness: Coding manual* (copy available from author)

Neil E. and Howe D. (2004) 'Conclusions: a transactional model for thinking about contact', in Neil E. and Howe D. (eds) *Contact in Adoption and Permanent Foster Care: Research, theory and practice*, London: BAAF

Parker R. (1999) *Adoption Now: Messages from research*, London: The Stationery Office

Parkes C. M. (2001) *Bereavement: Studies of grief in adult life* (3rd edition) Philadelphia PA: Taylor and Francis

Pearce N. (2006) *Adoption Law Manual*, London: Callow Publishing

Performance and Innovation Unit (PIU) (2000) *The Prime Minister's Review of Adoption*, London: The Cabinet Office

Quinton D. and Selwyn J. (2006) 'Adoption: research, policy and practice', *Child and Family Law Quarterly*, 18, pp 459–77

Reamer F. G. and Siegel D. H. (2007) 'Ethical issues in open adoption: implications for practice', *Families in Society*, 88, pp 11–18

Richards M. (1996) ' "It feels like someone keeps moving the goalposts" – regulating post-adoption contact: *Re T (Adopted Children: Contact)*', *Child and Family Law Quarterly*, 8:2, pp 175–9

Rushton A. (2009) 'Adoption support', in Schofield G. and Simmonds J. (eds) *The Child Placement Handbook: Research, policy and practice*, London: BAAF

Rushton A. and Dance C. (2002) *Adoption Support Services for Families in Difficulty: A literature review and UK survey*, London: BAAF

Ryburn M. (1995) 'Adopted children's identity and information needs', *Children & Society*, 9:3, pp 41–64

Sales S. (2002) 'Managing post-adoption contact through mediation', in Argent H. (ed.) *Staying Connected: Managing contact arrangements in adoption*, London: BAAF

Schofield G. and Beek M. (2006) *Attachment Handbook for Foster Care and Adoption*, London: BAAF

Sellick C. (2007) 'An examination of adoption support services for birth relatives and for post-adoption contact in England and Wales', *Adoption & Fostering*, 31:4, pp 17–26

Sellick C., Neil E., Young Y., Healey N. and Lorgelly P. (2006) *Supporting the Birth Relatives of Adopted Children and Supporting Post Adoption Contact in Complex Cases Stage 1 Report: Service Mapping, Interim Report to the Department for Education and Skills*, Norwich: University of East Anglia

Selwyn J. (2004) 'Placing older children in new families: changing patterns of contact', in Neil E. and Howe D. (eds) *Contact in Adoption and Permanent Foster Care: Research, theory and practice*, London: BAAF

Selwyn J., Sempik J., Thurston P. and Wijedasa D. (2009) *Adoption and the Interagency Fee, Department for Children, Schools and Families Research Briefing*, DCSF-RB149

Siegel D. H. (2003) 'Open adoption of infants: adoptive parents' feelings seven years later', *Social Work*, 48, pp 409–19

Sinclair I., Baker C., Wilson K. and Gibbs I. (2005) *Foster Children. Where they go and how they get on*, London: Jessica Kingsley Publishers

Slade A. (2002) 'Protection and supervision: making problematic contact safe and beneficial', in Argent H. (ed.) *Staying Connected: Managing contact arrangements in adoption*, London: BAAF

Smith C. and Logan J. (2004) *After adoption: direct contact and relationships*, London: Routledge

Smith F., Stewart R. and Cullen D. (2006) *Adoption now: law, regulations, guidance and standards*, London: BAAF

Spertus I. L., Yehuda R., Wong C. M., Halligan S. and Seremetis S. V. (2003) 'Childhood emotional abuse and neglect as predictors of psychological and physical symptoms in women presenting to a primary care practice', *Child Abuse and Neglect*, 27, pp 1247–58

Sturgess W. and Selwyn J. (2007) 'Supporting the placement of children adopted out of care', *Clinical Child Psychology and Psychiatry*, 12:1, pp 13–28

Sykes M. (2000) 'Adoption with contact A study of adoptive parents and the impact of continuing contact with families of origin', *Adoption & Fostering*, 24, pp 20–32

Tabachnick B. G. and Fidell L. S. (2007) *Using Multivariate Statistics*, (fifth edition), Boston, MA: Pearson/Allyn and Bacon

Thoburn J. (1996) 'Psychological parenting and child placement: "But we want to have our cake and eat it"', in Howe D. (ed.) *Attachment and Loss in Child and Family Social Work*, Aldershot: Avebury

Thoburn J. (2004) 'Post-placement contact between birth parents and older children: the evidence from a longitudinal study of minority ethnic children', in Neil E. and Howe D. (eds) *Contact in Adoption and Permanent Foster Care: Research, theory and practice*, London: BAAF

Thoburn J., Norford L. and Rashid S. (2000) *Permanent Family Placement for Children of Minority Ethnic Origin*, London: Jessica Kingsley Publishers

Thomas C., Beckford V., Lowe N. and Murch M. (1999) *Adopted Children Speaking*, London: BAAF

Triseliotis J. (1973) *In Search of Origins: The experience of adopted people*, London: Routledge & Kegan Paul

Triseliotis J., Shireman J. and Hundleby M. (1997) *Adoption: Theory, policy and practice*, London: Cassell

Von Korff L., Grotevant H. D. and McRoy R. G. (2006) 'Openness arrangements and psychological adjustment in adolescent adoptees', *Journal of Family Psychology*, 20:3, pp 531–34

Wade J., Biehal N., Farrelly N. and Sinclair I. (2010) *Outcomes for Children Looked After for Reasons of Abuse or Neglect: The consequences of staying in care or returning home*, Final Report to Department for Children, Schools and Families, SPRU, York: University of York

Wilson K. and Sinclair I. (2004) 'Contact in foster care: some dilemmas and opportunities', in Neil E. and Howe D. (eds) *Contact in Adoption and Permanent Foster Care: Research, theory and practice*, London: BAAF

Winkler R. and van Keppel M. (1984) *Relinquishing Mothers in Adoption: Their long-term adjustment*, Melbourne: Institute of Family Studies

Young J. and Neil E. (2004) 'The "Contact after Adoption" study: the perspective of birth relatives after non-voluntary adoption', in Neil E. and Howe D. (eds) *Contact in Adoption and Permanent Foster Care: Research, theory and practice*, London: BAAF

Index

scale 120
cost-benefit analysis 49–51
costs 10–11, 272–84, 301
    in contact
        for adoptive parents 202–3
        for birth parents 241–3
    contact support services
        282–3
    by model 36–8, 298, 299,
        300–2
    economic analysis 4–5,
        49–51, 307
court, directions for contact
    16–17

data analysis 48
diaries
    caseworkers 272–4
    service use 50–1
direct contact *see* contact
    meetings
domestic violence, in birth family
    59, 60
drug misuse, by birth parents 59,
    60, 93
dual connection
    adoptive parents
        emotions in contact 158–9
        promotion by 81, 83–4
    birth relatives
        acceptance by 101,
            107–12, 151, 188–9,
            292
        denial by 109–10
    contact benefit 160–1

emotional impact
    of adoption, birth parents
        112–17, 119
    of contact 287–9, 292
        on adoptive parents 158–9
        on children 27–8
        management 185–6
emotional problems
    of children 70–1, 135
    post-contact 148
emotional support 293–4
    for adoptive families 200–2,
        206–7
    for birth relatives 238–41,
        262–3, 269
    good practice 314
    individualised approach 297,
        298, 300, 301
    professional time commitment
        272–4
empathy
    for adopted child 82, 83–4,
        108
    for adoptive parents 108
    for birth relatives 82, 83–4,
        189–90
employment
    adoptive parents 54
    birth relatives 91–2
ethical approval for study 40
ethnicity
    adopted children 58, 96
    adoptive parents 53
    birth relatives 91
    language difficulty 225